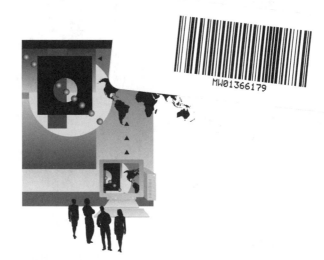

The Cybrarian's Manual 2

PAT ENSOR
EDITOR

American Library Association

Chicago and London   2000

While extensive effort has gone into ensuring the reliability of information appearing in this book, the publisher makes no warranty, express or implied, on the accuracy or reliability of the information, and does not assume and hereby disclaims any liability to any person for any loss or damage caused by errors or omission in this publication.

Trademarked names appear in the text of this book. Rather than identify or insert a trademark symbol at the appearance of each name, the authors and the American Library Association state that the names are used for editorial purposes exclusively, to the ultimate benefit of the owners of the trademarks. There is absolutely no intention of infringement on the rights of the trademark owners.

The paper used in this publication meets the minimum requirements of American National Standard for Information Sciences—Permanence of Paper for Printed Library Materials, ANSI Z39.48–1992. ∞

Library of Congress Cataloging-in-Publication Data

The cybrarian's manual 2 / [edited by] Pat Ensor.
    p. cm.
  Rev. ed. of: The cybrarian's manual. 1997.
  ISBN 0-8389-0777-6 (alk. paper)
  1. Internet (Computer network)—United States. 2. Library information networks—United States. I. Title: Cybrarian's manual two. II. Ensor, Pat.

Z674.75.I58 C933 2000
025.04—dc21

99-044215

Copyright © 2000 by the American Library Association. All rights reserved except those which may be granted by Sections 107 and 108 of the Copyright Revision Act of 1976.

Printed in the United States of America.

04 03 02 01 00   5 4 3 2 1

Contents

Preface v

1
The Cybrarian's Tool Kit
1–32

Internet News and Website Reviews   *Margaret Sylvia*   3

Searching the Future   *James Powell*   10

Netiquette, Hoaxes, and Scams! Oh My!   *Elizabeth A. Dupuis*   16

The New Library Demands a Closer Look at Ergonomics
Cindy K. Schofield-Bodt   24

2
A Network of Networks of Networks— Technical Underpinnings
33–58

The Basics of LAN Technology   *Caroline Higgins*   35

The Basics of a Nationwide Network for the Internet   *Aimee deChambeau*   42

Internet2 and the Next Generation Internet Initiative   *Steve Hardin*   51

3
Nothing Is Certain but the Web and Taxes
59–88

Guidelines for an Excellent Website   *JoAnn Sears and Andrew Wohrley*   61

Web-Based Markup Languages: HTML, DHTML, and XML
Martin R. Kalfatovic   68

Browser Plug-Ins: Customization for Multimedia   *Matthew Benzing*   77

A Day in the Life . . . Multimedia and Librarians in the Twenty-first Century
Brad Eden   82

4
The Document as Object and Commodity
89–121

Metadata 101: A Primer   *Priscilla Caplan*   91

Unique Identifiers on the Web for Documents, Sites, and Domain Names
Colby Mariva Riggs   99

Copyright in Cyberspace   *Gretchen McCord Hoffmann*   103

Cyber-Citing: Citing Electronic Sources   *Kristin Vogel*   113

5

Puttin' It Out over the Net: Sources and Services 123–175

Collecting Electronic Resources: What You Don't Know, You Can Learn
Kimberly J. Parker   125

Let's Put It All on the Web: Practical Information for Digital Imaging
Andrea Bean Hough   134

Digital Libraries   *Paul Jones*   145

In Search of the Elusive E-Journal   *Marilyn Geller*   152

Developing an Internet-Based Reference Service   *Blythe Bennett*   159

Electronic Reserves: Concepts and Models   *Jeff Rosedale*   170

6

The Library'd Be Fine if It Wasn't for All Those People! 177–218

Providing Web Access in Libraries: A Practical Guide   *Alicia Abramson*   179

Kids, the Internet, and All Those Adult Anxieties   *Walter Minkel*   190

The Iron Triangle of Privacy, Filtering, and Internet Use Policies
John A. Shuler   197

Licensed to Teach   *Ann Thornton*   206

You Gotta Go to School for That? Pac-Man in the Information Arcade
Jerry Seay   216

7

Cutting Edge or Bleeding Edge: You Make the Call 219–267

Security and Authentication Issues   *Marshall Breeding*   221

Wireless and Ubiquitous Computing   *Steve Cavrak*   233

Push Technology: Something New, Something Old   *Amira Aaron*   243

Virtual Reality Primer for Cybrarians   *David Mattison*   252

Quitting the "Technology of the Month" Club   *Ray Olszewski*   261

8

As the Librarian Turns 269–297

On the Lighter Side: . . . And a Small Child Shall Lead Them
Jim Johnston   271

Rupert Giles, Techno-Terror, and Knowledge as the Ultimate Weapon
GraceAnne A. DeCandido   276

Overcoming Image: Strategies for Librarians in the New Millennium
Jan M. Houghton and Ross J. Todd   282

Finding Things and Telling Stories   *Judy Myers*   291

Acronyms and Initialisms   299

Index   303

PREFACE

The threshold of a new millennium seems to be a suitable place to rearm ourselves with a "Cybrarian's Manual Version 2.0" to replace the 1997 publication. I am very proud of *The Cybrarian's Manual*, and I am pleased that it was so well received. In fact, I'll take it upon myself to say that parts of the first edition will still be worth reading in the years to come. However, the cybrarian also needs to be sure she has information that is timely as well as information that is timeless. To that end, I present to you *The Cybrarian's Manual 2*.

The Cybrarian's Manual 2 is almost entirely new. Two authors, Steve Cavrak and Kristin Vogel, updated chapters that were in the first edition. The scope of this edition has been broadened somewhat. Although still organized around librarians and cyberspace, the book goes beyond the purely technical to examine some of the social and management issues that have become inextricably entwined with the technology. As in the past, one of the main assets of this book is its inclusion of numerous sources of information for more extensive research.

The book is still intended to cover many of the practical, day-to-day aspects of a librarian's travels in cyberspace as well as to take a peek at some things to come. The audience is still the librarian with an intermediate knowledge of technology. Acronyms and initialisms that are commonly known might not be spelled out in the text, but are detailed in the Acronyms and Initialisms section at the end of the book.

It is interesting to see how much change has occurred in the topics needing to be included in order to accomplish the aim stated earlier. The browser wars of a couple of years ago don't seem that earth-shattering anymore, and widespread access to the Internet has become commonplace. Now we are more concerned with the library's place in cyberspace and how we can span the gap between "Web years" (known to the rest of us as "months") and "library years" (sometimes known to the rest of us as "decades"!).

Kids entering college in the fall of 1999 have never lived in a world where there was no MTV, videocassette recorder, compact disc, Sony Walkman, or cable television. In a world where entertainment and information have blurred—and where entertainment is of incredible importance—what place will libraries occupy, and how will they adapt to survive, while continuing to represent timeless values? And who will join us in this profession? I wish I could say this book answers those questions—then I could afford to retire and just think Deep Thoughts (interspersed with playing Tomb Raider). Instead, I hope *The Cybrarian's Manual 2* helps readers actively participate in working out the answers.

1 The Cybrarian's Tool Kit

Internet News and Website Reviews

Margaret Sylvia

Margaret Sylvia (*acadmarg@stmarytx.edu*) is the assistant director for Technical Services and a tenured associate professor at St. Mary's University Academic Library in San Antonio, Texas. She is also the library's webmaster. She has been an invited speaker at the Southwest Conference of the Special Libraries Association, the Texas Library Association, the American Library Association, and the Computers in Libraries annual conferences. Her publications and presentations range from topics of acquisitions and collection development to network administration with a particular emphasis on remote access to library services.

Keeping up with news about the Internet and new sites on the Internet can be a full-time job. The following annotated list of resources furnishes substantive Internet news and reviews of important new websites. Pat Ensor's excellent selection of resources in the first edition of *The Cybrarian's Manual* forms the core of this list. Although, as with all things Internet, some of them have ceased to be or have evolved into different sites, new sites abound.

I've divided the online sites into two groups—those oriented toward subject librarians or educators and those focused on the marketing and technology of the Internet. If you wish to locate good websites on particular topics, the first group will be most useful to you. If you are more technically oriented and need information on how the Internet is evolving, how to build cutting-edge websites, and where to find the latest software, the second set of sites will probably be more useful.

Most of the websites have e-mail options so that you can have new information delivered directly to you. Also, a large number of sites have browsable and searchable archives in case you have missed reading a few issues. These options are noted in the annotations.

Sites for Librarians and Educators

Ariadne Newsletter   *http://www.ariadne.ac.uk/*
This newsletter, based in the United Kingdom, is aimed at academic librarians and contains website reviews and articles on progress and developments in the electronic library community. Issued bimonthly, most of the articles on the site are also found in a print version of the newsletter, though the website may be updated more frequently. It is not available through e-mail, but back issues are browsable and searchable.

CIT Infobits   *http://www.unc.edu/cit/infobits/infobits.html*
From the Center for Institutional Technology at the University of North Carolina, this monthly publication is also available by e-mailing *listserv@ unc.edu* with the message: "subscribe infobits firstname lastname." The site includes reviews of educational software, multimedia resources, and websites.

Current Cites   *http://sunsite.berkeley.edu/CurrentCites/*
Current Cites, a monthly newsletter produced by the University of California-Berkeley Library, is also available through e-mail. To subscribe, send the message "subscribe Cites firstname lastname" to *listserv@library.berkeley.edu*. The newsletter is an annotated bibliography of new developments regarding information technology. The issues are archived and searchable. *Current Cites* is also distributed on the PACS-P mailing list along with *Public Access Computer Systems Review*, the *LITA Newsletter*, and the *Scholarly Electronic Publishing Bibliography*. To join PACS-P, send the message "subscribe PACS-P firstname lastname" to *listserv@listserv.uh.edu*.

D-Lib Magazine   *http://www.dlib.org/*
D-Lib is an organization that supports the advancement of research and communication regarding digital libraries. *D-Lib Magazine* is a monthly publication with articles and commentary on the state of digital libraries. The pointers to current events and publications are quite useful. An archive of back issues is browsable and searchable.

Edupage   *http://www.educause.edu/pub/edupage/edupage.html*
Published three times a week, *Edupage* is a digest of information-technology news items taken from newspapers and magazines. It is produced by EDUCAUSE, which, according to the website, is "an international nonprofit association dedicated to transforming higher education through information technologies." There is a searchable and browsable archive, and the newsletter is also available through e-mail. To subscribe, send the message "subscribe Edupage firstname lastname" to *listserv@listserve.educause.edu*.

Internet Resources   http://www.hw.ac.uk/libWWW/irn/irn.html
This monthly newsletter, produced by the Heriot-Watt University library in the United Kingdom, compiles and annotates lists of new Internet sites useful to the academic researcher. A browsable archive of previous issues is available as well as an alphabetized list of previously reviewed resources.

LII New This Week   http://sunsite.berkeley.edu/InternetIndex/
To be added to the *LII New This Week* mailing list, send the message "subscribe liiweek firstname lastname" to *listproc@sunsite.berkeley.edu*. This newsletter keeps its readers current on the latest websites added to the *Librarian's Index to the Internet*, a subject directory of websites selected and annotated by librarians. The sites annotated in the newsletter are incorporated into the *InternetIndex/* web page, which is searchable and browsable.

Net-Happenings   http://scout.cs.wisc.edu/scout/net-hap/
Produced and edited by Gleason Sackman, *Net-Happenings* is a service of the *Scout Report*, described later in this section. *Net-Happenings* distributes and archives daily announcements of Internet websites that may be of interest to K–12 librarians and educators. Between forty and sixty sites are announced each day, so the e-mail distribution list is in digest form. To receive *Net-Happenings* by e-mail, visit *http://scout.cs. wisc.edu/scout/lists/* or send the message "subscribe net-happenings firstname lastname" to *listserv@cs.wisc.edu*. Archives at the site are searchable and browsable.

Public-Access Computer Systems Review   http://info.lib.uh.edu/pacsrev.html
The University of Houston Libraries publishes this electronic journal focusing on digital libraries, document delivery systems, electronic publishing, expert systems, hypermedia and multimedia systems, locally mounted databases, network-based information resources and tools, and online catalogs. Back issues are online and are browsable and searchable. Publication of the journal is announced on the PACS-P broadcast list. To join PACS-P, see the instructions under the entry for *Current Cites*.

Scout Report   http://scout.cs.wisc.edu/report/
Saved the best for last; the *Scout Report* is my personal favorite for news of the Internet oriented toward librarians and educators. A general *Scout Report* is published weekly, and three additional subject-specific reports for business and economics, science and engineering, and the social sciences are published biweekly.

To subscribe to the e-mail notification service, visit *http://scout.cs. wisc.edu/scout/lists/* for the Internet Scout mailing list WWW gateway. Back issues are searchable and browsable. Each issue contains annotated and reviewed links to new and newly discovered websites of interest to educators and researchers. The *Scout Report* is published by the Computer Sciences Department at the University of Wisconsin–Madison.

Marketing and Technology News Sites

CNET http://www.cnet.com/
Oriented toward reviews of new hardware and software, *CNET* also reviews notable new websites. The site is searchable, and a "subscribe" page allows the user to select from various e-mail newsletters, including *Digital Dispatch*, which is a weekly update on new material from *CNET*. The site caters to computer professionals in many fields.

CyberAtlas: The Reference Desk for Web Marketing
http://cyberatlas.internet.com/
This site features a complete collection of Web statistics and articles on Web growth and advertising, particularly important for marketing on the Web. It includes current numbers of Internet websites and servers, user population, traffic patterns, advertising information, and lots of other demographics. The site is searchable but has no e-mail notification component.

HotWired http://www.hotwired.com/
This digital offshoot of *Wired Magazine* provides current news stories about the Internet and the computer industry as well as a huge amount of information on website development. *Wired News* is available in either ASCII text or HTML-formatted e-mail. The website has searchable and browsable archives.

InfoWorld Electric http://www.infoworld.com/
InfoWorld in its print edition is a source of reliable product news and reviews as well as commentary on issues related to the digital world. The *InfoWorld Electric* website continues that tradition and expands it by providing daily news updates and electronic discussion forums. The *InfoWorld Scoop* delivers new Web information by e-mail twice weekly. Archives are searchable with registration.

Internet World http://www.iw.com/
The digital counterpart of the weekly magazine *Internet World*, formerly titled *Web Week*, is a daily news reporter for the Internet. Back issues are browsable or searchable. The *Internet World Weekly Digest* is a news summary of articles from *Internet World* e-mailed to subscribers on the first business day of each week. The e-mail message provides links back to the website for the full articles.

Internet.com http://www.internet.com/
Internet.com is the host site for *Internet World,* the *Electronic Commerce Guide, Intranet Design Magazine,* and other resources for Internet business. Like *Internet World*, e-mail options are offered, and back issues are searchable and browsable.

Netsurfer Digest http://www.netsurf.com/nsd/
This weekly newsletter can be received by e-mail as well as read at the website. Back issues are searchable and browsable. Breaking news of

the Internet is highlighted first, followed by an eclectic mix of annotated websites encompassing both the weird and the wonderful.

Seidman's Online Insider   http://www.onlineinsider.com/
This semimonthly publication provides analyses of consumer online services, such as America Online, CompuServe, Prodigy, and the Microsoft Network, as well as the whole Internet. Browsable archives are available. To subscribe to a text version of the newsletter, send e-mail to *insider-text-on@seidman.infobeat.com*; for an HTML version of the newsletter, send e-mail to *insider-html-on@seidman.infobeat.com.*

TechWeb: The Technology News Site   http://www.techWeb.com/
Highlighting Internet and other computer technology news and analysis, *TechWeb News* is available by e-mail (subscribe at *http://www. cmpnet.com/delivery*) and on the website every weekday. Searchable and browsable archives are available.

Web Developer.com   http://www.Webdeveloper.com/
This site is of most interest to the website manager and HTML author. Book, website, and software reviews on HTML, Java, JavaScript, CGI, and other pertinent subjects are included as well as a headline news service on Internet developments. *WebDeveloper Weekly News* is e-mailed to subscribers on Fridays. To subscribe, go to *http://e-newsletters.internet. com/webdev.html* and fill out a form. A searchable and browsable archive is available.

Yahoo Internet Life   http://www.zdnet.com/yil/
Like the venerable Yahoo subject index/portal to the Internet, *Yahoo Internet Life* is almost too much of a good thing. Daily news, site reviews, and much more make this a must-read site. Back issues of *Yahoo Internet Life* are browsable and searchable. *Y-Life Daily Bulletin* is available by e-mail subscription by visiting *http://www.zdnet.com/yil/content/ misc/newsletter.html.*

In Print

Apparently print is not yet dead, though nothing in print can match the currency of the websites and e-mail news distribution lists. However, no battery, installation, or assembly are required for these. Listed here are some important periodicals that cover the various topics in this chapter, along with information for contacting the publisher.

EContent (formerly *Database*)
Online, Inc.
462 Danbury Rd., Wilton, CT 06897
(203) 761-1466
E-mail: *dbmag@onlineinc.com*
Website: *http://www.onlineinc.com/database*

According to its website, this magazine provides "practical, how-to advice on effective use of databases and systems. . . ."

InfoWorld
InfoWorld Publishing
155 Bovet Rd., Ste. 800, San Mateo, CA 94402
Phone: (415) 572-7341; (800) 227-8365
Fax: (415) 358-1269
Website: *http://www.infoworld.com/*

InfoWorld calls itself the Voice of Enterprise Computing. It provides news to support systems professionals in "mak[ing] important purchase and implementation decisions for large, enterprise computer networks" (website).

Internet World
Mecklermedia Corporation
20 Ketchum St., Westport, CT 06880
Phone: (203) 226-6967
Fax: (203) 454-8540
Website: *http://www.internetworld.com/*

The self-proclaimed "voice of e-business and Internet technology," *Internet World's* online version is updated daily.

Online
Online, Inc.
462 Danbury Rd., Wilton, CT 06897
Phone: (203) 761-1466; (800) 248-8466
Fax: (203) 761-1444
E-mail: *info@onlineinc.com*
Website: *http://www.onlineinc.com/onlinemag*

Online provides guidance on "selecting, using, and managing electronic information products," according to its site.

Wired
Wired Ventures Ltd.
520 Third St., 4th Fl., San Francisco, CA 94107
Phone: (415) 222-6200; (800) 769-4733
Fax: (415) 222-6209
E-mail: *editor@wired.com*
Website: *http://www.hotwired.com/*

Wired covers "the people, companies, and ideas that are transforming the way we live."

Yahoo Internet Life
Ziff-Davis Publishing Co.
One Park Ave., New York, NY 10016
Phone: (212) 503-4804; (800) 950-0484
Fax: (212) 503-5699
Website: *http://www.zdnet.com/yil/*

Explaining "how and where to get the best of the Internet" is the aim of *YIL*.

How to Find More

Of course, many other websites and periodicals contain Internet news and reviews of websites. The ones listed here are those I have found useful. For more lists of periodicals, try Yahoo at *http://www.yahoo.com* under its Computers and Internet: News and Media section. Most of the major Internet portals and search engines incorporate a similar section. Also, most of the websites listed in the first section of this chapter include lists and links to similar resources.

Searching the Future

James Powell

James Powell (*jpowell@vt.edu*) is the head of Distributed Information Systems at Virginia Tech. He has written extensively about digital library issues.

The future of information searching lies on the Web. Virtually any searchable collection of data can easily be made accessible through a simple HTML (HyperText Markup Language) form. In fact, the World Wide Web has exploded with searchable databases. Those that aren't on the Web are usually unavailable because of nontechnical reasons, such as the inability to protect intellectual content or ensure proper use.

Although the quality, capabilities, and presentations of search engines may vary, such services are maturing quickly. Such technologies as Java and JavaScript allow sophisticated search services to be provided with all the capabilities that were once only custom-made for proprietary clients. Fundamental similarities in the interfaces of search systems are allowing developers to implement such mechanisms as Apple's Sherlock to allow users to perform multiple site searches in parallel. Free search engines are providing indexes for more and more websites.

Web Searching Issues

Just as with websites themselves, a definite need exists for someone to help users sort through the search options and select good-quality resources. Searching on the Web is still defined as much by what is indexed as by what is not. Trends both interesting and worrisome are developing in the field of Web searching. With Apple's introduction of Sherlock, metasearching has stepped onto the desktop in a big way. *Metasearching* and *federated searching* (strategies that query multiple search engines simultaneously) seem to be the most promising developments in the realm of search engines.

Individual search sites all face the same problem—they cannot index everything on the Web. By applying sometimes secret proprietary rules to collecting and indexing documents, sites manage to present an appearance of completeness. However, indexing every website would require gathering site-specific information regularly. No technology has yet managed to entirely eliminate the need for some type of reconstructible representation of the indexed document to exist on the search server.

You can see the problem. Search systems must maintain some sort of search index, and no system indexes every document on the Web. In additon, these search systems often rely on indexing information provided by the website owner, who may embellish the site's substance. Some authors will misrepresent their content in order to ensure higher visibility, even going so far as to "spoof" search engines with keywords describing competitors or unrelated services. This is a big problem for Web search engines. Human-mediated portal sites, such as Yahoo, are still the only sure-fire solutions to this problem. Librarians acting as Yahooligan-style website catalogers will be increasingly valuable.

How Search Engines Work

Search engines themselves are available in many different implementations. Many are derived from the vector space search model, initially described by Gerard Salton. In its simplest form, the vector space search engine consists of a word set that encompasses all the words in all the documents in an indexed collection.

This collection represents a vector that is a line with an n-dimensional endpoint, where n corresponds to the number of documents in the collection. For example, if you had only three words in your document set, the endpoint of the vector for your wordset would have an x, a y and a z coordinate. Each coordinate value corresponds to the number of times each word occurs in all the documents. Each document is also represented by a similar vector.

Searches themselves are converted to vectors, and the vectors most similar to the search vector represent the best matches in the document collection. The beauty of this system is the ease with which relevance searches can be constructed. If you want more documents like one that showed up in your document set, the vector representing that document already exists, so it is simply converted into a query. This is probably more than you wanted to know, but if it isn't, a good place to learn more would be a linear algebra text (yes, math is good for something).

At the lower end of the search engine spectrum are brute force text scanners that do not build indexes. Many websites use these sorts of search engines. They are often based on or derived from system tools originally developed for Unix, such as grep (globally match regular expression and print), a program for finding specific character patterns within the content of a list of files. They tend to work fairly well for small document sets, providing basic single- or multi-word case-insensitive query capabilities. As a document collection grows, however, it takes longer for a search to be completed. A further drawback is that it is difficult to search content that spans multiple formats with text-scanning software, whereas most programs that build indexes of a document collection usually perform some type of format conversion during the indexing process.

Making text searchable is fairly well understood. Less well understood, however, is how users want to search the content. In addition to single- and multi-word queries, some users want to perform phrase queries, in which a string of words must occur exactly as specified in order to constitute a match. Many users expect to be able to perform Boolean queries, which allow them to indicate what combinations of words should be allowed in documents in the results set. More sophisticated users want to be able to perform "near," "with," and relevance feedback queries against the full text. Still other users prefer searching catalog records that consist of metadata describing each item in the collection. All these options and more can be found on the Web.

Search Problems and Possibilities

Recently, users have become aware of the shortcomings of various search engines. They are beginning to realize that the AltaVistas and HotBots of the Web do not index every single document ever published, or even all documents currently available on the Web. As a result, users have been seeking alternatives that allow them to search multiple sites in parallel. In fact, it is very possible that parallel, distributed Web queries will outnumber queries targeted at one specific search engine in the not-too-distant future.

Is this an indicator that search engines are not doing a good job? Maybe. But search engines have improved in many respects. They've gotten faster. They've remained free. They've combined searching with high-level categories to form "portal" sites, which have become very popular with users who have lost patience with Boolean searching, stemming operators, and "natural language" queries that use some obscure, stilted notion of natural language developed by twins raised by wolves.

Search engines have not improved in some areas. *They display result sets that list documents that no longer exist.* They've made very little real progress in the area of *multilingual searching.* Most boast of multilingual interfaces but that usually means someone translated the text of the search page into another language. However, both AltaVista and Yahoo have made significant contributions in this field. Yahoo provides geographically and linguistically distinct search sites like Yahoo Japan and

Yahoo Italia. AltaVista has collaborated with machine translation services to provide simple translations of documents between various languages.

No search site seems to provide *targeted query translation;* this really seems like a metasearch-level service and touches upon many areas of linguistic computation that are still being researched. Search engines are *sluggish in updating their content.* Changes in documents indexed by a site might not be reflected in a search engine's index for weeks, months, or ever.

But the *lack of standards* is perhaps the most frustrating characteristic of Web searching. It is true that some standards have been developed with the potential to allow interoperability between search engines and define a uniform search interface. But no widely supported protocol exists for search engines, or for search clients and search engines, to exchange information about breadth of content coverage, search features, or metadata. Projects like Dienst and STARTS both describe mechanisms for these types of services, but no major search engine vendors have implemented support for the protocols defined by these projects, nor for such tried and true standards as Z39.50, which allows the translation of search commands between various online systems.

The only near-term solution for allowing searches to span multiple search engines seems to lie in heuristic solutions that take advantage of some inherent similarities among search engines. As for interface design, the best practices are emerging from the field of human–computer interaction, such as Ben Shneiderman's four-phase framework for searching (see *http://ijhcs.open.ac.uk/shneiderman/shneiderman-t.html*). The closest thing to a standard now is the simple search, which consists of one fill-in field and one button. Plenty of work remains to be done to determine how to present advanced search features in a standard, universally understood way.

Metasearch Systems

The immediate future of Web searching will be defined by various heterogeneous metasearch or federated search systems. Such systems allow software to programmatically conceal and resolve differences between search engines, using heuristics that have been encoded in some manner. This allows such systems to even support prequery processing—such as use of a thesaurus to improve a query or the translation of a query into the primary language used by the collection before it is submitted to a search engine. It also allows for postquery processing to merge and possibly translate results.

What is metasearching all about? Most simply, it is the act of delivering query terms to more than one search engine in the format expected by each search engine. Some pseudo-metasearch systems present a set of prefilled forms at an intermediate stage and then expect the user to submit each query as desired. The user can achieve a similar effect by relying on a set of search engine bookmarks and a few open browser windows. True metasearching involves some form of query reformulation and automatic delivery. Beyond that, there are many additional tasks that can be performed.

Sherlock is an extension of Version 8.5 of the Mac OS for Macintosh computers (*http://www.apple.com/sherlock/*). It was the first integrated, extensible Web metasearch system ever provided as part of the services of an operating system. Sherlock employs a simple markup language that allows anyone with basic knowledge of HTML to build descriptions of almost any Web-accessible search engine. These descriptions can then be installed into a special folder, which Sherlock consults whenever a user attempts to perform a "find" action on the local hard drive's contents or the Web. The user selects a set of search engines to which a query should be sent, and Sherlock takes care of mapping between search engines, delivering queries, and merging results.

Several Web-based metasearch systems employ similar solutions. The *Global Federated Searcher* (*http://jin.dis.vt.edu/fedsearch/*) is a Web-based system that utilizes XML site descriptions to allow users to search descriptions of search engines and deliver queries to multiple sites. One additional feature of this system is the ability of the metasearch software to identify the primary language of each search engine targeted by the user. It then employs a mechanism to communicate with a dictionary-based word translation service to request translations of queries from, for example, English to Japanese before delivering the query to a Japanese search engine.

It is easy to underestimate the importance of such a feature. However, if you have ever tried to search a search engine in a language you do not speak well, particularly one that uses different characters and employs different techniques for query entry, encoding, and parsing, then you will probably appreciate being able to bypass these hurdles. This feature merely hints at the possibilities as networks and processors become faster, and applications and developers become smarter.

One big question in the emerging field of metasearching is: What will be the reaction of the major search engine sites? Until Sherlock appeared on the Macintosh, the threat to individual search engines was fairly small. But imagine if the next version of Windows NT supports a Sherlock-like mechanism that eliminates ads, conceals the complexity of a search engine, and seamlessly merges results from different search engines into a single set of links. Who will pay for search engines? Will royalties be associated with the use of such tools? Will this be decided in the courts? What could be a big win for end users will likely cost search engines in lost revenue and legal fees, so the battle over metasearches hasn't yet begun.

Intranet-based metasearches will likely lead the pack in terms of functionality. Linking large multinational companies will require overcoming various barriers to communication securely and seamlessly. A great opportunity exists for libraries to lead the unification of the scattering of search engines that inevitably crop up on campuses, in corporations, and around the Web. Schemes for classifying and describing search engines will require experts to evaluate and catalog them.

What Libraries Should Do

What does this mean for libraries? First, if you haven't made your website searchable, do it. A number of free search engines are available for indexing content stored on a single Web server. For indexing multiple servers, you will probably have to purchase some software. Or you can establish indexes for each site and build a page pointing users to the catalog. Or you can try out JavaScript or Perl-based metasearch systems that provide simple, transparent metasearching without a lot of bells and whistles.

Next, make sure your *online catalog is searchable through a Web interface*. That's not to say that you shouldn't also strive to provide support for Z39.50, but remember that many of your clients will have no idea what Z39.50 is or what its benefits are. By providing a Web-based keyword query, you can reach a wider audience than ever before.

Libraries can also contribute by performing the service they have traditionally provided when pointing users at specific books and journals: *directing users to search engines with more features or better interfaces*. This can take the form of traditional reference services, or a library-developed directory of search services, or even building custom metasearches.

For example, instead of merely pointing users to some of the best sites for information about traveling in Europe, libraries could build a metasearch tool that allows for parallel queries against those sites. At the same time, they could improve upon the search interface and the result-set presentation, as well as incorporating additional technologies, such as query translation and thesauri, to further improve searches. Libraries can also help improve existing search engine interfaces, capabilities, and result-set presentation, and work to encourage the implementation of standards. Finally, libraries can continue to generate metadata that include quality ratings about resources at both the collection and document levels.

Will users build their own custom metasearches as easily as they build their own Web pages? They already can. The tools will only continue to improve. But does this mean users will eventually be able to find everything they are looking for? Probably not. Savvy users who are able to construct their own custom metasearchers to address specific research needs will fare well in this environment. Other users will simply find that metasearch results are even more overwhelming and less useful than searching sites like AltaVista. For these users, their salvation still resides within the real or virtual walls of the nearest library.

Netiquette, Hoaxes, and Scams! Oh My!

Elizabeth A. Dupuis

Elizabeth A. Dupuis (*beth@mail.utexas.edu*) is currently head of the Digital Information Literacy Office and Acting Head of the Undergraduate Library at the University of Texas at Austin. Among other responsibilities, she coordinates the instructional programs for the General Libraries and initiates collaborative educational projects with faculty and other campus agencies. Over the years, Elizabeth has worked in public, scientific, legal, and academic libraries. Many of her recent publications and presentations focus on information literacy, the Internet, and user services.

Traversing the Internet is similar to embarking on a new adventure—it's best to be prepared and forewarned. The longer you spend connected, the more likely you are to encounter interesting people and unexpected situations. You'll get farther by bringing along respect for different perspectives, critical evaluation skills, and common sense. This chapter provides a discussion of proper etiquette as well as information about a variety of Internet hoaxes and scams.

Netiquette

Network etiquette, or netiquette, offers guiding principles that make living and working in the online world a bit friendlier for everyone. There are hundreds of rules of thumb when using e-mail, mailing lists, and newsgroups. Some rules are simply based on courtesy; others are designed to accommodate technological limitations. As the Internet matures, technology and legislation may set more definitive boundaries for all users.

You are probably familiar with the basic etiquette and conventions of e-mail. Experienced online writers always keep their audience in mind and pay attention to grammar, punctuation, spelling, and brevity. All things should be done in moderation, including use of acronyms, emoticons (images indicating feelings and made from punctuation marks), signature files, and even airing your opinions. Generosity and spite are usually paid back in kind.

Privacy, Courtesy, and Copyright

An array of things can happen to an e-mail message once sent. It can be misdirected, misunderstood, or forwarded at will. Because it is nearly impossible to recall a message once sent, heed this warning. Your e-mail may be personal, but it is not private. A message may be saved on backup disks, routed incorrectly, previewed by someone's secretary, or surreptitiously read by a system administrator. Before sending each message, ask yourself, "Would I say this to her face?" and "Would I mind others reading this?"

Some company policies allow monitoring of your actions and your e-mail during work hours. The 1992 case of *Borland v. Symantec* involved charges that a former employee of Borland relayed proprietary information to staff at Symantec. Borland officials searched e-mail files of the former employee and found proof of their suspicions. All questions of ethics and trade secrets aside, the best idea is to keep personal e-mail and opinions separate from your actions on work time and on office equipment. It's important to check with your organization to learn about its policies regarding e-mail privacy and Internet use.

When responding to messages, do so with care. Replies are most effective when they quote only the relevant parts of the original message along with a response. If you intend to forward messages, refrain from editing the original text. Because an e-mail message is generally meant only for the initial recipients, courtesy suggests you request permission before distributing it to a larger audience. Once approved, copy others thoughtfully, especially when blind copying (bcc) messages to other people without disclosing their identities. You should be aware that some consider blind copying a deceptive practice akin to electronic eavesdropping.

You are always welcome to post or forward copies of your own information. Be cautious, though, of posting others' e-mail messages, content from websites, or copies of published articles. To avoid infringing on copyright, request permission from the author or publisher before redistributing proprietary information.

If you ask members of a group for input or ideas about a topic, it's often most effective to have replies sent to you from which you can compile a summary. Summaries sent to lists or posted to newsgroups should be well organized, include only essential content, and give attribution for each reply. Replies that request anonymity should be respected—after all, anonymity is one benefit of the Internet!

Disruptive Behavior

Harassment. Sometimes other people create uncomfortable situations online. One of the most serious is *harassment*. Let's assume we don't need to explain why you shouldn't do this to others. If you receive harassing e-mail, you should first talk to your mail system administrator. He or she will need copies of the messages with the header information to accurately trace the sender, time, and date. (If the header information is not automatically displayed, there will be a toggle command somewhere within your mail program that allows its display.) In some states, online harassment is classified as stalking and may be pursued with the police as well.

Chain Letters. Although e-mail *chain letters* seem fairly innocent and sometimes humorous, they wreak havoc on mail servers. Imagine one letter being sent to five people, each of whom forward it to five others and so on. Within a day, thousands of people can be involved. It is poor etiquette to create frivolous Internet traffic. When you receive a chain letter, it's best to forward a copy to your mail administrator and ask the sender to cease sending them.

Cross-Posting. Another questionable behavior is *cross-posting*. If you'd like to post a message on numerous lists, choose them wisely and limit yourself to three or four. People often subscribe to numerous lists and will become annoyed seeing the same message posted on each. It is polite to note at the top of your message all the places you have posted that message. By sending a message to too many lists or by sending off-topic messages, you can be accused of spamming and have actions taken against you. (Spamming will be addressed in more detail later in this section.)

Mail-Bombing. A similar concern is *mail-bombing*, in which the culprit fills up a user's mailbox with endless messages and stresses the server for all users. This act is not only discourteous and disruptive, but also illegal and traceable. Some list subscribers have unwittingly caused this type of flooding when going on vacation for an extended period. They neglect to sign off a mailing list or set their subscription to "nomail," and their mailbox bounces the overload messages back to the list moderator or the list itself. If you experience this problem, notify your system administrator—though he or she will probably know about it before you do!

Flaming. As in any forum, there will be conflicting ideas of appropriate behavior. *Flames*—attacking or insulting language—often come from heated discussions—one person disagrees with another and the exchange moves beyond rational discourse. Flaming can lead to (at best) lively banter and (at worst) libel. Try not to begin or respond to these volatile exchanges. You may say something rash or unprofessional that you'll regret. Remember, many people subscribe to these lists, and many lists are archived—what you say may come back to haunt you.

If you feel compelled to respond, remain truthful, offer proof, state that it is your opinion, and combat the ideas, not the individual. It's also best to keep your exchanges private rather than continue on the list or in the newsgroup. Many readers won't care who started the fight, just that you are wasting their time.

If you have flamed and want to repent, a short message of apology is usually accepted. If you receive a message that is blatantly offensive, you can talk to the administrator or moderator of that forum or you can choose to ignore it. Many mail programs have filters that allow you to block out messages from specific addresses or with certain words in the subject line. If the flames are too hot for you, perhaps you should simply unsubscribe for awhile.

Friendly Reminders

Many different mail programs are on the market. Some offer special features, such as filtering, text formatting, multiple signature files, customizable address books, graphics displayed in text, and rich HTML coding. Some of these features simply make your life easier, while others require the receiving mail program to be able to interpret the same information. Before you use these features, consider whether the people you are e-mailing will have software that can accommodate them. When in doubt, use more traditional techniques to convey the information (such as emphasizing points with an asterisk) or let the recipient know that you can resend the information in a different format.

Once you become a seasoned subscriber, remember the mysteries e-mail, mailing lists, and newsgroups hold for new users. If someone makes a naive mistake, a simple message sent to that person's e-mail address will probably be most productive for both of you in the long run.

Hoaxes

Hoaxes have plagued the Internet for so long that they are often referred to as the "urban legends" of the online world. They are effective because they are difficult to disprove, emulate valid warnings, use technical-sounding language, and refer to credible sources. Although some hoaxes may not be intended to cause harm, investigation and follow-up at each of thousands of sites cost billions of dollars as well as a huge loss of productivity. Listed here are some well-known hoaxes and tips for handling them.

You may have received e-mail about the Good Times Virus, Irina Virus, Deeyenda Virus, or PKZ300. Each of these viruses has its own unique history. For example, information about the Irina Virus was finally traced to a publishing company that was promoting a book by the same name. The firm's ill-conceived promotion went awry, and company managers have since apologized for the incident.

In some cases, the original incident was real but has long been over. One famous e-mail, often titled "A Dying Boy's Last Wish," is about a young boy who has a brain tumor and a short time to live. He wants to get into the *Guinness Book of World Records* for receiving the highest number of get-well cards. Such a boy did exist. He did make the record, did have surgery, did recover, and continues to receive mail from people all over the world. Because most messages do not include a specific expiration date, each new user will probably encounter such legends at some point.

Each April 1 spawns many jokes, including some that turn into widespread hoaxes. For example, *PC Computing* published an article about a bill sponsored by Senators Leahy and Kennedy to eliminate intoxication on the information superhighway. Apparently, hundreds of people wrote their senators, furious that Congress was spending time on this issue; many were embarrassed to learn this was an April Fools' joke.

Another example is based on an *InfoWorld* article that discussed the "Metavirus AF/91." The Associated Press and *Nightline* picked up the story, and the virus itself was later attributed to an attack on Iraqi computers during the Persian Gulf War. None of this was possible, since the virus was just a joke. Although there is always potential for misinformation and exaggerations, be particularly skeptical on April Fools' Day.

Without too much trouble, a person can send mail messages that appear to be from another person. Stories abound of famous people appearing in newsgroups, such as Stephen Spielberg posting messages to *rec.art.movies*, or Bill Gates asking for favors in exchange for money or free software. All incidents of *spoofing* are illegal acts of misrepresentation. Before you respond to the hype, think, "How likely would it be for this person to post that message?"

There are many more hoaxes—Gerber supposedly offering $500 savings bonds to all babies born during certain years to repent for false advertising; Nike exchanging your old sneakers for new ones at no charge; organ thieves preying on unsuspecting travelers and performing operations in hotel bathrooms; and the list goes on.

If you receive a questionable e-mail, do not forward the message! You may have good intentions but would only be perpetuating the rumor. If you wish to pursue the issue, try contacting any individuals or companies mentioned in the message. You might also look at one of the archives about urban legends or viruses listed at the end of the chapter to see if the issue has already been documented. If you receive a message about viruses, always send it to your system administrator for verification and action.

Fraud and Scams

Internet fraud is an even more serious and sinister assault on Internet users' trust. Most schemes are based on timeless tactics that work in any community with trusting people. With new users logging onto the Internet every day, there is an endless supply of naive consumers; many of them believe all businesses on the Internet are legitimate. Unfortunately, this is not true.

Would you believe the number of consumer Internet fraud complaints to the National Fraud Information Center has increased 600 percent since 1997 (see *http://www.fraud.org./internet/9923stat.htm*)? Or that the Federal Trade Commission receives one hundred to two hundred online fraud complaints each month? (See *http://www.ftc.gov/os/1998/9806/test.623htm.*) Listed here are a few examples of the most prevalent Internet scams, tips to identify a scam, and suggested actions to take when you encounter one.

Pyramid Schemes. Pyramid schemes (also known as multilevel marketing or matrix scams) require each member to invest money and recruit new members. Money from new members is funneled to older members. Eventually the pyramid collapses, and often only the initial investors make money. These schemes are illegal and are pursued by the Federal Trade Commission (FTC). The most famous example to date is the Fortuna Alliance, which purportedly ensnared seven million consumers. The company was forced to shut down but reemerged as the Fortuna Alliance II offshore where it is more difficult to prosecute. Question any offers that have a limited time, require you to pay up front, use "special methods" that are not disclosed, and allow you to get in on a "ground floor opportunity." Check references, verify data, and be critical of testimonials.

Password Scams. Password scams can take many forms that leave a scam artist with your password and access to all other accounts on your server. In one scam, someone impersonates an employee of your computer services department or a billing service. Usually, this person claims to need your password for a short time for a testing procedure. Another scam involves the creation of a false screen where you are prompted to type your log-in and password. Instead of your identification information being sent to your server, it goes directly to the hacker's computer.

All sorts of illegal computer activities revolve around accessing people's passwords. Unfortunately, most passwords that are easy for you to remember will also be considered poor security choices. Choose passwords that are not names of friends, pets, or relatives. Be sure they are not the same as your log-in or words from the dictionary. It is best to mix cases and choose both letters and numbers. Never share this password with anyone. Any system administrator who needs to run a test will not need your account to do so.

Web Auctions. Web auctions create an environment where people bid for merchandise. The highest bidder is notified by the auction house and given the seller's contact information. The bidder is asked to send money and often never receives the goods. Most people pay with cash or money orders that are untraceable. Before finalizing any business transactions, verify the seller's identity. Ask questions about the refund policy, and get the offer in writing. If you decide to purchase an item, use a credit card or pay COD, and document your transactions.

Prizes and Offers. All sorts of prizes and offers are available online. In most cases, these companies tell you that you have been randomly selected as a winner and ask for your contact information and credit card number for verification and shipping charges. Some offer illegal services, such as tax evasion, postage fraud, and credit repair scams. Occasionally, they try to sell you information that is available free, such as phone numbers, credit information, government information, recipes, and advice. Question any unsolicited offers. Never give out personal information, such as your full name, address, credit card number, social security number, or financial information.

Misrepresentation. As mentioned in the discussion of hoaxes, it is possible for people to misrepresent themselves on the Internet. People can disguise their identities through spoofing, forged headers, or anonymous mail sites. Some people use their real identity but refrain from identifying themselves as a representative of a particular company. Some people are simply experimenting with alternate identities, while others have more unsavory motives. If you are communicating with a stranger, use healthy skepticism. Beware of e-mail messages that are written as if the sender is an acquaintance of yours, although you cannot recall who it is. In general, be as cautious of predators seeking personal information about you online as you would be in real life.

Spamming. Also prevalent on the Internet is electronic junk mail known as spam (after a Monty Python comedy sketch). The most infamous and egregious example of spamming was perpetrated by Canter and Siegel, two immigration lawyers who posted ads for their services in Phoenix to 6,000 mailing lists. Thousands of people were enraged and retaliated. Although Canter and Siegel were dropped by their service provider, they weren't apologetic, and neither are many spammers who have followed in their footsteps. Most reputable companies realize that spam violates business etiquette and refrain from wasting the resources of the recipients.

If you receive spam, you can simply delete the file. This will save you time but does little to discourage people from spamming in the future. You can attempt to reply to the message, although often the mailbox is full, or the address has been spoofed. Many spammers utilize the free trial accounts offered by large service providers and are, therefore, difficult to trace and shut down permanently. You may direct a complaint to the postmaster of the spammer's site or directly to the FTC by copying the spam message with all the header information. Although spamming is annoying and wasteful, the FTC has not decided to completely ban it yet, because of free speech claims.

The list of scams is too numerous to describe comprehensively. Others include work-at-home opportunities, health and diet scams, investment opportunities, guaranteed loans, get-rich-quick promises, and Trojan horses. Many scammers use harvesting programs that obtain a list of e-mail addresses from chat rooms, Web surveys, and membership lists.

One common characteristic is that all these scams rely on your naiveté. Be cautious of giving too much information to any site. Similarly, don't allow the look of a site to convince you of the company's professionalism;

sites can be created quickly by contractors and tell you nothing of the organization's intent. If you believe you have encountered a scam, contact the Internet Fraud Watch program and your state's attorney general. Both groups have histories of protecting consumers and prosecuting offenders.

Additional Resources

The following sites offer further information about these topics:

*Bandits on the Information Super-
highway*
*http://www.blazemonger.com/
bandits/*

Better Business Bureau
http://www.bbb.org

Computer Incident Advisory
Capability
http://ciac.llnl.gov/

Computer Professionals for Social
Responsibility
http://www.cpsr.org/

Computer Virus Myths
http://www.kumite.com/myths

Electronic Frontier Foundation
http://www.eff.org

Federal Trade Commission
http://www.ftc.gov

National Fraud Information
Center/Internet Fraud Watch
http://www.fraud.org

Netiquette Guidelines
*http://www.cis.ohio-state.edu/
htbin/rfc/rfc1855.html*

Red Rock Eater News
*http://dlis.gseis.ucla.edu/people/
pagre/rre.html*

Scambusters
http://www.scambusters.com

Urban Legends Archive
http://www.urbanlegends.com

Newsgroups

alt.comp.virus
alt.current-events.net-abuse.*
alt.folklore.urban.*
news.admin.net-abuse.*
news.announce.newusers

The New Library Demands a Closer Look at Ergonomics

Cindy K. Schofield-Bodt

Cindy K. Schofield-Bodt (*Schofield@scsu.ctstateu.edu*) is the head of cataloging at Southern Connecticut State University's Hilton C. Buley Library and an adjunct professor in Southern's library science program. She chairs the Resources and Technical Services Section of the Connecticut Library Association and has organized ergonomic workshops and awareness events.

Why Consider Ergonomics?

Finally, the computers have arrived—clear off the tables and start plugging things in! Such a scene has been repeated at libraries and research centers throughout the country and screams for the application of ergonomic theory to library work flow. Though resources will be at their fingertips, library staff and patrons are destined to experience discomfort and pain—often after their work on the keyboard is over—without the correct furniture, equipment, and training.

As more tasks are becoming automated and people spend increasing work and leisure hours in front of the computer, the field of office ergonomics has exploded. Coincidence? Probably not. Pain begets solutions, and the pain of repetitive strain injury (RSI) can be debilitating. Most ergonomic solutions offer affordable and effective ways to ensure that seeking information on a computer does not become hazardous to one's health.

Who could have predicted that library staff and patrons would suddenly find themselves deep in the rough and tumble world of work-related injuries?

Beginning in the 1980s, the nature of library work and research has undergone a steady metamorphosis from the large-muscle activities of stamping, reaching, filing, and thumbing through indexes and references to the quick, small, repetitive motions of keyboard tasks.

Because RSI is far easier to prevent than to cure, library personnel who use the computer should be aware of the hazards of repeated physical movements. Although carpal tunnel syndrome is probably the best-known RSI injury, it is only one of many injuries related to keyboard typing. The chance of injury to tendons, nerves, muscles, and other soft body tissues is great when technique or body position places undue stress on the hands, wrists, arms, shoulders, or neck.

The following sections are predominantly concerned with preventing RSI and increasing the general comfort of the work environment. Because keyboard-related injuries are difficult to reverse, you should run, not walk, to the doctor if any of the following symptoms occur: tingling or numbness in the hands and fingers; loss of strength in hands and arms; lack of coordination or control of fine movements; or sleep-disrupting, off-task pain. Keyboard users should also be concerned about general discomfort or soreness of the wrists, fingers, forearms, and elbows.

The Right Tools for the Job

The welder on a work site doesn't light the torch until all the proper equipment is in place—face mask, protective gloves, heavy boots, and a fireproof suit. Some of the equipment is OSHA-mandated; some of it is common sense. Workers at the keyboard do not yet have the strength of legislation to ensure their protection, but the growing body of knowledge and experience in the area of ergonomics should encourage many "commonsense" decisions about how to create a safe working environment.

Ergonomics ensures that a person can accomplish a task in the way that is least stressful to the body. It is important to note that individual comfort preferences can deviate from accepted ergonomic trends. Generally, individual comfort will fall within the ranges described here. It is advisable to try the settings suggested and then, with knowledge of the issues, reject what isn't comfortable.

The great temptation in libraries is to clear off the reading tables near the old card catalog in the public area, or move the clutter off the worktables and desks in the technical service department, and plunk down the new computers in the spot that's closest to an outlet. Unfortunately, this will only work for a short while.

Eventually, the convenience of quick setup will take its toll. In the early 1990s when 24 library staff members at Texas A&M University began complaining of the pain and discomfort of carpal tunnel syndrome, the library administration agreed to invest in correct chairs, adjustable computer desks, and ergonomic computer keyboards. The results of a case study conducted at the university clearly indicate that many health problems can be alleviated with ergonomically correct furniture and equipment.

Computer work generally occurs at an area consisting of a desk and a chair, which have to work as a unit to form a safe workstation. The keyword throughout any discussion on workstations is *adjustable*. This is especially true in situations where the workstation is going to be used by more than one person—whether in public or restricted areas of the library.

The Chair—Accommodating Comfort

The widely accepted ideal body position when seated is to have knees bent at a 90-degree angle, the back straight, elbows bent at a 90-degree angle, and wrists straight. Current research indicates that while the 90-degree rules are best for most people, it is possible for other body positions to be healthy and comfortable. The proper adjustable workstation will accommodate traditional as well as newer ideas.

Look for chairs with height adjustments that position the seat between sixteen and twenty-one inches from the floor. Although the traditional admonition is to sit with the feet flat on the floor and knees bent at a 90-degree angle, some people prefer to have their legs stretched out in front of them. The chair should accommodate the body height no matter how the legs are positioned. A footrest placed under the desk will be comfortable for some users, and an adjustable backrest with lumbar support will ease back strain and "force" good posture.

It is essential to be able to change positions throughout the day. One new idea is that a chair that allows one to lean backward will ease pressure on the intervertebral discs and allow the chair's backrest to take weight off the lower back. A word of caution about reclining, however—leaning the torso backward can force the head forward and put strain on neck muscles. Because the head is relatively heavy, it is important to keep it balanced between the shoulders at the top of a straight spine.

Chair armrests should be positioned so that they are actually below the elbow when a worker is sitting in keyboarding position and should only be used when taking a break from working at the computer. Pressure on the elbow over an extended period of time can inflame the ulnar nerve, causing pain and discomfort at the elbow and outer fingers of the hand.

Ergonomic chairs are available in a variety of styles and prices from office and library supply houses. Shoppers should consider how much use the chair will get—especially the adjustable mechanics. An investment in quality is always worthwhile when it comes to comfort and safety.

The Desktop: A Home for Monitor, Keyboard, and Mouse

The chair's partner at a workstation is the computer table or desk. Plan space for the monitor, keyboard, and mouse. The monitor can stand either on the desktop or on an adjustable-height shelf. Libraries that have old editions of LCSH have free monitor height adjusters readily available. More often than not, though, the monitor is too high and needs to be lowered rather than raised. The practice common in the past of putting the monitor on top of the desktop CPU case will likely make it too high.

A better solution is to put the CPU case on a shelf or in a rack under the desk. In most instances, the monitor is most comfortably viewed when set on the surface of the desktop. The top of the monitor should be at eye level or slightly below to avoid strain on the neck from looking up or down. The viewing angle can be changed easily by shifting the monitor on its base.

The recommended distance between the monitor and the eyes ranges from fourteen to twenty-four inches. New research indicates that monitors should be as far away as possible (while still readable) because longer viewing distances relax the eyes. In addition, although the physiological effects of electromagnetic (EM) exposure are not completely understood, it is known that EM radiation declines as the distance from the monitor increases.

Given the positioning goals of elbows and wrists, an adjustable surface on which to rest the keyboard is ideal. Many tables come equipped with a slide-out tray for the keyboard; trays can also be purchased and attached to tables. These trays can be raised or lowered and should allow the user to be at a reasonable distance from the monitor. The jury is still out on the effectiveness of split keyboards, though a recent Cornell University (CU) study concluded that the Floating Arms Keyboard, a split keyboard that mounts onto the arms of a chair, can help reduce RSI disorders. (Several reports from this study can be located through the CU ergonomics website at *http://ergo.human.cornell.edu.*)

Various keyboard designs are available through library and office supply companies. It is important to note that keyboard preferences tend to be very personal, and the keyboard preferred by one worker may be uncomfortable to another. A workstation that is being used by many different people throughout the day is best outfitted with a standard keyboard. One change from the normal configuration that should be comfortable to all users is to slant the keyboard away from the user, slightly lifting the wrists of the typist. The adjustable legs at the back of most keyboards lower the front of the keyboard, forcing the hands to bend up from the wrist when typing.

The mouse is being used more extensively in library work as applications become tailor-made to the current generation of computers. When using the mouse exclusively, it should be positioned in the center of the work area with the keyboard moved or stored. If the mouse is used along with the keyboard it should be positioned close to the side of the keyboard so the user does not have to reach for it. By focusing on keeping the elbow close to the body and the forearm and hand in a straight line, the user will be encouraged to position the mouse in a way that puts the least amount of strain on the arm and associated neck and shoulder muscles.

Wrist Rests and Keyboard Technique

Found under "wrist support" in catalogs and indexes, a wrist rest, used with the keyboard and mouse, is a resting place for the heel of the hand and alleviates pressure on the wrists and forearm. Raising the heel of the hand to form a straight line between the elbow and the fingertips leaves less chance for pinching nerves and straining muscles.

While actually typing, it is best not to rest the hands on anything. The best technique is to move the arms freely, constantly repositioning the hands over the keys. Use the wrist support to rest arms while not typing, but work to maintain a straight line from elbows to fingertips without it. New products in wrist care include gel-filled wrist rests that conform to the contours of each individual's wrist, and computer gloves that, when worn at the keyboard, absorb and divert pressure on the wrist so the median nerve is not compressed.

Lighting and Other Vision Issues

Everyone loves an office with a window, but the sunshine we crave will invariably cause eye stress and strain. Computer-related eyestrain (CRES) is another ergonomic problem that can be controlled by manipulating the work environment. Computer eyestrain can result from the position of the monitor, the brightness and contrast of the screen image, the size and color of the screen image, the quality of the image, and the surrounding room illumination.

Distance and screen elements should all be adjusted to maximum comfort. Users should be encouraged to use the adjustments that are available on most computer monitors, including focus, with the understanding that the next user may change those settings for his or her own maximum comfort.

Lighting is a common problem and is especially exacerbated when no natural light is available. Lighting should be indirect, ideally from above. Eyestrain from either reflection or backlight will occur if a computer screen is parallel to a window. Positioning a computer screen perpendicular to the window will greatly reduce glare. Older monitors are more likely to have glare problems that can be reduced with glare reduction shields that cover the screen. These are readily available from computer or library supply vendors.

Beyond Furniture

Ultimately, some of the responsibility for avoiding the painful injuries of RSI rests with the computer user. Simple hand exercises done throughout the workday are an excellent way to stay healthy. In addition to regular fifteen-minute breaks away from the workstation, workers should get in the habit of giving their hands and wrists short, thirty-second "breaks" every ten or fifteen minutes. The following simple hand exercises will help relieve stress and encourage good blood flow to the hand:

1. Back away from the keyboard and let your hands fall to your sides. Gently shake your hands as if you have just washed them and then found yourself without a towel. (Stop when you think they are dry!)
2. Hold one hand in front of your body with the fingers extending upward and palm out. With your other hand, gently pull on each finger, forcing the thumb to a right angle with the forefinger and bring-

ing the other fingers individually back toward the top of the wrist. Repeat stretching exercise with the other hand.

3. With palms turned up, gently squeeze a soft foam ball ten or fifteen times. Keep the ball nearby and reach for it several times a day.

4. Stretch your fingers by extending them as long as possible and spreading them as wide as possible. Relax. Repeat the stretch several times.

5. Finish by massaging the elbows, arms, hands, and fingers briskly and gently. Applying lotion to your hands will accomplish the motion of massage and force a short break from the keyboard until the lotion is absorbed into the skin.

In addition to periodically increasing blood circulation through exercise, it is important to continuously move and change positions. A list of exercises taped next to the computer will remind you to do them throughout the day. Intentionally interrupt keyboard work to stretch and wiggle, and make it a habit to move hands and arms while on the telephone, at the copy machine, and even while daydreaming.

Stretching and massaging need not be confined to arms and fingers. It is also a healthy habit to massage the neck between the base of the skull and the shoulders and to stretch by moving first to one side, then the other, then forward—ear to shoulder, chin to chest.

Gimmicks and associations can help make stretching into a routine. Some people make a habit of standing up before making a telephone call, or using time on the phone to push away from the desk and do foot exercises or head rolls. A goal of two sets of exercises before lunch and another two before going home is easily attainable and very beneficial.

Software and Websites

It seems appropriate that one tool for getting a handle on ergonomics is computer software that reminds and cajoles the user to be aware of his or her ergonomic performance and to make corrections as necessary. Many ergonomic programs can be downloaded from Internet sites for a trial period—they simply "uninstall" from the computer if the password is not purchased. The following is only a small sample of what is available.

1. ErgoMinder (*http://www.netspace.net.au/~thetwo/ergo.htm*) calls itself "an entertaining exercise reminder." This program can be as basic as a background timer reminding you to take stretch breaks at regular intervals, or as advanced as a personal coach with instructions on setting up a comfortable workstation and doing the exercises that prevent the pain of RSI.

2. ErgoSentry (*http://www.magnitude.com/*) and The Ergonomic Timer (*http://www.tropsoft.com/ergtimer/main.htm*) are also coaching-type software products that remind users of the need to take regular breaks by monitoring the use of the mouse and keyboard. These

programs offer stretching tips and inform the user of dangerous repetitive movements when they are detected.

3. ErgoStar (*http://www.ergostar.com/*) ergonomic software, according to its website, is designed to "prevent problems by educating computer users about the hazards associated with using an improperly adjusted computer work area." It includes instructions on how to adjust a computer workstation to fit individual needs.

4. The ErgoKit (*http://www.preventblindness.org/resources/catalog/cadults.html*) is an evaluative tool that guides the user through a set of questions and then generates a report analyzing the "ergonomics" of the workstation in question. Specific products are suggested to remedy shortcomings with emphasis on affordable improvements.

Many consulting firms specializing in occupational health and safety and workplace design have developed their own software packages that feature evaluation and instruction in ergonomic issues. Features include video clips of proper exercises, checklists for work site conformity, and timing devices to encourage healthy work habits.

For some users, simple screensavers are preferable to the comprehensive software packages on the market. These are available from many sources, especially office supply vendors, and serve as reminders to workers to take breaks, do exercises, and position their bodies correctly.

In addition to software to install on individual computers and networks, a plethora of information is available on the Internet to guide library workers and administrators in good ergonomic workplace design:

1. *ErgoLib* for safer library computing (*http://library.ucr.edu/ ergolib/*) is a great starting point for resources on the topic and includes links to related sites and support groups, an annotated reading list, and "cheap tips," as well as instructions and diagrams on equipment and exercises.

2. The General Libraries Ergonomics Task Force at the University of Texas at Austin (*http://www.lib.utexas.edu/Pubs/etf/*) maintains another excellent library site. The website was established as a staff resource and has detailed information on workstation design and use. In addition, there is an annotated list of other online resources on related topics and a book list for off-line reading about online stress.

3. The Ergonomic Resources Home Page (*http://www.geocities.com/CapeCanaveral/1129*) is a general ergonomics website with even more helpful information and links. The Conventional Ergonomics vs. Current Ergonomics website (*http://www.ur-net.com/office-ergo/conventi. htm*) is not concerned exclusively with library ergonomics, but presents an interesting summary of some of the current research in office ergonomics, comparing conventional wisdom with new research.

Discussion lists on ergonomics are another source of online information. Addresses for some of these are noted in the previously mentioned websites. Questions that are posted to these lists are answered by both experts and laypeople. One recent discussion concerned the merits of a roller-ball mouse substitute for disabled or younger computer users.

Common Sense and the Comfort Police

There are probably no "comfort police" in your library enforcing the ergonomic rules of the road. In a commercial environment, the profit incentive pushes managers to keep workers healthy, making the big bad world of business a potentially safer place to work than publicly funded libraries.

Profit or not, library managers do have a responsibility to provide workers and patrons with more than just a computer on which to do their work. The associated ergonomic tools and techniques must be there to ensure that as the nature of library work and research changes, people are able to operate in this new environment without risk of injury.

Ergonomic Checklist for Safe Library Computing

Chair

Safe:	Adjustable height; adjustable lumbar support; castors or wheels; armrest lower than elbows
Dangerous:	Fixed height; nonadjustable features
Correct Body Position:	Knees at 90 degrees; elbows at 90 degrees; wrists straight

Monitor

Safe:	More than fourteen inches from eyes; top of screen level with eyes or lower; adjustable brightness, contrast, color
Dangerous:	Screen above eye level; nonadjustable base
Correct Body Position:	Head level, centered over spine

Keyboard/Mouse

Safe:	Set at level of forearms when elbows at 90 degrees; slanted away from user
Dangerous:	Hands reaching up or down to use; wrists breaking through a level plane
Correct Body Position:	Wrists straight; arms move to propel hands around keyboard

Desk

Safe: Surface large enough for monitor and keyboard; adjustable surfaces; eye-level document holder

Dangerous: Limited surface area

Correct Body Position: No reaching, elbows close to body

Lighting

Safe: Natural, overhead electronic ballast fluorescent, incandescent lighting; monitor with high flicker rate

Dangerous: Low flicker rate of light or monitor; direct or backlight

Correct Body Position: Blink eyes twelve times per minute; wear corrective glasses if necessary

2
A Network of Networks of Networks—Technical Underpinnings

The Basics of LAN Technology

Caroline Higgins

Caroline Higgins (*higginsc@dt.uh.edu*) is automation librarian at the University of Houston-Downtown Library. Caroline has been providing support to automated library services for five years and has been trained as a Microsoft Windows NT administrator. She is currently occupied with issues regarding remote access and the cataloging of scholarly electronic resources.

Don't Skip This Chapter, Even If You Really Want To!

The inevitable use of local area networks and other network technologies in the library setting requires that all librarians, not just systems personnel, have a basic understanding of network operations. Without an understanding of networks and how they operate, librarians and other staff members will not be able to effectively communicate equipment problems and network difficulties to technical support staff, nor will they be able to define future equipment needs. With a sound grasp of network technologies and emerging electronic information products, librarians will continue to be perceived as a necessary and worthwhile resource for public and academic communities. Savvy librarians can help to ensure that libraries maintain a foothold in the future budget appropriations of school boards, city councils, and administrators.

What Is a LAN?

A local area network (LAN) is the physical connection of individual computers that allows shared resources within a limited (local) area. A LAN may exist as a multistation computer lab; a small reference area connected to a laser printer and a CD-ROM tower; or an entire library full of connected computers, servers, and printers.

Sometimes separate LANs coexist, or a LAN can even reside within another LAN. If you're in an academic library, perhaps your library LAN is a subset of the campus LAN; perhaps your circulation department uses the library LAN to circulate books and a separate administrative LAN to check student enrollment. LANs allow the sharing of a multitude of valuable resources and can even improve communication among coworkers and library departments.[1]

Information Resources Computers on a LAN Can Share

Computers on a LAN can share spreadsheets, documents, and program files, as well as printers and other peripheral hardware. Many libraries already make use of LANs in circulation, technical services, and interlibrary-loan departments. Reference librarians use LANs and networked information resources in the reference area to provide access to local CD-ROM products and proprietary databases.

Equipment That Can Be Attached to a LAN

Personal computers, Macintoshes, printers, file servers, print servers, scanners, CD-ROM towers, and more can all be connected to a LAN. When a computer has been attached to a LAN, it may still act as an individual computer, but it may also act as a network workstation, or client. (In peer-to-peer networks, it may even act as a server).

As a *network client*, the computer may share information and resources with other equipment, or devices, on the network. To access the network, the workstation client must have a network adapter and be connected with proper network cabling. To communicate with the rest of the network, the client will need to have the appropriate client software installed to match the network operating system software.

Most network operating systems require authentication and passwords to log on and access shared documents and programs. The network administrator uses network operating system utilities to control shared resources so that only authorized users will have access.

A *file server* is a network storage device with plenty of memory, or storage space. The file server can be compared to a centralized file room in a large corporation in which all the documents are kept, and users from all areas of the corporation may access the files by submitting a request.

In the case of a LAN, the user makes the request for documents (or files, or programs) at his or her workstation, then the file server retrieves the information from its own storage area and returns it to the requester. Unlike the corporate file room scenario, data housed on a LAN file server are stored in digital format and may easily be duplicated to provide simultaneous access to files for multiple users.

A *print server* allows network users to share one or more printers while it monitors the status of the printers and print jobs. A wide-carriage dot matrix printer, a label printer, and a laser printer may all coexist on the same network and be shared by all authorized workstations and users. Network users may access a printer if the printer is attached to a workstation and is installed on the network. A printer with a network interface card does not need a workstation and may be connected directly to the network with cables and the network card.

Hubs are connector devices used to organize network cables and wiring. Passive hubs simply organize and connect wires, while active hubs contain circuitry that can check for transmission errors and amplify transmission signals.

How Are Computers on a LAN Connected to Each Other?

All network hardware must have a network adapter, or network interface card (NIC), attached externally or plugged into an available internal slot. The NIC is a circuit board that communicates with hardware and software on the device and provides the ports for cables to connect the device to the network.

Several types of cables are commonly used to connect devices on a network, depending on the computing environment. Important factors to consider when choosing cabling include the maximum distance over which a given type of cable can effectively transmit data; capital outlay and maintenance costs; susceptibility to interference; and information capacity. Some general examples of cable types and their limitations are given in figure 1.

Computers and Peripherals—Physical and Logical Placement

The cables that connect network equipment are laid out in a particular arrangement, or topology. Star, bus, and ring are three of the most widely used network topologies today (see figure 2). Each is designed to suit a variety of networking needs.

FIGURE 1   Networking Cables and Their Features

Type	Transmission Distances	Cost	Susceptability to Interference	Transmission Speeds
UTP Unshielded Twisted Pair	feet/meters	low	high	100 Mbps
STP Shielded Twisted Pair	feet/meters	low	medium-high	10 Mbps
Coaxial	feet/meters	medium	low	500 Mbps
Fiber Optic	miles/kilometers	high	immune	100 Mbps–2 Gbps
Wireless	miles/kilometers	very high	high	2–3 Mbps

FIGURE 2   Commonly Used Network Topologies

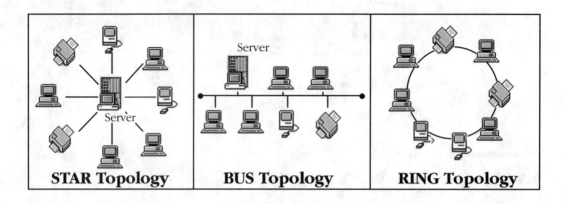

In a *star topology*, all workstations on the network are connected directly to a hub or a server, and all transmitted information passes through the central hub or server. The layout of a star LAN simplifies troubleshooting because failure of a single device, or node, will not disable the network. LANs with a star topology usually have a dedicated server and multiple workstations and are often used in client/server networks. Unlike peer-to-peer networks, a client/server LAN with a dedicated server can handle large files, connect to other LANs, and even replace mainframes in a large computing environment.

In a *bus topology*, all network equipment is connected along a single cable. As information passes down the cable, each network device checks the destination address of the information, or packet, to discern whether the workstation, printer, or other device is the intended recipient.

In a *ring topology*, all equipment is connected to a cable that forms a logical circle, rather like bus topology with the two ends of the cable brought together. Ring topologies are often used in peer-to-peer networks because peer-to-peer does not require a dedicated server, and any workstation on a peer-to-peer network may act as the server (if configured to do so). Windows for Workgroups and LANtastic are common peer-to-peer network operating systems.

How Do Computers Communicate with Each Other If They Don't Speak the Same Language?

As you probably already know, PCs and Macintoshes do not speak the same language. Similarly, Unix servers, Windows NT servers, and Novell servers do not speak the same language. Major manufacturers of computer equipment have had to agree on a standard way, or protocol, to send and receive data on their equipment. With the help of vendors and manufacturers of networking products, the International Organization for Standardization (ISO) has been able to create the Open System Interconnection (OSI) model for network construction.

Imagine the OSI model as a recipe for creating networks that will successfully transmit data internally and successfully communicate with other outside networks. The OSI model defines the following seven ingredients, or layers, that must appear in the recipe for anyone wanting to "bake a network cake":

Layer 7:   The Application Layer provides the user interface to the network. E-mail programs, File Transfer Protocol (FTP) programs, and Internet browsers are all members of the Layer 7 category.

Layer 6:   The Presentation Layer encodes and translates data so that the sending and receiving machines will understand each other.

Layer 5:   The Session Layer manages communication channels between computers and works with programs on each computer to help them communicate.

Layer 4:   The Transport Layer monitors the data that have been sent and checks to make sure that the data arrived.

Layer 3:   The Network Layer places data into packets and translates Internal Protocol (IP) addresses into physical addresses.

Layer 2:   The Data Link Layer performs packet switching. It sends the data packaged by the Network Layer.

Layer 1:   The Physical Layer contains electrical connections, hardware, and cabling, and provides the mechanical interface to the network.

At Layer 2, the access method, or data link protocol, regulates the movement of data across the network. Token Ring, ARCnet, and Ethernet are three of the most common access methods used today. Each method incorporates a variety of topologies and signaling for the transmission of data.

Token Ring gets its name from the way in which it controls data flow. A station must possess a token to transmit data, much like a runner in a relay race must possess the baton. Older versions of Token Ring transferred data at a rate of 4 to 16 Mbps, but vendors of second-generation Token Ring networks claim transfer rates of over 100 Mbps.[2]

ARCnet (Attached Resource Computer Network) transfers at a rate of 2.5 to 20 Mbps and controls data flow by allowing computers to transmit in turn.

Ethernet networks use "Carrier Sense Multiple Access with Collision Detection" (CSMA/CD) to control the movement of data across the network and to decide which station gets to transmit at a given time. Ethernet has traditionally had a transfer rate of 10 to 100 Mbps, but gigabit Ethernet, an emerging technology, can transmit up to 1,000 Mbps.[3]

FDDI (Fiber Distributed Data Interface) is a high-speed data link protocol that transmits at a speed of 100 Mbps on fiber optic networks.

NetBEUI (NetBIOS Extended User Interface) allows fast transmission of data and is relatively easy to administer. It establishes sessions among nodes on the network and handles flow control of messages. It has good error-checking resources and is an excellent choice for small networks that do not require communication with any other networks.

TCP/IP (Transmission Control Protocol/Internet Protocol) at Layer 3, the Network Layer, is more difficult to set up than NetBEUI, but it works well with computers of all types. It controls data flow by setting up a session between sender and receiver to control the delivery of transmitted data. The ability to allow centralized control over a network makes TCP/IP an excellent choice for client/server networks.

IPX/SPX (Internetwork Packet Exchange/Sequenced Packet Exchange) regulates the routing of information in Novell NetWare operating systems. It checks for transmission errors and can force the retransmission of data when necessary.

AppleTalk is a peer-to-peer network protocol that provides file transfer capability, printer access, and a data transmission protocol for Apple computer networks.

Software to Control a LAN

Just as a desktop computer or Macintosh requires an operating system, so does a LAN. The operating system on a LAN is known as the Network Operating System (NOS) and is installed on all network servers and workstations. The NOS controls all network components so that they may act as a single unit. The LAN administrator can use NOS administrative applications to control user accounts, add and remove hardware, troubleshoot network problems, and communicate with other networks.

The network server uses part of the NOS to store and access large amounts of data held in files, programs, databases, and so on. The server uses another part of the NOS to adhere to one of the several different types of protocols that enable communication among network devices. The NOS uses network protocols to regulate routing of information and provide error checking on the network and uses transfer protocols to control the actual delivery of the information.

Three of the most commonly used network operating systems are Microsoft Windows NT, Microsoft Windows for Workgroups, and Novell NetWare. Windows NT Server is a client/server LAN operating system that organizes network users and resources into "domains." Group and user profiles determine the rights of users on the network. Windows NT allows administrative control of directory and file rights and organizes printing services through print queues.

Windows for Workgroups is similar to regular Microsoft Windows (95 or 98) but includes peer-to-peer network functionality. It enables workstations to share files, printers, and e-mail.

Novell NetWare uses the proprietary network protocol IPX/SPX. NetWare services include the ability to control user and group rights to directories and files. It also supports DOS, OS/2, Macintosh, and Unix.

What Will Networking Be Like in the Future?

Wireless LANs will provide the resource sharing of computers, printers, fax, e-mail, and so on over a limited physical area with the use of radio waves or infrared light. Users will be able to connect to the network wherever they are, as long as they are within range. Wireless radio or infrared receivers/transmitters must be installed on all remote network devices and on the wired portion of the network. Transmission of data on wireless networks is still a relatively slow 2 to 3 Mbps, but the potential transmission speeds of future wired networks is astonishing. (See the chapter titled "Wireless and Ubiquitous Computing" on page 233 in this book.)

The National Science Foundation and MCI WorldCom have come together on a project to provide a medium for very high speed data transmission called the *Backbone Network Service (vBNS)*. The vBNS connects five supercomputing centers, and, as part of the Internet2 project, connects 150 universities at speeds of at least 155 Mbps or higher![4] (See the chapter titled "The Basics of a Nationwide Network for the Internet" on page 42 in this book.)

Libraries may expect to reap tremendous benefits from the *Internet2* project. (See the chapter titled "Internet2 and the Next Generation Internet Initiative" later in this book.) The technology being developed will enhance multimedia applications, distance learning, telemedicine, and much more. CNN's Ann Kellan recently reported, "Abilene, one of the many networks that will make up Internet2, is up and running, connecting 150 universities and research centers with high-speed fiber optic cable. It is 45,000 times as fast as the average modem, which means it could transmit the entire Library of Congress in just twenty seconds."[5] In that case, beam me up, Scotty!

Online Resources

Brundin, Michael. *Local Area Networks in Libraries: A Librarian's Guide to LAN Technology.* (1998). *http://www.ualberta.ca/~mbrundin/lans.*

Meyer, Chris. *Networking Essentials Cram Session.* (1997). *http://www.meyercs.com/network_study.html.*

Notes

1. Neil Jenkins and Stan Schatt, *Understanding Local Area Networks,* 5th ed. (Indianapolis: SAMS, 1995).
2. Cisco Systems, *Second-Generation Token Ring Switching Solutions* (1997). *http://www.cisco.com/warp/public/731/token/trsdg_tc.htm.*
3. Gigabit Ethernet Alliance, *Gigabit Ethernet Comparison Summary* (1998). *http://www.gigabit-ethernet.org/technology/overview/compsum.html.*
4. vBNS from MCI and NSF, *The Next Generation: A History of the vBNS* (n.d.). *http://www.vbns.net/press/history.html.*
5. Ann Kellan, "Internet2 Holds Promise of Technological Leap" (1999). *http://www.cnn.com/TECH/computing/9902/24/internet2/.*

The Basics of a Nationwide Network for the Internet

Aimee deChambeau

Aimee deChambeau (*daimee@uakron.edu*) is assistant professor of bibliography at the Science and Technology Library of the University of Akron.

In the preceding chapter ("The Basics of LAN Technology"), you learned about the "layers" of software programs and hardware components that make up a network. This chapter examines the Internet's architecture, focusing primarily on the physical connections that define the Net. Although software may be used in a part of the architecture, ultimately it is the physical connections that make this worldwide communication possible.

Today's Internet is based on a Network Access Point (NAP) architecture created by the National Science Foundation (NSF) in 1994. Under this scheme, commercial network backbone operators directly interconnect with one another at a series of access points rather than connecting separately along an intermediary backbone as regional networks had done with NSFNET.

A *backbone* is a network that connects two or more other networks together. Backbones occur at various physical levels. For example, the PC in my office is connected to the local area network (LAN) in our building. The LAN is then connected to the university's backbone network, the one that links all the university's smaller networks together. The university network, in turn, is connected to our regional network, which provides a backbone for various university (and other) networks in our state. The regional network then connects to a national backbone provider's network, which ultimately transports our data over long distances. There is no single backbone to connect to in order to be "on the Internet"; it is a combination of all the networks just described.

Slicing Up the Internet

The physical support structure of the Internet can be divided, with much crossover, into five categories (see figure 1). This division presents a framework for focusing on each of the different services. Many network providers operate in more than one of these categories, supporting their own access to several different markets. The five categories are:

1. The Interconnect level
2. The National Backbone/National Service level
3. The Regional Network level
4. The local Internet Service Provider level
5. The Business/Consumer Market level

The Interconnect Level

At the very top of the Internet structure are the Network Access Points, generally referred to as NAPs. The NAP is a place where online traffic is exchanged between Internet service providers. This meeting and exchanging of traffic between providers at a NAP is called *peering*.

The service providers may make selective peering agreements with other providers at a NAP regarding the exchange of traffic, or they may

FIGURE 1   Internet Structure Levels

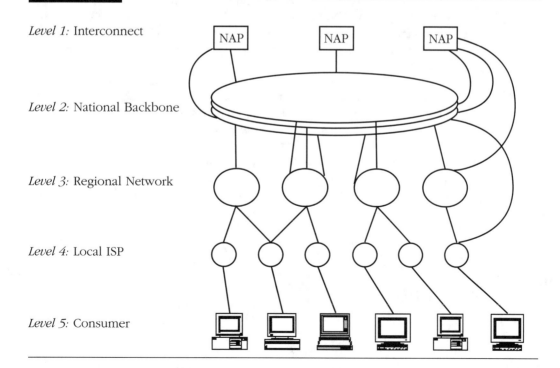

elect to sign a MultiLateral Peering Agreement, which outlines acceptable rules for the exchange of traffic among multiple providers interconnecting at the NAP. The NAPs are not connected to one another with dedicated telephone lines; if a service provider wishes to interconnect at more than one NAP, it must build its own backbone network to make the connection from one NAP to another.

The NSF originally designated four NAPs. Three of the original NAPs are the San Francisco NAP, operated by Pacific Bell; the Chicago NAP, operated by Ameritech and Bellcore; and the New York NAP, operated by SprintLink. The fourth original NAP is MAE-East, a metropolitan area network in Washington, D.C., which was operated by Metropolitan Fiber Systems (MFS) at the time of the NSF designation. Because MAE-East was already in operation and working well when the NAPs were first specified by the NSF, it seemed natural to include it as one of the four.

These four NAPs were not the first major Internet exchange points in existence. The Commercial Internet Exchange (CIX) was an exchange point in Santa Clara, California, developed by commercial operators, such as MCI, Sprint, and AT&T, to interconnect themselves because commercial traffic was not permitted on the NSFNET backbone. The CIX was recently migrated from the Santa Clara site to Palo Alto. There were also two Federal Internet Exchanges (FIXes): FIX-East, located in College Park, Maryland; and FIX-West, located at NASA Ames Research Center in California. Still in operation today, the FIXes exist primarily to interconnect federal networks.

In addition to the CIX and the FIXes, more MAEs were in operation than just the MAE-East NAP in Washington, D.C. (At that time, MAE was an acronym for Metropolitan Area Ethernets. It has since been changed to Metropolitan Area Exchanges to better reflect their status as major interconnect points.) MFS merged with WorldCom in December 1996, and the MAE services are now offered through WorldCom.

Seven MAE sites are in operation today: MAE-East NAP, located in Washington, D.C.; MAE-West, located in San Jose, California; MAE-Chicago; MAE-Dallas; MAE-Houston; MAE-Los Angeles; and MAE-New York. MAE-East and MAE-West are considered by WorldCom to be national interconnect points, or Tier 1 MAEs, deemed such because higher-speed connections are available and because one or more of the major national service providers, such as Sprint and PSINet, maintain a presence there.

The MAEs other than MAE-East and MAE-West are designated as regional interconnect points, or Tier 2 MAEs, by WorldCom. These MAEs have few major service providers interconnecting through them while more regional network operators maintain a presence there. Tier 2 MAEs have slower connections than the Tier 1 MAEs. All in all, there are approximately twelve major interconnect points: the four original NAPs, the additional MAEs, the CIX, and the FIXes (see figure 2).

The National Backbone Level

Currently, there are about forty or so national backbone operators, also known as national service providers. Because the NAPs do not provide any type of dedicated connection to each other, the national service

| Figure 2 | Major Internet Interconnect Points |

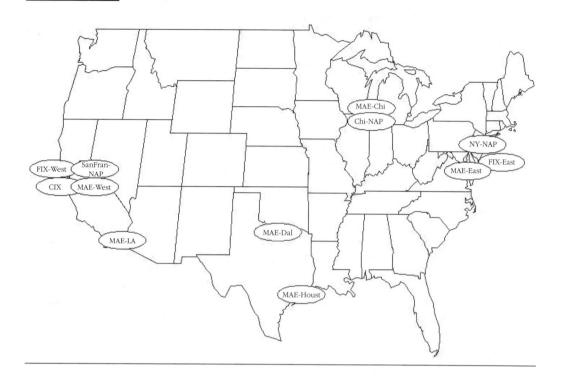

providers must use their own backbone networks to connect themselves to more than one NAP. These operators have created their national backbones by installing high-speed routers in major cities across the country (usually at a Central Office Switching Station) and connecting them with high-speed, leased lines. In actuality, these providers may have more than one router in a given city and may lease their high-speed lines from more than one long-distance carrier, thereby introducing redundancy into their network. Multiple routers and lines enable an operator to reroute traffic under many different circumstances, such as a cut in one long-distance carrier's main trunk line or a network overload.

Many of the national service providers actually lease lines from themselves, from their parent company, or from a subsidiary. Ironically, they may even lease lines from (or to, depending on which side you're on) their biggest competitors. In an often repeated net-story, it appears that AT&T, for a while at least, relied upon the services of MCI. This is how it happened: While AT&T was developing its own national backbone infrastructure, the company leased its lines from BBN Planet. BBN Planet, originally Bolt, Beranek, and Newman, the developers of ARPANET, was acquired by GTE while GTE was forming GTE Internetworking. AT&T was still leasing lines from BBN Planet after BBN Planet became part of GTE Internetworking. GTE Internetworking, in turn, was leasing some of its lines from MCI (now MCI WorldCom). So MCI was leasing lines to AT&T while AT&T strengthened its own network operations.

The national backbone operators generally maintain a presence at most, if not all, of the major interconnect points. Most operators interconnect through at least three of the original NAPs and most of the MAEs, but this is not a firm rule. PSINet, for example, is a large national service provider that only interconnects at CIX, MAE-West, San Francisco NAP, and MAE-East. From their size, however, one would expect them to maintain a presence at more of the major exchange points.

Some of the well-known giants in the national backbone arena include MCI WorldCom, AT&T, PSINet, SprintLink, and GTE Internetworking. WorldCom, though known by different names, has literally been devouring telecommunications and networking companies for the past ten years. By May 1995, when LDDS (Long Distance Discount Service) officially changed its name to WorldCom, it had already absorbed at least fourteen communications companies.

In August 1996, MFS, the Metropolitan Fiber Systems of MAEs fame, acquired UUNET, the largest Internet service provider at the time. That same month, MFS and WorldCom announced their intention to merge and, in December 1996, the shareholders of both companies approved the merger, with UUNET becoming a WorldCom subsidiary. One year later WorldCom announced that not only would it buy CompuServe, but that it would also acquire ANS Communications, the primary network service provider for America Online (AOL).

ANS was one of the original NSFNET participants, having been spun off by the Merit/MCI/IBM team in 1990 specifically to upgrade and run the NSFNET backbone. AOL signed a five-year contract with WorldCom, making WorldCom its primary network services provider. In exchange, WorldCom gave CompuServe's Interactive Services division and $175 million to AOL. CompuServe's Network Services division (CNS) was retained by WorldCom. The WorldCom/CompuServe merger was completed in January 1998.

In September 1998, WorldCom merged with MCI to form MCI WorldCom. Because the merger was between the first- and third-largest national backbone providers, it was opposed by such companies as Simply Internet, GTE Service Corporation, Bell Atlantic, and BellSouth, and such organizations as the Communications Workers of America, the U.S. Internet Providers Association (USIPA), and the AFL-CIO.

Regional Network Providers

During the days of NSFNET, the National Science Foundation supported the formation of regional networks around the country. These networks concentrated the traffic from research and educational institutions in a particular geographical area and channeled it to the NSFNET backbone. Funding from the NSF was only seed money, and the regional networks were expected to become self-sustaining when the funding period ended.

Many of the regional networks today have their roots in those supported by the NSF in the 1980s and 1990s. PSINet, now a national backbone operator, actually began as a for-profit spinoff of NYSERNET, the New York State Regional Network. NYSERNET was one of the first re-

Figure 3   Layout of OARNet

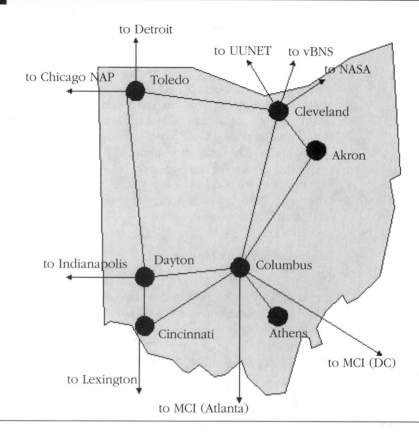

gional networks. Some of the other original regional networks were MIDnet in Lincoln, Nebraska; BARRNet in Palo Alto, California; and SURANET at Georgia Tech. OARNet in Ohio is a regional network that currently provides services for schools, universities, government agencies, and businesses in Ohio (see figure 3).

Regional networks usually have a statewide backbone, or a backbone for adjacent states, and connections to one or more national service providers. Some may maintain a presence at a NAP or MAE. If a regional network maintains a presence at a NAP, it is generally a NAP that is located within, or very close to, the area covered by the regional network.

A wider range of connection options is offered by regional networks for their clients, combining T-1, fractional T-1, and 56K leased lines, and often even modem banks for dial-in connections. An original benefit of connecting institutions to a regional network was the shared cost for expensive resources. This is still true today, where a regional network essentially pools the resources of many organizations in order to provide them all with a higher level of service than a single organization could afford on its own.

Local Internet Service Providers

The local Internet Service Providers (ISPs) range from very small to quite large, with all sizes in between. In general, however, local Internet Service Providers do not operate a backbone or regional network of their own. Instead, they lease their lines from a regional or national provider. Local ISPs may operate leased-line services for their own business customers but mainly provide dial-up connections for individual users. Usually these ISPs operate in a relatively small geographical area covering a single area code or a few contiguous area codes. Simply stated, the local ISPs are those you would find in your yellow pages if you were looking for an Internet service to connect to from your home.

Of course, some of the large backbone providers have services from the very top level all the way down to the local ISP level. Sprint, MCI World-Com, and AT&T all offer local Internet connections for individuals and small businesses.

Consumer/Business Market

The very last level is the end user. When businesses, schools, or individuals connect to a local provider, they are bringing the Internet into their offices, classrooms, or homes. To some extent you might say that businesses and schools operate as de facto ISPs when employees and students are permitted dial-up access, but this level really represents you and me and the pizza shop down the street whenever we dial in to our local ISP and connect ourselves to the Internet.

Blurring the Lines between These Levels: Sprint

Sprint operates at each of the top four levels of our structure of the Internet. Sprint itself has been involved in the development of the Internet since the early days of NSFNET. In 1991, Sprint entered into a cooperative agreement with the NSF to operate a network service connecting NSFNET in the United States to research and educational institutions overseas as the NSF International Connections Manager (ICM). Sprint remains the ICM today. When the NSF designated the original four NAPs, Sprint was awarded the New York NAP. Operation of the New York NAP puts Sprint within the first level, the interconnect level.

Sprint also maintains major backbone router presences in eleven U.S. cities. In addition to its own New York NAP, Sprint interconnects with other backbone providers at the Chicago and San Francisco NAPs, MAE-East, FIXes East and West, and CIX. As a national backbone operator, Sprint falls into the second level of our Internet structure.

Sprint has points-of-presence in over two hundred locations in the United States. This means that Sprint maintains more than two hundred nodes across the country, each of which offers a range of connection services. Therefore, we could say that Sprint is functioning at the third level as a regional network service provider operating many separate regional networks across the country, each of which is funneling traffic to Sprint's backbone.

Finally, at the fourth level, Sprint also offers leased lines for small businesses and dial-up access to individuals as a local Internet Service Provider.

Sprint is by no means unique in the way its services cross over many of the divisions in this five-level Internet structure. In the AT&T and MCI example discussed earlier, AT&T was operating at the fourth level as a local ISP while leasing lines from BBN Planet and, ultimately, MCI. IBM Global Network, a national backbone operator, also offers leased-line services at the third level and dial-up services to consumers at the fourth level.

On the other hand, DataXchange Network, Inc., is a national backbone operator that concentrates on providing backbone network services to regional networks and local ISPs at the fifth level only. @Home Network is a different example altogether. @Home Network maintains its own national backbone and interconnects with other backbone operators at several major interconnect points. @Home Network, however, concentrates mainly on cable modem connections from subscribers' homes; this puts @Home Network at the second level as a backbone provider and at the fourth level as a local ISP.

Conclusion

The current Internet architecture is based on a series of interconnect points—NAPs—where national backbone operators meet and exchange network traffic. This architecture differs from that of its precursor, the NSFNET. At the time, NSFNET was the national backbone; it was the connection to make to be "on the Internet." Today there is no single Internet backbone to connect to.

We are able to divide the Internet into five levels of service, the highest level being the NAPs and the lowest level being the end-user. Knowing that these different levels exist and making distinctions among them is useful when choosing a provider for yourself or your organization. Although we haven't addressed network speeds or capacity at all in this chapter, common sense tells us that we would not want to connect two high-speed networks with a slower speed network; the network's weakest performance link, so to speak, will be its slowest link.

As a practical example, if you were tracing your connection, or a potential connection, backward through these levels and discovered that the regional provider (the third level) operated at slower speeds than the local ISP (the fourth level) connecting to them, you might then question the use of that particular ISP. Shopping around, you might then find and choose one that connects through a faster regional provider. As you move through the levels from fifth to first, you would want each interconnecting network to operate at the same or higher speed than the preceding one.

Online Resources

http://www.boardwatch.internet.com
Boardwatch publishes the ISP Directory as well as articles about the Internet Service Provider business. It is a great starting point for learning about national backbone providers.

http://www.navigators.com/internet_architecture.html
Russ Haynal's online article "Internet: The Big Picture" is a clever representation of the levels of the Internet, with plenty of links to other information sources.

http://www.cybergeography.org/atlas/isp_maps.html
This site is filled with maps and other representations of backbone networks.

http://www.isoc.org/home.html
The Internet Society site is a good source of historical and current information about the Internet.

http://www.cs.washington.edu/homes/lazowska/cra/networks.html
Dr. Vinton Cerf's article "Computer Networking: Global Infrastructure for the 21st Century" can be found here.

http://www.mci.com/cerfsup/
"Cerf's Up." See what Dr. Cerf has to say about the Internet.

http://www.isoc.org/guest/zakon/Internet/History/HIT.html
"Hobbes' Internet Timeline" provides a chronological look at the development of the Internet.

Internet2 and the Next Generation Internet Initiative

Steve Hardin

Steve Hardin (*S-Hardin@indstate.edu*) has served as a "holistic" librarian at Indiana State University since 1989. In the University Library's Electronic Information Services Unit, he works with the World Wide Web, deals with user interface issues, helps maintain a CD-ROM network, and serves as a traditional reference librarian. He also works in Technical Services, where he has served in turn as acting head of Acquisitions, Monographic Cataloging, and Serials Cataloging and Catalog Management. He has written widely on electronic information and telecommunications topics.

We've all experienced it. You get access to a hot new computer—one with blinding speed and bushels of RAM—and you try it out on the World Wide Web. But your favorite web page still takes five minutes to load. You stare as the page slowly forms on your lovely new monitor, thinking of possible stand-up comedy routines: "I wouldn't say the Web is slow, but last night I read half of *War and Peace* while loading my library's home page. Maybe WWW really does stand for 'World Wide Wait.'" As you get more frustrated, you start asking yourself, "What good is having access to so much stuff if I'm going to die of old age waiting for it to make its way to my computer? Why doesn't someone do something about this? How about an Internet where pages in cyberspace load as quickly as a file on my hard drive? Maybe there's a way to make those teenage gamers wait for their files while my serious research takes priority? I wonder . . . ."

Well, a lot of other people have wondered, too. With Internet traffic quadrupling roughly every year, performance has deteriorated to the point where people in education, industry, and government are devoting some serious planning and funding to the Net's future. The academic community—with help from industry and the government—has come up with the Internet2 project. And the government—with help from industry and academia—is working on the Next Generation Internet Initiative. As we'll see, the two projects have a lot of overlap. And it's impossible to discuss them without first discussing two other items: the very High Performance Backbone Network Service (vBNS) and Version 6 of the Internet Protocol (IPv6).

The Very High Performance Backbone Network Service

It all began back in 1993, when the National Science Foundation realized the Internet wasn't going to be able to handle the research challenges of the future. Traffic on the Web that year increased dramatically with the National Center for Supercomputing Applications' release of the Mosaic browser. By 1995, the NSF had concluded a cooperative agreement to make MCI Telecommunications Corporation the provider of the vBNS. The vBNS was established on April 1 of that year.

MCI provides networking protocol services for the vBNS using Asynchronous Transfer Mode (ATM) and Synchronous Optical Network (SONET) technologies. Traffic flows along this more-than-14,000-mile network at OC12 speeds—622 megabits per second (Mbps)—and the speeds may well be faster by the time you read this. In addition to the speed, the vBNS is designed to have a high degree of stability and a low level of congestion. A very nice map of the backbone may be found at *http://www.vbns.net/backbone.html*. A "logical" map of the vBNS is available at *http://www.vbns.net/logical.html*.

Needless to say, the congestion level on this network would soon rise to unmanageable levels if every interest clogging the current Internet could get into it. The NSF awards access to this backbone service through its high-performance connection program. The vBNS connects supercomputing centers as well as some of the nation's leading research institutions.

And what use are researchers making of this high-speed, low-congestion network? The vBNS is ideal for people trying to do collaborative work across distances. For example, researchers at Carnegie Mellon University in Pittsburgh are working with colleagues at the University of Southern California to learn more about earthquakes. There's a lot of data to be analyzed, and the vBNS permits it to be shared quickly to produce computer simulations of quakes with varying magnitudes and locations. In another project, the University of Illinois at Chicago and the University of Pennsylvania are studying "cluster computing," in which systems are linked to produce a sort of virtual supercomputer.

In addition, the vBNS provides backbone service for Internet2. And some of the innovations created by the vBNS will make possible the realization of some of the Next Generation Internet Initiative's goals. More information on the vBNS can be found at *http://www.vbns.net*.

Internet Protocol Version 6

Not all the present Internet's problems result from congestion and speed. The Internet Protocol itself—the collection of "rules" that permit the various parts of the Internet to work together—has placed limits on who gets what traffic when and the number of addresses available for use. With this in mind, efforts are under way to upgrade Version 4 of the Internet Protocol (IPv4) to Version 6. You may have heard of IPv6 by its earlier moniker, "IP next generation" (IPng).

Prioritizing Traffic

Traffic moves along the Internet under IPv4 without regard to urgency. No distinction is made between an e-mail message that can arrive at its destination fifteen minutes late without causing any real problems, and data in a video stream, in which a fifteen-second delay can degrade display quality. Every packet gets the same "best level of effort" treatment.

IPv6 takes care of this problem by requiring packets to carry an indication of their priority. Network routers facing congested traffic conditions can decide to give precedence to the packets with higher priority. Routine traffic can then gracefully yield to more urgent traffic. The video display is produced quickly and well, and the e-mail message gets to its destination a little later with no harm done. Assuring a certain "quality of service" level is a much more realistic goal under IPv6 than under IPv4.

Alleviating Traffic Jams

Another improvement IPv6 makes over IPv4 involves broadcast messages. Under IPv4, these multiple messages can cause traffic jams as they wander the Internet, especially if they're intended for a bad address and do some bouncing. The result is slower performance. But IPv6 makes use of single "multicast" messages; that is, a single message is delivered to a specified group of recipients. This approach requires fewer messages, results in less traffic, and contributes to speedier performance than is attainable under IPv4.

Relieving the Address Shortage

Yet another IPv6 advance involves addressing. IPv4 addresses are 32 bits long, and the numbers are arranged in various classes, allocating a few very large networks more than 16 million addresses, other sites more than 65,000, and everyone else a mere 254 apiece. The problem with this scheme is that precious few organizations have need of 16 million addresses. In fact, not too many need 65,000, but a lot of sites could use more than 254. Because addresses are allocated and reserved in blocks in accordance with the classes, the places that need more than 254 can't use the unused part of the 65,000 or 16 million addresses other sites may have.

In other words, there's an address shortage. IPv6 addresses are 128 bits long—which alone greatly increases the number of possible addresses— and the allocation of addresses can be much more flexible. The bottom line for librarians is that under IPv6, no one need fear running out of possible Internet addresses for awhile.

IPv6 and vBNS

The vBNS we mentioned a few paragraphs back carries IPv6 traffic. In fact, the vBNS is connected to the 6Bone, an experimental network designed to provide a place for the development of IPv6. You can find more information about it at *http://www.6bone.net/*. Some of the Internet2 and Next Generation Internet Initiative traffic makes use of IPv6 as well. As the protocol becomes more widespread, chances are the rest of us will be able to take advantage of it sooner or later.

There's much more to say about IPv6. Take a look at:

http://playground.sun.com/pub/ipng/html/ipng-main.html

http://www.ietf.cnri.reston.va.us/html.charters/ipngwg-charter.html

Internet2

Internet2—originally called "Internet II" and often abbreviated I2—began in October 1996, when representatives of thirty-four universities met in Chicago to begin coordinating the development of new network services and network-based applications to enhance research and education. (Its website is *http://www.internet2.edu*.) Now administered by the University Corporation for Advanced Internet Development (UCAID), the project has grown to include more than one hundred member universities, not to mention more than a dozen "corporate partners." Each participant contributes both funds and expertise to the project.

Internet2 has nine stated goals (you can find the full list at *http://www.internet2.edu/html/mission_and_goals.html*). They're consistent with many of the projects the general public expects major research universities to be pursuing. For example, one goal is to "demonstrate enhanced delivery of education and other services . . . by taking advantage of 'virtual proximity' created by an advanced communications infrastructure." Sound familiar? How often have we heard about the great possibilities the Internet offers for collaborative work in education and research? Internet2 represents a directed effort to realize that potential.

Another I2 goal calls for facilitating "development, deployment, and operation of an affordable communications infrastructure, capable of supporting differentiated Quality of Service (QoS) based on applications requirements of the research and education community." Once again, this goal should have a familiar ring. As we saw earlier, IPv6 is addressing just such a QoS differentiation. It's scarcely a coincidence that many I2 members also have access to the vBNS, which runs native IPv6.

Other goals call for setting up partnerships with government and the private sector, coordinating standards and practices, and studying the impact of all this on higher education and the Internet community. The best news for those of us not affiliated with high-powered research institutions or major industry players comes from the goal to "encourage transfer of technology from Internet2 to the rest of the Internet." Sooner or later—it's hoped—these I2 innovations will work their way down to the rest of us.

Separate Internet2 work groups explore issues relating to IPv6, measurement, multicast, network management, network storage, quality of service, routing, security, and topology. These groups include representatives from academia, industry, and other affiliated organizations.

A special UCAID project related to I2 is Abilene (*http://www.ucaid. edu/abilene/home.html*). A joint project with Qwest Communications International Inc., Nortel, and Cisco Systems Inc., Abilene is another high-speed network, intended to serve as a backbone for Internet2, supplementing the vBNS. Providing a separate network will permit testing of new services before they're introduced to the Internet community at large. Planners hope for fully operational speeds of as much as 9.6 Gbps.

What are people doing with Internet2? The applications are many and varied. For example, researchers at Texas A&M University, the National Museum of Natural History, and the Smithsonian Institution are working on "Massive, Distributed On-line Digital Libraries as Resources for Curriculum Development in K12 and Higher Education." This project intends to use the bandwidth and speed of I2 to make curriculum developments available to as broad an audience as possible.

Other researchers and staff at the Block Museum at Northwestern University, the U.S. Holocaust Museum, and at the Auschwitz-Birkenau Museum in Poland are putting together an electronic exhibit of art produced by Auschwitz prisoners. The advanced network capabilities will be used, among other things, to transmit video and audio interviews with survivors and historians and provide video tours of the camp. Many other projects are underway using I2's resources, cutting across disciplinary boundaries and ranging from pure research to dissemination of research results.

The Next Generation Internet Initiative

If Internet2 represents academia's most extensive effort to modernize the Internet, the Next Generation Internet Initiative (abbreviated NGI; *http://www.ngi.gov*) represents the government's effort. Like I2, NGI made its public debut in October 1996, when President Clinton and Vice President Gore announced their support for the initiative.

Calling NGI a "government effort," though, is a bit misleading. Many of the academic and industry players involved in Internet2 are also involved in NGI. In fact, the NGI concept paper of July 1997 (*http://www.ccic. gov/ngi/concept-Jul97/*) states: "The initiative will be built on partnerships: partnerships between researchers developing advanced networking technologies and researchers using those technologies to develop advanced applications; and partnerships between federally funded network testbeds and commercial network service and equipment providers that participate in these testbeds. . . ."

The Next Generation Internet Initiative has three main goals:

Experimental research for advanced network technologies: This goal includes research in such areas as quality of service, robustness, security, protocols, and application environments.

Next Generation network fabric: This goal includes the oft-quoted twin objectives of connecting at least one hundred sites at speeds one hundred times faster than 1997's Internet and connecting about ten sites at speeds one thousand times faster than 1997's Internet. (The concept paper assumes a 1997 speed of 1.54 Mbps.) Some observers consider the first of these twin goals has already been met—by Internet2.

Revolutionary applications: This goal involves the demonstration of "a wide variety of nationally important applications that cannot be achieved over today's Internet."

Just as for I2, the "revolutionary applications" (*http://www.ngi.gov/apps/*) cover a range of disciplines. For example, the National Oceanic and Atmospheric Administration (NOAA) is sponsoring a project on "Advanced Weather Forecasting." It's a good example of how a fast network can be put to timely use, as forecasts coordinate data from a half-dozen or so NEXRAD radar sites, updated at least every fifteen minutes over a 2,500-square-kilometer area. Couple this data with observations from satellites, aircraft, and other sources, and you get an idea of the mammoth amounts of information being processed.

Another NGI application is "Real-time Telemedicine," sponsored by the National Institutes of Health. Here, the network makes possible remote medical consultations, incorporating "real-time observation and analysis of objects in motion." This arrangement can bring the expertise of a specialist to any place with a network connection. The possibilities for health care are intriguing, to say the least!

Several high-performance networks have relationships to NGI. We've already discussed the vBNS. There are also the NASA Research and Education Network (NREN), the Defense Research and Engineering Network (DREN), and the Advanced Technology Demonstration Network (ATDnet). Other involved networks include the Multiwave Optical Networking network (MONET), the Collaborative Advanced Interagency Research Network (CAIRN), Energy Sciences Network (ESnet), and the NASA Integrated Services Network (NISN). Although these networks have different missions and characteristics, they share the high-performance characteristics needed to meet NGI's goals.

Relationship between I2 and NGI

There's a lot of confusion about the relative roles of Internet2 and the Next Generation Internet Initiative. Some people use the terms interchangeably, thinking, perhaps, that "next-generation Internet" is a generic term to describe the improved Internet of the future. The problem is significant enough that the websites for both projects contain discussions of the relationship.

As mentioned earlier, I2 began in the academic community; NGI had its genesis in the federal government. Both projects make use of the vBNS; both are working with IPv6. Both projects are also developing applications for a variety of disciplines. Both also make use of federal funding, although neither is supported entirely by tax dollars. As the I2 website says, the two are "complementary and interdependent" (*http://www.internet2. edu/html/internet2-ngi.html*).

Issues and Problems

The present Internet is not without controversy. (Just say "regulation" or "commercialization" to a roomful of net surfers and watch the reaction.) So it only makes sense that efforts to improve the Internet are meeting with controversy and even opposition in some quarters.

Take quality of service, for example. We've already discussed how high-priority traffic can be expedited at the expense of lower-priority traffic. This ability raises several questions. First, how do you determine what priority to give an Internet packet? Obviously, the time sensitivity of certain applications requires that they be handled more speedily than routine traffic. And while it's important not to ask more of a protocol than it can deliver, let's try to take the concept to its logical extreme.

Most of us can agree that two surgeons involved in a collaboration with life-or-death consequences should take precedence over a couple of youngsters trying to play a game. But how do you decide whether it's more important to move the large amounts of data needed in a chemistry experiment or the large amounts of data needed to transmit an innovative new musical work? And who should make the decision? The user? How do you keep people from always claiming the highest priority for whatever they're doing? Should the people who request higher QoS be made to pay more for it? If so, how do you make sure the "haves" don't keep the "have nots" from ever getting the best service?

Then there are those who believe the NGI is a waste of taxpayers' money. "Let private industry modernize the Internet," they say. After all, some of the Internet's innovations have come from "netrepreneurs" who saw a need, filled it, and stimulated the economy by providing jobs and capital. On the other hand, NGI supporters maintain the NGI is a quite appropriate project for government because it represents the kind of long-term R&D investment that government can risk more easily and readily than can the private sector. Who's right?

A related objection comes from people in areas of the United States not served by a major research institution. Why should the citizens of these areas be taxed to support a project with no direct benefit to them?

Supporters of the NGI counter that whatever improves the Internet helps everyone in the long run. Who's right?

Because NGI and I2 share so many objectives and members, should they merge? Should some of the other projects merge, too?

And what about people who don't happen to work for a big-time research institution or for one of the large industrial players? What good will a 9.6 Gbps network do you if you're still dialing in from home on a modem? How much of this innovation will trickle down to that "last mile" of Internet access? Are these questions even relevant for this discussion?

You get the idea; there are no easy answers here.

Conclusion

There may not be any easy answers, but after all, these efforts are very much works in progress. It's a well-worn phrase, but "time will tell" how well these efforts pan out. Frankly, time has already told pretty well. Consider this: In 1989, most people had never heard of the Internet. There was no World Wide Web. Today, not only have those two concepts been developed, but they're struggling with the traffic brought on by their success.

Even though it's frustrating to wait forever for a web page to load, if you take a broader view, it's sort of a nice problem to have. It means people are trying to get the maximum use out of the network and are testing its limits. In fact, here's something else to consider: As higher speeds make possible the transmission of ever increasing numbers of packets, and as people try to do increasingly complex things with the Internet, will we still be complaining in ten years about "low" speeds that would seem incredibly fast today? It's a distinct possibility. But think of all the fun we'll have getting there!

3

Nothing Is Certain but the Web and Taxes

Guidelines for an Excellent Website

JoAnn Sears and Andrew Wohrley

JoAnn Sears (*searsjo@lib.auburn.edu*) is currently a science and technology reference librarian at Auburn University. She has a degree from Purdue University in Mathematics Education and recently completed her MLS at Indiana University.

Andrew Wohrley (*wohrlaj@lib.auburn.edu*) is a reference librarian at Auburn University. He earned his MLS from Indiana University and his BA from Valparaiso University.

The qualities people value in websites vary from web page to web page and from person to person. Some people focus on content, while others prize the nebulous notion of "coolness." The qualities outlined in this paper are: purpose, audience, authority, comprehensiveness, accuracy, ease of use/design, currency, and legality. These eight criteria should be familiar to librarians because they follow William Katz's *Introduction to Reference Work* (McGraw-Hill, 1997). Together, these eight criteria are the basis for excellence in web page design. Each will be discussed, with examples.

Purpose

A clear purpose, or mission statement, should provide the basis for everything uploaded on the site. To evaluate the purpose, two questions must be answered: What is the website's purpose? Does the website meet its objectives? Without clearly stating a purpose, focusing on a goal is impossible for a website creator. Formulating a purpose statement has occasionally been disparaged as a bureaucratic formality by those who prize the creative impulse in Web construction. A formality it might be, but a good statement of purpose clarifies a website's mission.

When one asks, "What is the purpose of a website?" one should look for a statement that serves the same purpose as a business's mission statement. The purpose could be just one sentence long, but it should state what the site will cover and, if needed, what it will not cover. The *New York Times* (*http://www.nytimes.com*) declares on the front page of every print issue "All the news that's fit to print." These seven words, the longest of which is five letters long, constitute a remarkably specific statement of purpose that website developers would do well to keep in mind as an example of brevity. The U.S. Army website, on the other hand, goes to the opposite extreme in its purpose statement (see *http://www.army.mil/DA_Web_guidance.htm*).

The question "Does a website meet its objective?" is critical to website evaluation. The question can be clouded by many factors, not the least of which is the clarity of the website's purpose. If the creator was clear on his or her purpose, the evaluation becomes more straightforward. If a site does not meet its objective, the failure will appear in a variety of ways, such as irrelevancies, gaps in data, a lack of coherence, and conclusions that are not supported by facts in the website.

Although purpose is easy to define, it is challenging to implement effectively. For the essayist, the writer, and the webmaster, there may always be just one more detail that could illustrate another facet of the topic, yet it is just outside the scope of the essay, book, or website. As Shakespeare said, "Brevity is the soul of wit."

Audience

The audience is a critical part of every website. The web page creator would be extremely foolish to antagonize the very people that he or she wishes to attract! Web pages should be created with a particular audience in mind, whether they are cooks, college students, or chemists. The webmaster can hope to meet the needs of his or her target audience only by knowing who that target audience is.

Meeting the needs of the audience requires that the information be relevant. Note that comprehensiveness can exist with relevance. The Weather Channel website (*http://www.weather.com/*) has information of relevance to everyone from pilots to commuters, and no information that is not weather related.

If a site is devoted to children, the evaluator must look at the site through the eyes of a child. Is the site intuitive to a child? Does the site load quickly so the child does not get impatient and lose interest? Will the software entertain the child? Finally, is the content aimed at the child's level? A website of interest to a 12-year-old is different from a site designed for an 8-year-old.

The advantage of the Web is that it provides the ultimate in narrowcasting to a select audience, such as through a fanzine. Fanzines, or 'zines, are narrowly focused magazines or websites that cover an aspect of popular culture. However, just because one is creating a fanzine is no reason to gush. Excellent website creators should trust that the facts alone are sufficient for the audience and should understand that they need not embellish those facts.

Authority

Authority on the Web has had a checkered history. Internet old timers can remember—around 1992—when cyberpunk authors celebrated the anarchic energy of the Web. The cyberpunks believed that the state would be smashed under a tidal wave of packets that would carry their message to the world and thereby signal the end of mass media. Well, a funny thing happened. A sort of inverse Gresham's law of information set in, in which "good" information drove out "bad" information. For example, the multitude of NASA websites (*http://www.nasa.gov*) provide the most credible information about space science available to the public.

That is not to say that government-sponsored information equals authoritative information. Few sites posted by organizations will admit to faults in those organizations. However, institutional bias can be detected, and the intelligent reader can determine whether the site is authoritative. The caution here is to make sure of your source and, if in doubt, do more research.

Ideally, authoritative information has been filtered by someone that the reader can trust to make a sound judgment, thereby sparing the reader the need to check every fact. For example, The NIST WebBook (*http://Webbook.nist.gov*) provides an excellent interface to authoritative information detailing the physical properties of compounds. Peer review provides an institutionalized process through which all facts are checked by experts; it is the foundation of science and technology literature. Peer-reviewed scientific journal literature is moving onto the Web for the benefit of scientists. A good example of a peer-reviewed journal online is the Science Online site at *http://www.sciencemag.org/*.

Although bias has always existed in the marketplace of ideas and shows no signs of going away, a website creator puts his or her biases online only at personal peril. If a site is to be perceived as authoritative, the creator must carefully scrub it clear of all bias or suffer the consequences of being considered partisan. Put another way, information on a website must be backed up by stronger evidence than just the preconceived notions of its creator.

Comprehensiveness

Comprehensiveness is another component of an excellent web page. An example is found in the Census Bureau's electronic TIGER mapping website (*http://tiger.census.gov/*). There, the entire United States is laid out with roads, rivers, and political boundaries, and the scale for each is available as menu options for the user. A driver could travel from Seattle, Washington, to Key West, Florida, with maps from this service as the only guide.

The primary question to ask when examining for comprehensiveness is this: Does the site do what it claims to do? The *Washington Post*, for example, has compiled a thorough resource on the bombing of Baghdad during the Persian Gulf War (*http://www.washingtonpost.com/wp-srv/inatl/longterm/fogofwar/splash.htm*). The site's focus is narrow: It covers only the military air strikes on Baghdad. It doesn't include all aspects of the war (political, economic, and so on). The resource, however, does what it says and is very thorough.

One way to discover the comprehensiveness of a website is to examine subject guides provided by authoritative sources. For example, the International Society for Plant Pathology provides a link to the comprehensive *Plant Pathology Internet Guide Book* (*http://www.ifgb.uni-hannover.de/extern/ppigb/ppigb.htm*).

Accuracy

Some levels of accuracy are easily evaluated, such as obvious spelling errors and poor grammar. Others may be more complicated: Does the resource represent some bias that is reflected in the website? For example, the U.S. Nuclear Regulatory Commission (*http://www.nrc.gov/*) promotes the safe handling of nuclear power for energy, while Greenpeace (*http://www.greenpeace.org/*) opposes nuclear power. The information in a website supports the mission of its originators and may include a slant toward the group's purpose. Spotting such biases may take more than a first glance, and it may require some additional research.

The information in the resource should be accurate, regardless of the mission of the organization. To verify this, you may have to do some fact checking in other respected resources or have a subject expert analyze the website. Verification could include checking statistical or other information in standard reference books. You should also be cautious of sites that use such phrases as "it is always true" or "as everybody knows."

One key component of accuracy is logical consistency throughout the site: The resource should not contradict itself. One exception to this would be a resource that attempts to include opposing viewpoints on a controversial subject. In such a case, providing contradictory views can allow for more education about both sides of an issue—and may include both provable facts and opinions. Often accuracy is compromised by what is left out rather than by the inaccuracy of what is included.

Website users should keep in mind that determining the accuracy of a web page involves more than fact checking; it also involves checking for clichéd thinking, straw man arguments, sweeping generalizations, and shaky credentials.

Ease of Use/Design

Users should consider three major components of design when evaluating a Web resource: the physical layout of the interface; the organization of the information; and technical options, such as sound, video, or interactivity.

For more detailed information about good Web design, check out the excellent site Web Pages That Suck (*http://www.Webpagesthatsuck.com*).

Interface Layout

The layout of the interface is one of the first items that the user encounters; the use of color, space, and graphics will cue the user how to proceed with the resource. Often a crisp, clear interface is noted for its design; too many icons and pictures may distract the user and make the web page confusing.

An example of good design is the Ovid (*http://www.ovid.com*) interface for networked databases. The screen has both graphics and text describing the purpose of various features, such as author searching, title searching, and combining searches. The icons are small and clear, and the screen is simple. Additional options, such as date limiters and full-text restrictions, are obvious, and the screen does not include any bright colors that would distract from the searching; even a beginning searcher has little trouble knowing how to use the resource.

Content Organization

How the content is organized will contribute directly to how easily you can navigate, or work through, the resource. Categories used for information and the number of hierarchical levels will affect how many "clicks" of the mouse you will have to use to get to the desired page. For example, to search the Carl Uncover database (*http://uncWeb.carl.org*), you must click through a few pages before arriving at the search screen. Other websites, such as the *New York Times*, permit keyword searching of the entire site from the home page.

Technical Options

A third area to consider when evaluating the design of the resource is how the medium is utilized. The World Wide Web offers considerable options for including sound, video, and images. A high degree of interactivity can be added, including choices for the user or even a quiz after working through a tutorial. Many libraries are now examining—and implementing—tutorials on basic library skills, such as how to locate items within the library environment or how to cite resources in a paper. One example of this is James Madison University's "Go for the Gold" (*http://library.jmu.edu/library/gold/modules.htm*). This program includes an exercise set after each module that gives immediate feedback to the user about how well the skill has been mastered.

The different kinds of computers and browsers must be considered when evaluating websites. Some individuals may have access only to a textual browser, such as Lynx, and cannot make use of images and sound; a well-designed system will accommodate both types of browsers. In addition, lower-level systems may work very slowly in loading pages that have sophisticated design elements. Most people are impatient with sites that load pages slowly and will not wait. In some cases, providing "mirror sites" (that duplicate content) can speed load times. In addition, some people have strong preferences about whether or not pages have frames (a design feature of web pages that divides the page and may make printing and other functions more difficult).

A final consideration is providing users with the ability to print the information from the web page when appropriate. Printing can become time-consuming and frustrating, depending on the structure of the website. A nice feature for sites that have many pages is to include a single file containing the information; for example, the Patent Searching Tutorial web page at the University of Texas at Austin (*http://www.lib. utexas.edu/Libs/ENG/PTUT/ptut.html*) provides a PDF (portable document format) file for printing all the information rather than forcing selection of several pages throughout the site.

Some users may prefer to select individual pages to print or download—especially if they do not have the Adobe Acrobat Reader installed, so it is wise to provide download and print options. It is also a good idea for the page to be designed for a 480-by-640 pixel screen (or be flexible for the size that is needed). Pages that are designed for larger screens may yield printouts that have portions of information chopped off by the printer.

Currency

Web information should be more current than what can be found in print. Currency depends on how frequently the information becomes available. For example, because patents are issued only once a week, it would be illogical for resources to add new patents on a daily basis. Stock quotes, on the other hand, may be updated every fifteen minutes or as quickly as the price changes in real time. Regardless of the topic, the resource should keep up with new developments in the field being covered by the source, and these updates should be clearly visible to the user.

You should not assume, however, that because a page was published recently on the Web, the information in it is the most current available. For example, you can locate *Roget's Thesaurus* easily on the Web, but, because of copyright restrictions on the more recent editions, it is only the 1911 version. This resource can be accessed at a couple of locations, including Project Gutenberg's website (*http://promo.net/pg/*). Although some may consider this information obsolete, others may value it for historical purposes. Similarly, a web page discussing the four food groups may not be useful because the USDA has replaced them with the food pyramid (*http://www.usda.gov/fcs/library/961001.pdf*).

You must also anticipate the stability of the resource; in other words, does it seem like the kind of resource that will still be available—with updates—tomorrow, next week, or at some other date in the future? Some sites go one step farther—they provide archived versions, not just the most current version. For example, the *Scout Report* (*http://scout.cs.wisc.edu/report/index.html*) provides access to previous issues—both in PDF files and as Web links.

A final note is to check for outdated links. Some webmasters continually add links and change the "last updated date," but they do not check to see if existing links are still working properly. These existing links should be checked routinely. More important than the updating of links to other resources is the currency of the local links—the links used to navigate within the same resource. The site manager has full control over these links and should provide them in working order for users.

Legality

Legality is one topic that should not be ignored when evaluating websites. Generally, material that has a copyright or trademark cannot be legally copied. If the Web manager has any doubt about whether the material may be used legally, courtesy alone should compel him or her to request permission before posting the information.

The only exception to this rule involves publications of the United States government, which are not subject to copyright. Users must check the laws of other nations before posting information generated by all other governments. In any case, the source, whether private or governmental, must be cited lest the Web manager be accused of plagiarism. Although this paper is too brief to cover copyright in depth, more information can be obtained by consulting the chapter titled "Copyright in Cyberspace," later in this book.

Conclusion

There is no reason that everyone cannot have an excellent website. The principles laid out here can guide anyone interested in establishing a Web presence. Over the past five years, the Web has grown from an academic curiosity to a force that Wall Street follows avidly. What was once a crude and energetic environment now attracts the attention of such giants as Disney and Microsoft. For a website creator to grab the attention of the public, she or he needs an excellent website.

Online Resource

Alastair Smith, *Evaluation of Information Sources* (*http://www.vuw.ac.nz/~agsmith/evaln/evaln.htm*).

Web-Based Markup Languages: HTML, DHTML, and XML

Martin R. Kalfatovic

Martin R. Kalfatovic (*mkalfato@sil.si.edu*) is the information access coordinator for Smithsonian Institution Libraries, a position he has held since 1993. Editor of the *Library Information Technology (LITA) Newsletter*, he is a frequent contributor of articles and reviews to various publications. He is also an adjunct faculty member at the Catholic University of America's School of Library and Information Science where he teaches library automation and museum librarianship.

Just when it seemed that the world of markup languages was beginning to settle down, along comes a plethora of new tagging schemes to upset our tidy little apple carts. In the world of the Web, Hypertext Markup Language (HTML) created a minipublishing boom that rivaled the explosion of printed documents created by the introduction of mimeograph and photocopy machines. The basic concepts and tag sets of HTML were easy enough to learn, and the handy "reveal codes" feature of Web browsers enabled the rest of us to "borrow" the markup of pages we liked.

The Standard Generalized Markup Language (SGML), the basis for HTML, was relegated to second-class Web citizenship. SGML was accepted in the publishing industry, though, and in the world of libraries and archives, the SGML document type definition (DTD) for the Encoded Archival Description (the EAD DTD) seemed the perfect solution for creating digital finding aids. By late 1998, however, the convenient duo of SGML and HTML had become obsolete in the markup world. First in the Web-conscious public's eye was Dynamic HTML (DHTML), which was soon followed by XML (or eXtensible Markup Language). What do these latest markup language developments mean to Web developers, and, more importantly, to the Web-using public?

WEB-BASED MARKUP LANGUAGES: HTML, DHTML, AND XML   69

SGML: The Parental Unit of All (Web-Based) Markup Languages

It has been waggishly noted that SGML is neither standard, generalized, nor a markup language. Be that as it may, SGML or *ISO 8879:1986. Information processing—Text and office systems—Standard Generalized Markup Language (SGML)* has become an indispensable tool for structuring and formatting documents. As a markup language, SGML is able to describe the document's content structure in a logical way and creates the ability to define what physical characteristics those elements possess (font, margins, spacing, and so on).

SGML documents consist of three layers: structure, content, and style. For the structure, SGML works with an application file called the Document Type Definition (DTD). The DTD describes and provides a framework for the structure of the document. The content element of an SGML document is the actual text with added tags that are defined in the SGML DTD. The third element, style, defines how the document will appear on the screen or in print. A number of style formats are supported within SGML, but the Document Style Semantics and Specification Language (DSSSL) is the preferred ISO standard for SGML documents.

Besides SGML, other widely used markup languages include PostScript and TeX (and its derivatives, such as RevTeX and LaTeX). These have taken their place in the publishing world but have never been widely implemented across disciplines or on the Web. SGML itself, with the exception of the EAD DTD mentioned above, has not achieved widespread use on the Web. Though SGML documents are readily downloaded and viewed through special viewers (for example, Panorama), they have not reached the same level of acceptance as other special formats, such as the Adobe Portable Document Formats (PDF).

For the Web, SGML has manifested itself in the form of HTML. HTML, the primary method of delivering documents by way of the Web, is simply an SGML Document Type Definition that pertains to the markup of HTTP delivered documents. The current version, HTML 4.0, is not a standard of its own, but rather a DTD of SGML.

HTML: Hypertext Markup Language

Simple, ASCII-based HTML documents began appearing in 1991 shortly after the creation of the hypertext transfer protocol (HTTP) by Tim Berners-Lee the year before at CERN (European Laboratory for Particle Physics). With the release of the GUI (graphical user interface) Web browser Mosaic in early 1993, the potential of Internet delivery of hypertext dawned on a host of net users.

The concepts of HTML were based on notions of hypertext that had been floating through computer science and other fields for a number of years. The original tags and format for HTML were created by Berners-Lee at the time of his development of HTTP. HTML originated as an application of SGML. By November 1995, Berners-Lee and David Connolly had completed work on HTML Version 2.0, the first standard for HTML that incorporated most of the work that occurred in the intervening years.

With the rapid, worldwide acceptance of the Web and the HTTP and HTML standards, the number of Web documents increased at an exponential rate. As browser developers, most notably Netscape, began adding new tags and extensions to HTML (for example, the often mocked <BLINK> tag), the 2.0 standard was quickly left behind. Among the key elements introduced were the <FONT> and <TABLE> tags, which gave content developers much more control over the look of their pages. With the rapid and often confusing pace of HTML development, work on Version 3.0 of HTML was scrapped and the Internet Engineering Task Force, led by Dave Raggett, switched gears to work on a new version of HTML, code-named "Wilbur." This version, endorsed by the World Wide Web Consortium (W3C) in January 1997, was released to the world as HTML 3.2.

In his introduction to the HTML 3.2 document type definition, Raggett notes, "HTML 3.2 aims to capture recommended practice as of early '96 and as such to be used as a replacement for HTML 2.0 (RFC 1866). Widely deployed rendering attributes are included where they have been shown to be interoperable. SCRIPT and STYLE are included to smooth the introduction of client-side scripts and style sheets."[1]

A number of Web purists consider HTML 3.2 to be the final word in the HTML standard. As browser developers and content creators kept pushing the HTML envelope, it mutated from a simple markup language to a display and page layout tool, something never planned by HTML's originators. However, in mid-1997, Raggett and others began work on HTML 4.0, which would incorporate even more of the Netscape- and Internet Explorer-specific tags.

Among the more controversial tags HTML 4.0 accepted was the <FRAME> tag, which allowed multiple navigable pages to appear on the user's screen. HTML 4.0 also standardized the use of scripts, more fully supported style sheets, and made documents more accessible to users with disabilities. The earliest codified version of HTML 4.0 appeared in late 1997 and minor revisions continue on the document.

Dynamic HTML

Dynamic HTML, building on the work done for the HTML 4.0 standard, is nothing more than that most dreaded of beasts, the paradigm shift. No "official" standard for DHTML exists. Rather a host of concepts and technologies work together within the HTML 4.0 environment to create pages with which the user can interact after the page has loaded into the client with no need to call on the server again.

The key components of DHTML are the standards and tags developed for HTML 4.0. These include client-side scripting (for example, JavaScript [*http://www.irt.org/script/faq.htm*], VBScript [*http://msdn.microsoft.com/*

scripting/default.htm?/scripting/vbscript/], ECMAScript [*http://www.ecma. ch/STAND/Ecma-262.htm*], JScript), the Document Object Model (DOM), and the use of style sheets (particularly cascading style sheets).

Document Object Model (DOM)

The DOM is predicated on the notion that a document or web page can contain objects (elements, links, etc.) that can be manipulated. The document creator will be able to delete, add, or change an element; change its content; or add, delete, or change an attribute.

A DOM may be done in two ways: using JavaScript or VBScript; or using an external application, such as a plug-in or ActiveX control that accesses the document through your browser. In the first instance, pages will need to have embedded JavaScript or VBScript; in the second instance, there will be no need to change the pages.

For more information, see "Document Object Model FAQ" (December 11, 1998), *http://www.w3.org/DOM/faq.html*.

Style Sheets

The primary purpose of a markup language (such as HTML or XML) is to define the structure of a document. The development path of HTML, however, blurred the distinction between structure and appearance. In the current HTML 4.0 and in future XML developments, control of the document structure will return to the markup, and appearance will remain in the control of the style sheet.

Among the style sheet standards currently in use or under discussion are Cascading Style Sheets (CSS), Document Style Semantics and Specification Language (DSSSL), and Extensible Style Language (XSL).

For more information, see "Web Style Sheets," *http://www.w3.org/Style/*.

Using these components, page designers now have the ability to make pages both interactive (with different elements changing as the user moves around the page) and more visually attractive (though one of the most popular implementations of DHTML, creating images that fly across the screen, is also one of its more silly uses). DHTML is fully supported only by the 4.0 (and above) generation of the Netscape and Internet Explorer browsers and, because of different implementations of the elements of DHTML, cross-browser compatibility of DHTML documents leads to problems reminiscent of those seen in the early days of HTML.

So, will DHTML solve all the problems of Web development, bring better-structured documents to the Web, help me find all the information I want, and give me whiter, brighter teeth? Sadly, no. HTML (even the DHTML flavor) has become so encumbered with nonstandard tags that developers feel it's just as well to stop adding elements and start from scratch. Or if not quite scratch, to go back to SGML and create a markup language that can meet the needs of more complex Web documents.

XML: Extensible Markup Language

Just what is this latest markup language that's planning on hitting all the websites and making webmasters feel both powerful and helpless? Nothing more than XML, or eXtensible Markup Language. Though only approved as a standard in October 1998 (and lacking any full-blown applications), XML is beginning to take the online world by storm.

XML is a markup language built from the start to be extensible, meaning that you, the creator, can make up any tags you like (as long as you specify them in your XML DTD). XML is designed to enable the use of SGML on the World Wide Web in a more robust manner than was ever possible with HTML. In November 1996, the first XML Working Draft was announced and since that time the World Wide Web Consortium (W3C) has taken on the responsibility of helping to define the standard.

XML: SGML or HTML, Either or Both?

Well, both and neither. A very basic definition of XML is that it's a document type definition of SGML for WWW delivery of information. You might even think of it as a dialect of SGML. But wait, you say, isn't that what HTML is? Yes, but the key difference is that XML offers the following three benefits not found in HTML:

Extensibility. HTML does not allow users to specify their own tags or attributes in order to parameterize or otherwise semantically qualify their data.

Structure. HTML does not support the specification of deep structures needed to represent database schemas or object-oriented hierarchies.

Validation. HTML does not support the kind of language specification that allows consuming applications to check data for structural validity on importation.

Through a number of extensions—many of them browser-specific—HTML has been made to "look" like it can handle more complex format/structure elements than it really can. As noted in *HTML Unleashed:* "If we strip away for a moment the innumerable struts, crutches, and sophisticated gizmos that make the HTML golem walk and speak and look alive, what we'll see will be a pretty simple (not to say primitive) markup language designed for basic documents of a quite predictable structure."[2]

XML, by allowing the page creator to define any number of tags (and how they will look and behave), avoids the problems of HTML. Another key element of XML is that it supports Unicode. By employing ISO 10646, the international standard 31-bit character set that covers most human (and some nonhuman) written languages, XML documents (as well as the XML tags themselves) can be "written" in nearly any language.

Best of all, unlike the SGML specification that runs to over five hundred (print) pages, the specification for XML is under thirty pages in length. By trimming the specifications to the bare-bones minimum, the principles and application of XML will be much more widespread than was possible with SGML. But if ease of use is a goal, hasn't HTML already become easy enough for all but the most novice user? Well, yes, HTML has become easy to use, but even with all the proprietary and often incompatible extensions, HTML is unable to handle some of the more important elements of document markup.

The ability of XML to handle industry-specific markup (through the use of specially created DTDs) allows for logically and tightly structured documents that can be employed in a number of ways. Already, a number of industries are completing work on XML DTDs for their documents. A few of these are:

XML for the automotive industry (SAE J2008):
http://www.xmlxperts.com/sae.htm
Bioinformatic Sequence Markup Language (BSML):
http://visualgenomics.com/sbir/rfc.htm
Chemical Markup Language Version 1.0 (CML):
http://www.ch.ic.ac.uk/omf/cml/
Mathematical Markup Language Version 1.0 (MathML):
http://www.w3.org/TR/REC-MathML/
Weather Observation Definition Format (OMF):
http://zowie.metnet.navy.mil/~spawar/JMV-TNG/XML/OMF.html

XML, Java, DSSSL, and the DOM

"XML gives Java something to do" is a cry of XML developers. The functionality of XML will allow Java to move beyond the realm of useless, if catchy, banners and pale rip-offs of Tetris to more interactive and useful Web applications. In addition to Java, XML will take better advantage of the Document Object Model of software development and the latest expansion of Document Style Semantics and Specification Language.

Goodbye HTML?

With millions of copies of today's browsers likely to be on desktops well into the twenty-first century, XML will not put HTML out of business tomorrow. Just as SGML documents can be used to generate HTML documents (on the fly or in batch mode), the same can be done with XML documents. For that not so distant future when the XML user agent (also known as a "browser") comes to dominate the desktop, it is important now to create HTML documents that are "XML-compliant." When considering creating XML-compliant documents, keep the following points in mind.

1. XML tags, unlike HTML tags, are case sensitive; thus <ul> is a different tag (and will be rendered differently) than <UL>. Note: you can use either style, as long as you remain consistent!

2. XML offers much more complex linking capabilities than HTML; in addition to a linear link between two documents, XML will offer the ability to link documents in complex, bidirectional ways.

3. HTML documents can be easily "converted" into XML as long as the HTML documents are "well formed" (meaning, minimally, that the tags are uniform in case and that all open tags have matching closing tags).

4. Just as in SGML where the author creates and declares a Document Type Definition for each document, in XML, the header information will declare the associated XML DTD—for example, <?xml version="1.0" standalone="yes"?>.

So, What's It All Mean to Me?

XML offers content creators the opportunity to make all information free. Not free in the monetary sense, but free from the constraints of various proprietary or platform-specific applications. Microsoft Word and WordPerfect will no longer have the ultimate control over how our documents look. Additionally, this control of the look and feel of the document will no longer be limited to the printed page or the screen; XML will eliminate the problem of documents that (as is the case with HTML or even some word processors) look good on one screen (or printer) and terrible when the document is ported to another platform.

At the same time, XML is much simpler to use and implement than full-blown SGML and offers numerous advantages over the more limited HTML. At this point, the advantages of XML are clear, and it's just a matter of time before the standard becomes more fully implemented.

Conclusion

Growing out of SGML, Web-based markup languages have enabled content developers to deliver a variety of information using the most user-friendly Internet protocol. HTML, the first of the Web-based markup languages, has become burdened by nonstandard extensions. Dynamic HTML has stepped in to allow the creation of Web pages that emulate many of the effects of programmed displays.

The advent of the eXtensible Markup Language (XML) promises to incorporate the latest advances of HTML (including style sheets) and DHTML in a standardized manner. The flexibility and standardization offered by XML will allow content developers much the same layout and output options available to print publishers.

Resources

SGML

ArborText. "SGML: Getting Started: A Guide to SGML (Standard Generalized Markup Language) and Its Role in Information Management." *http://www.arbortext.com/Think_Tank/SGML_Resources/Getting_Started_with_SGML/getting_started_with_sgml.html.*

Bradley, Neil. *The Concise SGML Companion.* Reading, Mass.: Addison-Wesley, 1997.

Marchal, Benoît. "An Introduction to SGML." *http://www.pineapplesoft.com/reports/sgml/index.html.*

Seaman, David. *About SGML. http://www.lib.virginia.edu/etext/sgml.html.*

The SGML/XML Web Page. *http://www.oasis-open.org/cover/.*

Von Hagen, Bill. *SGML for Dummies.* Indianapolis: IDG Books Worldwide, 1997.

World Wide Web Consortium. "Overview of SGML Resources." *http://www.w3.org/MarkUp/SGML/.*

HTML

Berners-Lee, Tim, and David Connolly. "Hypertext Markup Language* 2.0 (RFC 1866)." (November 1995). *http://www.cis.ohio-state.edu/htbin/rfc/rfc1866.html.*

Graham, Ian S. *HTML 4.0 Sourcebook.* New York: Wiley, 1998.

Raggett, Dave, ed. *Raggett on HTML 4.* Reading, Mass.: Addison-Wesley, 1998.

Raggett, Dave, Arnaud Le Hors, and Ian Jacobs. "HTML 4.0." *http://www.w3.org/TR/REC-html40/.*

DHTML

"DHTML, HTML & CSS." *http://www.microsoft.com/workshop/author/default.asp.*

Dynamic HTML Index. *http://www.all-links.com/dynamic/.*

The Dynamic HTML Zone. *http://www.dhtmlzone.com/index.html.*

Goodman, Danny. *Dynamic HTML: The Definitive Reference.* Sebastopol, Calif.: O'Reilly, 1998.

Hyman, Michael. *Dynamic HTML for Dummies.* Indianapolis: IDG Books Worldwide, 1997.

Inside Dynamic HTML. *http://www.insidedhtml.com/.*

Mudry, Robert J. *The DHTML Companion.* Upper Saddle River, N.J.: Prentice Hall Computer Books, 1998.

XML

Bosak, Jon. "XML, Java, and the Future of the Web." (March 10, 1997). *http://metalab.unc.edu/pub/sun-info/standards/xml/why/xmlapps.htm*.

Bradley, Neil. *The XML Companion*. Reading, Mass.: Addison-Wesley, 1998.

"Extensible Markup Language (XML) 1.0: W3C Recommendation 10-February-1998 (REC-xml-19980210)." *http://www.w3.org/TR/REC-xml*.

Flynn, Peter. *Understanding SGML and XML Tools: Practical Programs for Handling Structured Text*. Boston: Kluwer, 1998.

"Frequently Asked Questions about the Extensible Markup Language: The XML FAQ Version 1.41." (October 6, 1998). *http://www.ucc.ie/xml/*.

Goldfarb, Charles F., and Paul Prescod. *XML Handbook*. Upper Saddle River, N.J.: Prentice Hall, 1998.

Kalfatovic, Martin. "What the <?XML!>: Extensible Markup Language, Making the Web Safe for SGML." *LITA Newsletter* (fall 1998). *http://www.lita.org/newslett/v19n4/19–4tx7.htm*.

Leventhal, Michael, et al. *Designing XML Internet Applications*. Upper Saddle River, N.J.: Prentice Hall PTR, 1998.

McGrath, Sean. *XML by Example: Building E-Commerce Applications*. Upper Saddle River, N.J.: Prentice Hall, 1998.

Pfaffenberger, Bryan. *XML for Web Publishing in Six Easy Steps*. San Diego: AP Professional, 1998.

St. Laurent, Simon. *XML: A Primer*. Indianapolis: IDG Books Worldwide, 1998.

Wiggins, Richard. "XML: What Every Webmaster Should Know." *Internet Buzz* (March 18, 1998). *http://www.webreference.com/outlook/column19/*.

"The World Wide Web Consortium Issues XML 1.0 as a W3C Recommendation XML 1.0 Fact Sheet." *http://www.w3.org/Press/1998/XML10-REC-fact*.

Notes

1. Dave Raggett, "HTML 3.2," *http://www.w3.org/MarkUp/Wilbur/HTML32.dtd*.

2. Rick Darnell et al., "Introduction," *HTML Unleashed* (Sams.net Publishing, 1997), *http://www.webreference.com/dlab/books/html/38–0.html*.

Browser Plug-Ins: Customization for Multimedia

Matthew Benzing

Matthew Benzing (*benzim@rpi.edu*) is the information systems librarian for Rensselaer Polytechnic Institute Libraries. This position entails the management and continuing development of RensSearch, Rensselaer Libraries' Web interface. He also maintains and optimizes library computer hardware, provides consultation and training in the use of library software, and investigates new technologies and their possible applications to the library environment.

In the beginning was the text browser, and it was good. Well, good enough for what CERN needed, anyway. Then came Mosaic, and its patricidal offspring, the Netscape Navigator. Once browsers like these made the World Wide Web safe for images and graphical content, suddenly a multitude of uses for the Internet became apparent, some good, some questionable, some downright perverse.

As Web pages made of text and images became commonplace, a desire began to develop for incorporating more types of media: video, sound, music, interactive content. The Web was beginning to explode into a wider cosmos with a richer palette. There was only one problem with this: Although theoretically it was possible to transmit any type of computer file across the Internet and use it on the World Wide Web by building the appropriate capability into each browser, actually doing this would create a severe case of software-bloat. It was difficult to justify multiplying the size of browsers in order to accommodate each and every type of file that someone might find useful. One way around this involved using helper applications.

From Helpers to Plug-Ins

Helper applications are programs that browsers can be trained to "whistle for" when they run into an unfamiliar file type. For example, the Netscape Navigator browser does not display BMP image files. If you try to open such a file with the Navigator, it will launch Microsoft Paint or any other program that you have specified for handling these types of files.

The helper application method gives the Web wanderer a richer and more useful online experience, but it still falls short of being an ideal solution in many cases. Opening an entire program for each unknown file type makes for a much clunkier ride than most of us would prefer. It also limits the content provider's ability to integrate different file types directly into web pages.

Plug-ins developed as a more graceful way to handle a multitude of file types without bloating browsers to a Rabelaisian scale. The principle is simple and elegant: Create miniprograms that plug in to a browser the same way an expansion card plugs in to a motherboard. Each plug-in expands the capability of the browser so that it can handle a new type of file or files. This allows the user to essentially customize a browser to his or her needs.

The types of content that plug-ins can handle are varied. Everything from displaying various document formats, to streaming audio and video, to embedding interactive multimedia in a page, to providing a virtual reality environment is possible with plug-ins. Plug-ins are useful for content providers who wish to make various types of information available, and they are useful to content consumers who wish to partake of all the variety of formats that populate the Web. As both providers and consumers, libraries are in a position to doubly benefit from the advantages that plug-ins offer.

What Does a Plug-In Do, and Why Would a Library Want One?

Libraries have a history of providing information in a variety of formats. Books, serials, various audio and video containers, maps, manuscripts, and other ways of containing and transmitting information have found their way into library collections. With the advent of online information gathering and the digital library, the situation has not changed; just because more and more information is contained in bits rather than atoms does not mean that we are faced with a simpler apparatus for storing and disseminating that information. Rather the difficulty is in working with a multitude of file types rather than an assembly of physical formats.

Plug-ins allow various file types to be used through the same browser. One common example is the Adobe Acrobat plug-in that has found its way into many library browsers. Often electronic journals, government documents, and other online materials in which libraries are interested are available in some sort of rich-text format, such as Adobe's PDF file type.

These formats allow content providers to create a product that more closely replicates the look and utility of a paper document than is possible with HTML. It is also much easier to convert a physical document into a rich-text PDF than it is to convert to HTML.

Of course, library users could not care less about all this. They just want the information they are seeking with as little fuss as possible. The Acrobat plug-in makes the incorporation of these file types as seamless as possible. The user does have to learn a bit about navigating in the Acrobat environment, but it is very similar to the point-and-click environment of the Web browser. There are also plug-ins for handling other specialized text files, such as TeX and LaTeX.

It is the same with other file formats. The VivoActive and RealPlayer plug-ins, for example, allow the user to view streaming video through their browsers; this video content can even be incorporated into a window that exists within the web page that launches it, creating an even more seamless viewing experience. Similar plug-ins allow users to experience MIDI music and other audio file types in an integrated manner.

Plug-ins also allow the user to experience interactive content in real time. The Shockwave plug-in allows you to invoke presentations and tutorials that have been created with Macromedia's multimedia authoring systems. Many plug-ins also allow the user to interact with virtual worlds that have been created with the VRML standard or other virtual reality formats. Again, as with the Acrobat plug-in, these miniapplications have controls of their own and users may need assistance in learning to use them; still, they are usually intuitive to anyone familiar with using a browser.

As consumers of information, libraries are, of course, going to be interested in those plug-ins that are associated with the information sources they wish to make available to their patrons. Plug-ins broaden the range of materials that a library can consider in its online collection development plans by making file types a less-important factor in decision making.

Making Plug-Ins Available to Library Users

Once a resource has been located that a library wishes to make available through its website, the appropriate plug-in must be downloaded and installed on library machines. Locating the appropriate plug-in is usually simple: Most websites that contain plug-in–dependent content post this fact and link to the appropriate site for downloading the necessary software. (For more information on plug-ins on the Web, see Yahoo at *http://dir.yahoo.com/Computers_and_Internet/Software/Internet/World_Wide_Web/Browsers/Plug_Ins/*.)

Also, Netscape has on its site (*http://www.netscape.com*) a list of plug-ins that work with its browser as well as detailed information concerning what file types each plug-in works with, what operating systems it works with, and where to download it. Microsoft (*http://www.microsoft.com*) has a similar list for plug-ins that work with its browser, Internet Explorer.

Trying to open a web page that contains a plug-in–dependent browser will usually bring up a window in either browser that will give you the option of letting the browser search these lists for appropriate plug-ins. However, this feature doesn't always work that well; sometimes it will suggest an incorrect plug-in. Your best bet is usually to go ahead and browse the whole list of plug-ins at the Netscape or Explorer websites and make your own decision.

Often there is a choice of different plug-ins for the same file type. In these cases, you must choose which plug-in best suits your needs, taking into consideration the platform from which you are going to be working (not all plug-ins are ported to all operating systems), system requirements, and features of each plug-in.

If you are providing this resource for use by distant patrons outside the library, keep in mind that they will need to download the plug-in and install it on their own computers, so you may want to choose one that provides the most flexibility in operating systems and has the most forgiving system requirements. You should also post a notice on your own web pages notifying patrons that the resource you are pointing to requires a plug-in, and provide a link to a site where the latest version of the plug-in can be downloaded.

The Library as Content Provider

If you are acting as a content provider, you will have a different set of concerns when it comes to using plug-ins. The first question that you will want to ask yourself as a library is whether or not a plug-in is really necessary for the type of information you wish to make available. Libraries should be concerned first and foremost with supplying information in a fashion that benefits the most people; technologically glitzy solutions may be acceptable for websites whose sole aim is marketing and sales, but for libraries, simplest is always best.

In many cases, it may be possible to share data over the Web using HTML and the built-in features of standard browsers. However, if, after a careful evaluation, you decide that you need to present your data in a format that requires a plug-in, your next step is to decide which plug-in to recommend to your viewers. Again, often more than one plug-in is available for the same file type, so you may have plenty to choose from.

Also keep in mind that some of your viewers may choose to use a different plug-in than the one that you suggest, either because they already have another loaded that can handle the same file type, or because they prefer certain features that your choice does not offer. With this in mind, try not to rely on features in a particular plug-in that may not be supported in others that handle the same file type.

Having decided on a plug-in, your next step will be to decide how you want it to be launched. It is possible to launch a plug-in within a page, to launch a plug-in that takes over the whole browser window, or to run a plug-in in the background. One simple HTML method for launching a plug-in from within a page is to use the EMBED tag. The EMBED tag incorporates the "plugged" data right into the page, in the same way that other tags display images and text.

Using the EMBED tag, you can also describe the size of the area that you want the data to display in. As an example, if you wanted to display the spreadsheet data in the file usedcars.xls in a web page, you could do it using this tag:

<EMBED SRC=usedcars.xls WIDTH 0 HEIGHT 0> </EMBED>

This will display the file in a 100-by-100 pixel square within the web page. Depending on the plug-in used, the viewer would then be able to enter and alter data within the form and obtain results. Of course, keep in mind that embedding does not work well with all plug-ins. Some are really designed to take advantage of a full screen. You might wish to try it out with a few differently sized perimeters.

Other times you may not wish for a file to be visible at all. For example, if you have an audio file that you want to play in the background as a page is viewed, you could add a tag like this:

<EMBED SRC=nebraska.mid HIDDEN=true></EMBED>

This tag would launch an appropriate plug-in and play the MIDI file "Nebraska." Because the HIDDEN attribute has been set to "true," no plug-in would be displayed. If the HIDDEN attribute were left out (making it "false"), the plug-in may or may not display some sort of console, depending on how it was designed.

An even simpler solution is to link directly to the desired file:

<A HREF="thundercrack.pdf">Thundercrack (PDF file) 50K</a>

This will usually open the file in a full-screen version of the plug-in. It is usually a good idea to post the size of the file, so that viewers will have an idea of how long they will have to wait for it to load.

Conclusion

Plug-ins greatly enhance the ability of libraries to make diverse formats of information available over the Web. As long as you are judicious in their use and have a firm understanding of what you want to accomplish, they can broaden the reach of your library's site.

A Day in the Life... Multimedia and Librarians in the Twenty-first Century

Brad Eden

Brad Eden (*beden@ccmail.nevada.edu*) is the head of cataloging at the University of Nevada at Las Vegas.

Bob

The year is 2020, and Bob is waking up to another exciting day as Multimedia Cybrarian at State-of-the-Art University. Although there are many terms for Bob's job throughout academia, he doesn't really care what he's called, as long as he can do everything that he is currently doing in his work.

As Bob gets out of bed, he says "On." Immediately the lights turn on. His multimedia communication device, or MCD, starts and runs his preselected program of morning television programs and computer and financial updates, and checks his voice- and e-mail for any current important messages; his kitchen begins cooking its automated breakfast menu. After his shower, Bob eats breakfast, answers important voice- and e-mail messages, checks his financial portfolio and makes any necessary changes, watches his favorite cartoon, and finishes the final draft of his five-year technology plan for the multimedia information center.

On the monorail on his way to work, Bob accesses the interactive work center available to all commuters and hears that his aggressive growth stock is down for the fourth day in a row. He initiates a sell order that is confirmed by the time he reaches work. He also peruses a summary of the day's current news stories, checks his online day planner, and contacts his director by videomail to update him on the technology committee agenda for the afternoon.

By the time Bob arrives at the Interactive Library and Learning Center, he realizes that his headache has gotten worse and that he really does not feel very well. In his office, Bob contacts his holodoctor through the Telemedicine Network in Human Resources. A computer scan reveals a virus, which is immediately eradicated, and Bob feels much better within minutes.

He then has an interactive multimedia conference with the university's seven worldwide distance learning facilities, making sure that all faculty and student needs are being taken care of in the area of multimedia resources. A quick look at his MCD gives him current worldwide, financial, and workplace news before he puts on his virtual reality (VR) helmet and continues virtual construction of the university's telecommunications infrastructure for the five-year plan.

After lunch, Bob presents his technology plan to his director and the university administrators in the main conference room. Once everyone has a VR helmet on, he presents the five-year technology needs and goals for the multimedia information center, along with 3-D animation and high-resolution graphics. University administrators revise and adapt the virtual presentation to budget and infrastructure projections on the spot and remind Bob and his director to address the needs of virtual students of the university in the completed draft.

Back at his office, Bob glances at his staffs' daily reports, examines current news and stock markets, and updates his virtual calendar for the next two weeks. On the monorail going home, Bob connects the interactive work center with his home MCD in order to activate the dinner program in his kitchen and check the entertainment subject keyword database for interesting television and live local shows that evening. He decides to program an evening of various interactive and virtual sitcoms and game shows. Once home, Bob receives a video call from his mother, who reminds him about the virtual family reunion planned for the coming weekend and says that his sister on the Mars colony will be attending as well.

After a relaxing evening, Bob programs his MCD for the next day, checks up on current world and local news, does some shopping on the virtual Webwide Shopping Network, and video-calls some colleagues around the world about the Worldwide Multimedia Library Conference to be held next month in Sydney, Australia. As Bob says "Off" and shuts down his MCD, he thinks how exciting his profession has become in the past thirty years and anticipates the possibilities and promises that technology holds for the next thirty years.

Multimedia Today and Tomorrow

Although the preceding scenario is obviously only one vision of the future, the world of multimedia is rapidly and with deafening speed overtaking everything that human beings encounter at home, in the workplace, and in the world. Providing access to and, sometimes more importantly, an understanding of new technologies and resources has become the mantra of a number of occupational and service industry professionals, not the least of which are librarians (in any of their current title manifestations).

Although there are numerous, current definitions for the term *multimedia*, the following definition by Nicolas D. Georganas will be used throughout this chapter:

> "Media" refers to a form of human interaction that is amenable to computer capture and processing, such as video, audio, text, graphics, images . . . whereas "multi" signifies that several of those "media" are present in the same application. We like the definition given by some authors that an application will be considered as "multimedia," if it involves at least one time-continuous medium, such as video and audio, and at least one discrete one, such as text, image, or graphics.[1]

Today's librarians have to deal with a number of multimedia items and systems, from the Internet to web pages to interactive encyclopedias to CD-ROM databases to integrated library systems. Librarians are having to discover, describe, classify, load up, provide access to, and maintain these resources, training users in the process. And although many reference sources exist to help librarians do all of the above, can librarians prepare themselves for the continued explosion in technology and information resources? If so, how? What challenges in multimedia does the twenty-first century hold for librarianship?

Looking into the future, most experts agree on a number of multimedia developments that have a high probability of success:[2]

Interactive "strips": Discs based on popular half-hour TV formats, such as sports programs, game shows, sitcoms, and soap operas, in which users participate in game-like simulations

Interactive movies: Movies that encourage participatory multiple plot developments similar to "Dungeon and Dragon" games

Infotainment: News and information shows that are dressed up with multimedia components to attract greater popular attention

Music videos: MTV-like, cutting-edge graphics and live action combined with play-along MIDI music tracks to create a karaoke format

Edutainment: PBS-style shows that will be enhanced to appeal to both adults and children with popular learning titles and multimedia animation and graphics

Simulations: Virtual reality video games and computer programs that require high-resolution television screens, laser, and peripheral equipment designed for interactive game participation

The purpose of this chapter is to inform librarians about current developments in the computer and media industries that will undoubtedly affect our ability to deliver information. Although most libraries are not actively involved in strategic planning and futuristic philosophy, especially in the area of media resource development, it would behoove our profession to seek partnerships with technology leaders.

Multimedia and the Internet

What does the Internet (or its future manifestations) hold for digital multimedia? Not only do they enhance one another, but new communications paradigms become possible. They are complementary: While multimedia has brought the Internet into the mainstream, the Internet promises to make multimedia more widely available and practical.

Three important points can be made regarding the Internet's capacity to impact multimedia computing. First, the Internet allows content vendors virtually unlimited storage capability for their applications and data. Currently, vendors are restricted by the high storage demands of digital video and audio on such distribution methods as floppy diskettes or CD-ROMs. Second, the addition of communication as an important new multimedia application domain means that networks can enable real multiway applications for multimedia that will allow for interactive television and radio.

Finally, the Internet gives the general public broad access to sources of digital audio, video, and images. Current technologies, such as RealAudio, the Internet Multicast Backbone (MBONE), and the Real-time Transport Protocol (RTP), have helped to develop WebTV, WebOnCall, and Internet conferencing tools, such as CoolTalk, Internet Conference, and Video-Phone.

A number of multimedia/Internet futuristic applications are already available. Many sites feature sound and music editors, video and animation editors, 3-D paint programs, and authoring programs. Interactive websites like Virtual Frog Dissection (*http://george.lbl.gov/ITG.hm.pg.docs/dissect/info.html*), the 3-D Abulafia Gallery (*http://www.cgrg.ohio-state.edu/~mlewis/Gallery/gallery.html*), and Virtual Antarctica (*http://www.terraquest.com/antarctica/*) are but a glimpse of what the future holds.

Probably the most exciting new development is multimedia demonstration sites where users can access cutting-edge software in adventure games, interactive movies, simulations, role-playing games, action games, and sports games. Of these, the most popular by far is Happy Puppy (*http://www.happypuppy.com*), where users can play game demos from the major computer software corporations.

Two other recommended sites for current multimedia development are FreewareWeb Online! Newsletter (subscription information at *http://www.freewareweb.com*) and the NODE Learning Technologies Network, "multimedia online: primer" at *http://node.on.ca/tfl/multimedia/primer/*, which describes the hows and whys of working with online multimedia tools and helps users understand the terminology and technology behind online audio, video, desktop conferencing, and animation.

Future Scenarios

Medium-range future multimedia applications are currently in beta testing. With high-definition television (HDTV) already a reality, these other multimedia developments will not be far behind:

Ubiquitous television: Screen-based devices, both stationary and portable, for personal communication

3DTV: Translation of the movie theater experience into the living room, with screen enhancers and special goggles

Flat-panel television: Being developed especially in Korea and Japan, along with flat-panel technology in other areas

Holography: Movement from flat, two-dimensional media representations to round, three-dimensional ones

Electronic picture frames: Replacing traditional paper-based presentation media, this new genre of visual display will create posters, photos, paintings, and other visual displays

Virtual reality: Challenging multimedia as a powerful performance and simulation medium, VR will transform action and video games, as well as the corporate and business community.

Along with these technologies, *participatory publishing* will change the meaning of "publishing" a work as well as the relationship between author and reader. This is currently happening on the Internet, where readers are able to influence and contribute to the content of publications. Together, editors and writers of multimedia publications will be able to create, customize, and deliver documents according to individual tastes. Personalized news and innovative advertising as well as dynamic annotations to web pages are just some of the functional applications possible with participatory publishing.

Webspace in three dimensions, using such languages as the Virtual Reality Modeling Language (VRML) currently available on some Web browsers, allows users to "fly" through doors, buildings, rooms, and spaces. WWW sites would become actual places one goes rather than just information one downloads.

A *total integration of WWW technology with traditional broadcast media* is definitely possible in the near to medium-range future. Not only will television stations have to incorporate Internet multimedia into their programming, but WWW-based stations will begin to compete with broadcast and cable television stations for popularity, advertising, and audience ratings.

Universal messaging systems will incorporate fax, voicemail, and e-mail, resulting in a universal mailbox as a single repository for voice, image, and text data, as well as any other media that become popular. A replayable workspace is another form of messaging that will allow users to record a session in their workspace, then deliver the product as an online help system, as a tutorial to train new employees, or as virtual policy and procedures manuals.

Finally, *enriched multimedia databases* will provide access not only to text documents, but also to all manner of audio and video clips, allowing for a kind of "Web multimedia search service" that can handle such requests as "Find pictures similar to this picture," or "Match audio clips similar to this piece of music." Not only will these databases be able to find all manner of multimedia, but users will be able to create and construct their own multimedia databases, personalized for their own daily use or transportable for work or school. Wrapped media encapsulates multimedia objects so that text, video, and audio can all be related to one another and presented with their own content-links. These wrapped media packages become independent compositions and documents in and of themselves.

For these visions of the future to be realized, the gap must be bridged between the information rich and the information poor. A next-generation video literacy must be achieved because, as has become obvious to many industry observers, people are moving away from a print-based literacy toward a video literacy.

The traditional universe of twenty-six letters and an ordered linear sequence will be replaced by something revolutionary—icons, graphical user interfaces, and symbolic images. The eye—and hence the brain—will be flooded by symbols, sounds, representations, text, data, color, and collage that will engender a new intellectual consciousness having nothing to do with print. How completely this happens depends on public awareness, public policy initiatives, and government direction and funding.

Librarians and Multimedia

Where do librarians fit into the multimedia of the future? Just as multimedia development is in a continuous state of change, so librarians must continue to provide access to new technologies. However, in order to become catalysts for and partners in future multimedia developments, librarians must initiate a number of changes. These concepts should be taught in library and information science schools; embraced by library associations; and encouraged by library administrators, supervisors, and mentors. Librarians need to be:

- Proactive in the development and testing of multimedia; in the direction and future of our profession; and in our participation and partnership with technology, industry, and business in planning and implementing multimedia packages.
- Creative in designing and implementing multimedia developments; in forming relationships with technology leaders; and in taking leadership roles in information technology.
- Cooperative in working with community, school, university, and government leaders in the implementation of the multimedia future; and among ourselves in the metamorphosis of our profession.

- Open-minded in dealings with technology and industry leaders regarding future multimedia developments; about the future development of the library profession; and about the evolution of the library into whatever manifestation(s) it may assume.
- Focused on the preservation of all past, present, and future information packages that humans have developed; on actively directing the destiny of the library profession; and on developing partnerships and open discussion in all areas of technology development.

In sum, librarians must begin to take charge of our own future, rather than let the future take charge of us. We need to actively communicate with the people and industries that are determining the future of technology, so that the needs and concerns of users are not forgotten or ignored in the inevitable multimedia explosion.

Additional Resources

Dean, Damon A. *A Pocket Tour of Multimedia on the Internet*. San Francisco: Sybex, 1996.

Dillon, Patrick M., and David C. Leonard. *Multimedia Technology from A to Z*. Phoenix: Oryx, 1995.

Dowling, Thomas. "Using Multimedia File Formats." In *The Cybrarian's Manual*. Edited by Pat Ensor. Chicago: ALA, 1997.

Nielsen, Jakob. *Multimedia and Hypertext: The Internet and Beyond*. Boston: AP Professional, 1995.

Reed, W. Michael, et al. *Multimedia and Megachange: New Roles for Educational Computing*. New York: Haworth, 1994.

Reisman, Sorel. *Multimedia Computing: Preparing for the 21st Century*. Harrisburg, Pa.: Idea Group Publishing, 1996.

Notes

1. Nicolas D. Georganas, "Multimedia Applications Development: Experiences," in *Multimedia Technologies and Applications for the 21st Century: Visions of World Experts* (Boston: Kluwer, 1998).

2. David Rosen, "Multimedia and Future Media," in *Multimedia: Gateway to the Next Millennium* (Boston: AP Professional, 1994).

4 The Document as Object and Commodity

METADATA 101: A PRIMER

Priscilla Caplan

Priscilla Caplan (*p-caplan@UCHICAGO.EDU*) is assistant director for systems at the University of Chicago Library. She is chair of the National Information Standards Organization Standards Development Committee and the author of the column "Casting the Net" in *Public-Access Computer Systems Review*.

In 1998, a joint LITA/ALCTS Institute titled "Managing Metadata for the Digital Library" sold out; the OCLC, Inc., Institute launched "Understanding and Using Metadata"; and a number of special interests, from the International Digital Object Identifier Foundation to the biodiversity community, initiated their own metadata efforts. Metadata is clearly a hot topic, and, equally clearly, it means many things to many people. For some, it implies description of network-accessible resources, although most metadata schema can be applied to nondigital materials. For others it means breaking away from traditional, rule-bound methods of description, although many of the emerging metadata specifications are enormously complex.

A good working definition of metadata that allows for a broad interpretation is "structured information about an object or event." A specification for a related set of metadata elements is called a *schema*. A schema defines the semantics or meaning of the metadata elements. Dublin Core (a schema), for example, defines an element called "Title" as "the name given to the resource by the Creator or Publisher." Some schema also prescribe syntax, or how the content should be encoded for use or exchange. Other aspects that may or may not be specified by schema include labels for display, methods of content representation (for example, using an authority list or thesaurus), and rules regarding the structure or use of the elements (for example, optionality, repeatability).

For convenience, we distinguish several different types of metadata, including descriptive, administrative, technical, rights management, and structural. *Descriptive metadata* depicts the content of a resource for such purposes as discovery, retrieval, and identification. Author and subject could be elements of descriptive metadata. *Administrative metadata* is information useful for managing a resource—for example, an accession or modification date. *Technical metadata* is a subset of administrative metadata describing technical aspects of the digital object, such as the compression scheme. *Rights management metadata* allows the terms and conditions of use to be identified for a particular object, user, and use. *Structural metadata* indicates how digital objects are put together so that constructs like pages and chapters can be identified for computer processing. This discussion will focus on descriptive metadata, although no clear distinction really exists between this and other types, and a single semantic element often has multiple uses.

A Metadata Sampler

MARC/*Anglo-American Cataloguing Rules 2*

Most descriptive metadata created by libraries for both digital and nondigital resources is still what we would call "traditional" cataloging using MARC, AACR2, and related rule interpretations and guidelines. Catalogers have aggressively pursued the application of traditional cataloging to Internet resources of all types, and libraries typically catalog remote resources that they license, subscribe to, or otherwise pay for, including individual electronic journals, journal collections, index and citation databases, and all manner of online services. Increasingly, libraries are also cataloging resources that they do not license or own, including free e-journals, websites, and digital collections created by other institutions.

The ability to describe Internet resources required changes to both US-MARC and to the cataloging rules and guidelines. The major change to US-MARC was the definition in 1993 of the 856 field for electronic location and access. Interestingly, this was defined before the Web (more accurately, the Hypertext Transfer Protocol or HTTP) became the dominant form of access, so the field carries much overhead for the description of Telnet, e-mail, FTP, and other services. Currently, however, the 856 is most frequently used to record a URL. Now that many library OPACs have Web front ends or gateways, it is possible to link from a URL contained in a MARC record directly to the electronic resource.

Primary sources for traditional library cataloging include *Anglo-American Cataloguing Rules*, second edition, 1988 revision (AACR2) and the 1993 Amendments, and the USMARC Format for Bibliographic Data. Electronic resources are addressed specifically in AACR2 Chapter 9, which contains special provisions for remote access computer files, and ISBD(ER), the *International Standard Bibliographic Description for Electronic Resources* (1997). Modules 31 and 33.18 of the *Conser Cataloging*

Manual give guidelines for electronic serials and electronic newspapers, respectively (*http://lcweb.loc.gov/acq/conser/issues.html*). (Conser, or Cooperative Online Serials, is an international cooperative serials cataloging program.)

Detailed guidelines on the use of the MARC field 856 are available from the Library of Congress (*http://lcweb.loc.gov/marc/856guide.html*). The best overall set of guidelines for general use is Nancy Olson's *Cataloging Internet Resources: A Manual and Practical Guide*, second edition (*http://www.purl.org/oclc/cataloging-internet*).

Traditional cataloging for Internet resources has many benefits for libraries, including widely available applications software for creating, modifying, and exchanging these records, and integrated access through the library's online public access catalog. How well Internet resources can be described using traditional mechanisms is subject to debate. AACR2 rules for computer resources still reflect their origin in the description of social science data sets, later updated to accommodate physical publication media, such as CD-ROM and floppy diskette; changes needed to describe remote electronic resources have not yet been fully integrated. ISBD(ER) is generally more progressive.

Dublin Core

Even in the early days of the Web explosion, it was clear that the vast majority of network-accessible materials would never be cataloged by traditional library methods, either because of the expense of cataloging or because the materials were outside the scope of library interest. At the same time, automatically generated indexes used by Internet search engines often contained too little information to be useful and resulted in huge numbers of irrelevant hits. In March 1995, OCLC and the National Computational Science Alliance (NCSA) cosponsored a meeting of librarians, software designers, and network specialists to see whether something couldn't be done to facilitate discovery on the Web. The result was the Dublin Core metadata element set (schema) for simple resource description.

The original Dublin Core was intended to be a simple, easily explained, and easily applied standard for creating descriptive metadata. It was designed to encourage authors and publishers to provide metadata for their own documents as they posted them on the Web. Almost immediately, however, other uses for the Core became apparent. Digital library projects are adopting the Core as a relatively inexpensive method of describing the collections they are making available. Some communities find the Core, which can be represented in HTML, to be a more "native" mode of network expression than MARC. Others are interested in the Core as a *lingua franca* for cross-domain searching. Most recently, the idea has emerged that the Resource Description Framework representation of the Core (described below) may provide a generic data model for description on the Web, usable as a component of electronic commerce and rights management applications. As a result, the Dublin Core is evolving to meet a range of quite different and sometimes conflicting needs.

The development of the Dublin Core has been a highly international and highly participatory enterprise. The Dublin Core discussion list has more than 500 subscribers, a substantial proportion of whom actively contribute, and there are active projects in at least twelve countries. As of fall 1998, six Dublin Core workshops have been held in four countries on three continents, and topical working groups continue development of the specification between workshops.

Version 1.0 of the Core consists of fifteen data elements and their high-level definitions. It is reasonably stable and has entered official standards processes in the United States and Europe. A second version, 2.0, is being considered to address some of the problems identified in 1.0 and to provide a better framework for generalized network applications. A mechanism for specifying the content and meaning of the base elements more precisely is also under development. For example, the Core includes an element called "Date," but one might want to specify that the particular date supplied should be the date the object was created and that it be formatted according to the ISO 8601 standard. The mechanism, called qualification, would be applicable to both 1.x and 2.x versions of the Core.

The Dublin Core itself is a purely semantic standard, meaning that it defines only the meaning of the data elements and not the format for encoding them. However, there is a recommended representation of 1.0 in HTML, where Core elements are given in META tags that can be either embedded in the HEAD portion of a document or stored separately. There is also an emerging representation in XML that is closely aligned with the RDF data model for the Core and that is better suited than HTML for representing qualification.

The best source for information about the Dublin Core is the DC home page at *http://purl.org/dc*, which contains the current reference definition of the specification as well as links to projects, publications, and information on the workshop series. The site also contains a link to *A User Guide for Simple Dublin Core*, a working draft from the User Guide working group. A number of editors, both freeware and commercial, include templates for entering Dublin Core data and will output Dublin Core elements in HTML. General-purpose Internet search engines can be used to harvest, index, and search Dublin Core metadata so long as they can be configured to support specific META tags (not all of them can). Some organizations have assembled Dublin Core toolkits, which include software for data entry, index and search, and conversion to other formats. A good collection of tools is referenced from the Dublin Core home page.

Encoded Archival Description

Archives and manuscript repositories have long relied on paper finding aids to describe their collections. The development of the USMARC AMC (Archive and Manuscript Control) format in the 1980s made it possible to represent such collections in online catalogs, but only in summary descriptions. Access to individual series or items required reference to detailed inventories and registers kept at the archive itself.

In 1993 the Berkeley Finding Aid Project was initiated to develop an Internet-accessible version of the paper finding aid. Using examples of paper finding aids contributed by a number of institutions, the project developed a draft set of encoding rules in the form of a Standardized General Markup Language DTD (Document Type Definition). The early DTD then entered a process of wide review and revision by museums, libraries, archives, and special collections, during which it was named the Encoded Archival Description (EAD). The beta version of the EAD was released in December 1996, and Version 1.0 was released in September 1998.

The EAD is now jointly maintained by the Society of American Archivists, which produces the EAD help pages (*http://jefferson.village. virginia.edu/ead/*), and the Library of Congress, which maintains the official tag library and documentation (*http://lcweb.loc.gov/ead/*). The EAD has been widely implemented in America, Europe, and Australia; institutions and projects using the EAD can be found listed on the LC site and at the Berkeley Digital Library SunSITE (*http://sunsite.berkeley.edu/ead/ proj.html*). In September 1998, the Research Libraries Group (RLG) launched a new service called Archival Resources, which creates a virtual union catalog of EADs by maintaining a searchable, central index of EADs housed at the contributing institutions.

The EAD, like the MARC record, is generally stored separately from the resources to which it points. However, an interesting aspect of the EAD is that in addition to describing nondigital resources, it also can embed pointers to digital resources, so collections that have been wholly or partially digitized can be integrated within their own finding aid. The EAD can be created and edited by any software that can manipulate SGML, and it can be viewed with an SGML viewer, such as Panorama. It is often converted to HTML for display on the Web using Perl scripts or software designed for SGML to HTML conversion, such as Inso's DynaText/DynaWeb.

TEI Header

The Text Encoding Initiative is an international project to develop guidelines for encoding electronic texts in SGML for interchange and scholarly research. The first draft release of the guidelines appeared in 1990, and the current edition, *TEI Guidelines for Electronic Text Encoding and Interchange (P3)*, in 1993. There are two versions of the 1994 TEI DTD: a complete version that covers all aspects of encoding various types of prose and verse, and a simpler subset called "TEI Lite." Both versions require the encoding of metadata in the part of the document known as the TEI header.

The TEI header consists of four major segments. The *File Description* segment contains full bibliographic data for both the electronic version of the text and the printed source, including such elements as author, title, publisher, and file size. The *Encoding Description* contains a detailed description of how the document was marked up, including the level of encoding applied, whether spelling was normalized, and so on. The *Text Profile Description* provides a detailed description of nonbibliographic aspects of the text, specifically the languages used and how the text was produced. The *Revision History Description* gives a place to record the changes in each version of the electronic text.

TEI-encoded texts should be prefixed with embedded TEI headers, but the headers may also be extracted and processed separately, in which case they are known as independent headers. Like EAD files, TEI headers can be processed by any software that supports SGML; a mapping also exists for converting headers to MARC for use in MARC-based systems.

Comprehensive information on the TEI can be obtained from the Text Encoding Initiative home page (*http://www.uic.edu/orgs/tei*). A searchable version of the guidelines along with other information is maintained by the Electronic Text Center at the University of Virginia (*http://etext. virginia.edu/TEI.html*).

Other Metadata Schema

GILS. The Government Information Locator Service is a federally mandated initiative to help the public locate and use government information. It has been adopted for international and nongovernmental use under the name Global Information Locator Service. GILS specifies how servers must support searching at the protocol level, independent of user interface or underlying data management systems. The specification also includes about one hundred metadata elements, known as the GILS Core, which are semantically tied to commonly used bibliographic data elements. Information about GILS can be obtained from the GILS home page at *http:// www.gils.net/*.

FGDC. The Federal Geographic Data Committee issued the draft Content Standards for Digital Geospatial Metadata (*http://geology.usgs.gov/tools/ metadata/standard/metadata.html*) in 1994 and is moving toward codification of these as an ISO standard in 1999. Use of the Content Standards is mandated for U.S. federal agencies collecting geospatial data and has been widely adopted elsewhere. The Content Standards are designed not only to facilitate the identification of appropriate geospatial datasets, but to help the user determine the availability, quality, and suitability of a dataset and how to access and transfer it.

VRA CC. The Core Categories for Visual Resources was developed by the Visual Resources Association and can be accessed at *http://www.oberlin. edu/~art/vra/guide.html*. The Core Categories contain two sets of elements: those describing works (defined as a physical entity or an event that can be captured in physical form) and those describing visual documents (defined as any image that depicts a work). They do not prescribe any particular syntax.

IMS. The Instructional Management Systems Project (*http://www. imsproject.org/index.html*) is an EDUCAUSE initiative aimed at building the Internet architecture for education. One of the IMS subprojects is the joint development of a metadata schema with the European ARIADNE project. The IMS Metadata Specification (*http://www.imsproject.org/*

md_overview.html) is designed for the description of various types of learning resources (items, modules, and tools) and includes many elements for describing educational content and taxonomy of knowledge. The prescribed syntax for the IMS schema is XML.

Crosswalks

The preceding list by no means exhausts the number of metadata schema in use or under development, but it probably covers the majority of those likely to be encountered in libraries. With so many schema in use by so many different communities, it should be no surprise that the need exists to map data from one schema to another. For example, a library with a MARC-based catalog may want to convert TEI headers to MARC for retrieval. An organization with multiple metadata files in different schema may translate them all to Dublin Core for searching. Even where there is no need for physical conversion, relating the elements of one schema to another can aid in the understanding of both.

A specification for mapping data from one metadata schema to another is called a *crosswalk*. Many crosswalks have been developed, including mappings from GILS, FGDC, VRA CC, Dublin Core, and TEI headers to USMARC, from MARC to FGDC, and from IMS to Dublin Core. Formal crosswalks are difficult to construct because different schema are often incompatible in scope, content, and/or format. A good discussion of the problems of crosswalk construction is given in the NISO White Paper, "Issues in Crosswalking Content Metadata Standards," by Margaret St. Pierre and William P. LaPlant Jr. (*http://www.niso.org/crsswalk.html*).

The ABCs of the Resource Description Framework (RDF)

No discussion of metadata would be complete without some mention of RDF, the Resource Description Framework under development by the World Wide Web Consortium (W3C). RDF is exactly that: a framework for the description of resources in the Web environment. It consists of a suite of specifications, including a formal data model; syntaxes for expressing the data model; a schema model; and a syntax for machine-understandable schema. In the future, the development of query and profile protocols is planned.

The purpose of RDF is to provide structured, machine-understandable metadata for the Web. The data model at the heart of RDF gives a formal, unambiguous way of stating the relationships between resources, their properties, and the values of those properties. So, for example, in natural language you can state that John Updike is the author of *Rabbit Run*, or that *Rabbit Run* was written by John Updike, or that the author of *Rabbit Run* is John Updike. The RDF data model provides a formal way to represent that the resource "Rabbit Run" has a property type "author" with the value "John Updike." This relationship can be expressed graphically, using circles, arrows, and boxes, or in XML.

A major advantage of the RDF data model expressed in XML is that it provides a way for different metadata schema to be used together to describe the same resource. This is useful in an environment where there may be different sources for the various types of metadata (for example, descriptive, technical, rights). It is also useful for extending schema with elements from other schema; thus, for example, a Dublin Core description could be extended to include an edition statement (which is not part of the Core) by taking this from another set.

In addition to the data model, a schema model and syntax were also under development at the time of this writing. An advantage of the RDF schema model is that it will provide a standard way of representing diverse metadata schema, and, as such, it will support the development of crosswalks, the development of machine-understandable schema, and the interoperability of metadata specifications.

The current draft of the RDF data model and syntax specifications can be found at *http://www.w3.org/TR/WD-rdf-syntax*. Other RDF-related drafts are referenced on the W3C Technical Reports and Publications page (*http://www.w3.org/TR*). Eric Miller provides a good, simple introduction to RDF in "An Introduction to the Resource Description Framework," *D-Lib Magazine*, May 1998 (*http://www.dlib.org/dlib/may98/miller/05miller.html*).

Conclusion

There are any number of websites with good pointers to metadata standards and projects. One place to start is Yahoo (*http://www.yahoo.com*), which indexes metadata under Computers and Internet: Information and Documentation: Metadata. The IFLA page Digital Libraries: Metadata Resources (*http://www.ifla.org/II/metadata.htm*) is a particularly good general aggregation. The UKOLN Metadata page covers projects in the United Kingdom and European Community specifically (*http://www.ukoln.ac.uk/metadata/*).

The proliferation of metadata schema provides libraries with a wonderful opportunity to provide resource description tailored to the particular needs of different types of users and objects. In a broader context, the increasing awareness of the need for resource description by the Web and wider Internet communities has led in turn to an increasing recognition of the value of cataloging and classification skills traditionally associated with librarians.

At the same time, the complexity of this new environment raises new problems for libraries and their users: How do you search across multiple repositories of metadata, each with their own structure and syntax? What is the appropriate architecture for metadata on the network, and how well do solutions designed in other communities suit the needs of libraries, museums, archives, and similar institutions? Becoming knowledgeable about metadata is a valuable beginning to answering these questions.

Unique Identifiers on the Web for Documents, Sites, and Domain Names

Colby Mariva Riggs

Colby Mariva Riggs (*cmriggs@uci.edu*) is a systems librarian at the University of California, Irvine. Her current interest is in information technology training and helping others use information technology to enhance their productivity. She has been active in the Library and Information Technology Association (LITA) of the American Library Association as interest group coordinator, chair of the Emerging Technologies Interest Group, coordinator of LITA's "The Connection," and member of the Program Planning Committee.

The development and expansion of the Internet over the past five years has increased dramatically. This growth has placed strains on users of the Internet as they attempt to locate and retrieve documents and related content. The disjointed manner in which information is structured and identified is stressing the basic retrieval tools of the Internet, making them almost useless and irrelevant. Unique identifiers are, therefore, becoming increasingly important as we move further into the digital age. As the collected body of digital information expands, it is clear we need a practical scheme to identify documents, sites and domain names on the World Wide Web. This chapter will discuss some of the significant efforts toward the development of a universally accepted unique identifier system.

Domain Name System

Early in the life of the Internet, very few locations existed for users to contend with. A user simply knew where desired information was located and could successfully retrieve it from an Internet site. Either a numeric IP address or a character string identified the site. As the quantity of Internet-connected sites grew, the Domain Name System (DNS) evolved as a means of dynamically indexing obscure numeric IP addresses with the hierarchical mnemonic strings in common use today.

The conventions established in the Domain Name System help users intelligently "guess" a location from which they may be interested in retrieving information. Beginning with the Top Level Domains (TLDs), the last component in an Internet name, a user can focus in on the name of the desired site. However, the most common TLDs, such as .com, .net, .org, .gov., and .edu, have burgeoned to contain such massive numbers of second-level domains that the hierarchical design of DNS has effectively been negated.

To compound this confusion, the granting of domain names in the United States is the responsibility of an impartial entity, Network Solutions. The agency has willingly registered domain names on a first-come, first-served basis. In the process, domain names recognizable as trademarks or as product names have been issued to entities not affiliated with the rightful owners, and arguments have occurred over the use of common and ambiguous names. The resulting chaotic environment of domain names has done little to help users surmise the location of the information they desire.

Many commercial entities that viewed uniquely identifiable domain names as necessary for their entry onto the Internet could not secure domain names that appropriately identified their product or service. As a result, alternate name space providers have emerged with the goal of achieving direct access to sites in a way that DNS is not able to accomplish. Such services as RealNames (*http://www.realnames.com/*) use company names, brand names, and advertising slogans as an alternative to long, complex URLs. With RealNames, a user can search by a unique company name, brand name, product name, or advertising slogan and retrieve the desired Web destination. Because there are few controls over who can register a particular name, RealNames has established a set of guidelines, Namespace policy, to ensure the uniqueness of the RealName.

An inherent issue is that the Internet per se is a carrier of information rather than a collector or organizer. The greatest technical aptitude of the Internet is its ability to reach a known location, not to find where specific content exists. This creates significant problems for users who know what they want to retrieve but don't know where it is located. Unfortunately, Internet users have often used domain names as their basic directory system with the flawed assumption that the domain name itself is strongly related to a company name or service.

Although most people search by domain name or search engine, the result still points to a specific location on the Internet by way of Uniform Resource Locators (URLs), which are subject to change. The URL system was designed to identify a location on the Internet, not give a description or title for the content. Developments in defining digital objects so as to further refine location identifiers are significant because using a URL to locate content is ineffective and depends largely on the Domain Name System, which has the problems of ambiguity and contention.

Solutions

Although there are limitations to the current Internet, solutions have been developed to build enhanced identification systems for unique Internet resources. Improvement in the DNS has brought some equity and common sense to domain names. Standards are being developed that can be used by various communities to further refine Internet resource retrieval. To be widely accepted and therefore useful, the standards that are under development must have the stability to be consistent and applicable to a diverse constituency. A wide variety of random standards should not be formulated to answer the same problems. Rather, a small number of universal standards should be established that can provide efficient retrieval of unique digital information.

There have been various developments to uniquely identify Internet resources. These systems enable users to navigate from the identifier to the location of the resource. The Internet Engineering Task Force (IETF) has been developing a system for Uniform Resource Names (URNs) designed to persistently identify actual information resources rather than their Internet locations (see *http://www.ietf.org/html.charters/urn-charter.html*).

A URN has three main components. A *naming scheme* includes policies and procedures for creating and assigning URNs within a particular domain. A *resolution system* translates the URNs into their location-specific identifiers (for example, URLs). Once unique identifiers have been established for digital objects, they will be registered and stored in a network-accessible service that can connect them to their locations. The third component, therefore, is a set of *global directories or registries* that provide information with which resolution systems can translate any particular URN.

OCLC developed the Persistent Uniform Resource Locator (PURL), which is similar to, but more limited than, the URN system (see *http://purl.oclc.org/*). Instead of pointing to an Internet location, a PURL points to an intermediate resolver service, which maintains a database linking the PURL to its current URL and returns the URL to the user client, similar to e-mail aliases. In this way, references expressed as PURLs should remain viable as long as the resolution service continues to operate.

Digital Object Identifiers (DOI) being developed for the Association of American Publishers by R. R. Bowker and the Corporation for National Research Initiatives (CNRI) are both identifiers and a routing system (see *http://www.doi.org*). URN-compatible and similar to the PURL system, the DOI system is designed to provide a persistent way of identifying and linking to electronic documents. At its core is the "handle" system developed by CNRI, which uses a directory to link the permanently assigned DOI to the URL containing the object.

These emerging improvements and modifications are encouraging and will likely provide better access to unique Internet resources. The downside to the progressive enhancements is that these are all technological in nature. There are many social and political factors that still need to be addressed. The Internet has been characterized as a self-regulated entity, but with its exponential growth and global application, much more needs to be accomplished to bring the various interested parties—commercial, political, legal, and operational—to consensus. Let's hope in this vibrant transitional period that we do not develop a wide variety of random standards and policies, but, rather, address the essential concerns and roles in a methodical and timely manner.

Resources

Arms, William Y. "Digital Object Identifiers (DOIs) and Clifford Lynch's Five Questions on Identifiers." (1997). *http://www.arl.org/newsltr/194/arms.html.*

Green, Brian, and Mark Bide. *Unique Identifiers: A Brief Introduction.* (1998). *http://www.bic.org.uk/bic/uniquid.html.*

Lynch, Clifford. "Identifiers and Their Role in Networked Information Applications." *American Society for Information Science Bulletin* 24 (December 1997/January 1998): 17–20.

Payette, Sandra. "Persistent Identifiers on the Digital Terrain." *RLG Digi-News* 2 (April 15, 1998): 2.

COPYRIGHT IN CYBERSPACE

Gretchen McCord Hoffmann

Gretchen McCord Hoffmann (*GMHoffmann@hotmail.com*) is currently working on a law degree at the University of Texas School of Law. She worked for two years as a reference/instruction librarian at the University of Texas at San Antonio, and from 1994 to 1998 was the coordinator of library instruction at the University of Houston Libraries. Gretchen has been very active in legislative and advocacy activities for libraries, participating in several national and state legislative days and serving on the Texas Library Association Legislative Committee and the Texas Libraries Political Action Committee Executive Board. Among her publications are two articles in *Texas Library Journal* encouraging librarians to become involved in the legislative process.

I'm a Cybrarian, Not a Lawyer; Do I Really Need to Know about Copyright?

The Internet, although a powerful tool for researchers, poses a new set of problems relating to permission and use. What is legal? Test yourself on the following questions.

1. Can a library download citations from a database to create a bibliography that will be distributed to the public?
2. Can a library put an unpublished manuscript into digital format to provide electronic access?
3. Can a library scan materials into a database to make them available to distance education students at remote sites?
4. Can an art library digitize a slide collection to make it more easily accessible to students?
5. Can a library digitize serials to make interlibrary loan of those materials easier?
6. Who owns the e-mail I write on my account at work?[1]

If you answered yes to any of these questions, you are one of the majority of cybrarians who are not as knowledgeable about copyright as they should be to protect their users' rights, their libraries, and themselves. The references cited at the end of this chapter will provide a thorough discussion of these questions; in a nutshell, the answers are: (1) it depends; (2) no; (3) generally no; (4) no; (5) no; and (6) undecided.

You might wonder how important it is to know the answers to these questions. Is anyone really going to sue a library or a librarian for copyright infringement? The Copyright Remedy Clarification Act of 1990 makes it clear that all defendants in copyright infringement suits can be held liable for monetary damages.[2] It may sound like overkill to suggest that an author or publisher would go after Marian the Librarian for copyright infringement, given that Marian's unlawful act was probably not for commercial purposes. This idea—that no one is going to take the time or spend the money to go after a public servant for a noncommercial violation of copyright law—is probably what has kept the majority of librarians not only in the dark about copyright, but unconcerned about it.

Perhaps it was unlikely in the past that a librarian, dealing only with print, would be sued for copyright violation. However, the proliferation of electronic forms of information has made it very important for librarians to be knowledgeable about copyright law. Copyright owners—authors and publishers—are at the least concerned, at the worst panicked, about the infringement possibilities created by cyberspace. The Internet makes it easier, quicker, and cheaper not only to make copies of almost anything, but to make an unlimited number of copies and to distribute those copies ad infinitum.

Aren't cybrarians and cyberspace users covered by fair use rights? Right now, the answer to that question is: It depends. It depends on who you ask, on the specific situation, and on what happened in the court system and on Capitol Hill last week. To understand why copyright law isn't as simple as it might once have seemed, let's look at the original intentions of the law.

Copyright Law—History and Purpose

The key to American copyright law, and indeed its focus over our entire history as a nation, is the balance between the rights of copyright owners and the necessity to provide access to information for the good of society. The United States Constitution in Article I, Section 8, Clause 8 states that "[Congress has the power to] promote the Progress of Science and the useful Arts, by securing for limited Times to Authors and Inventors the exclusive Right to their respective Writings and Discoveries." In the *Federalist Papers* No. 43, James Madison emphasizes that "the utility of this power will scarcely be questioned. . . . The public good fully coincides in both cases with the claims of individuals."[3] One of the first acts of the first United States Congress was to pass the Copyright Act of 1790, which granted authors and proprietors certain rights "for the encouragement of learning." Clearly, *protection* of information has been a major concern from the beginning of our nation, in order to promote the *production* of information for the public good.

Copyright law has been revised four times, most recently in 1976. These revisions have focused on extending copyright protection to a greater variety of formats (such as works of art); expanding the rights protected (such as performing the copyrighted work); increasing the length of copyright protection; and refining the process of obtaining a copyright. Case law as well as legislative law make clear that the purpose of copyright is to encourage individual contributions to knowledge, art, and society by protecting and promoting personal economic rewards.

It is also clear that throughout our history, copyright protection has been intended to apply to works in any medium. Each copyright revision has extended protection to an ever-widening variety of formats. The language in the current law makes this clear:

> Copyright protection subsists, in accordance with this title, in original works of authorship fixed in any tangible medium of expression, now known or later developed, from which they can be perceived, reproduced, or otherwise communicated, either directly or with the aid of a machine or device.[4]

Under the current law, exclusive rights of copyright owners include the rights to reproduce the copyrighted works; prepare derivative works; distribute copies to the public; perform the work publicly; and display the work publicly.

As a cybrarian, however, should you have to worry about copyright violations as long as you are making and distributing copies in the course of your job as a public servant and information professional? Perhaps. Section 107 of Title 17 of the U.S. Code delineates "fair use" limitations to the exclusive rights of copyright holders. It defines "fair use" as:

> . . . including such use by reproduction in copies or phonorecords or by any other means specified . . . for purposes such as criticism, comment, news reporting, teaching . . . scholarship, or research . . . .[5]

Section 107 also includes specific guidelines for what would be considered "fair use." The bottom line, however, is that fair use is determined on an individual basis and depends on four factors:

1. The purpose and character of the use, including whether such use is of a commercial nature or is for nonprofit educational purposes
2. The nature of the copyrighted work
3. The amount and substantiality of the portion used in relation to the copyrighted work as a whole
4. The effect of the use upon the potential market for or value of the copyrighted work

Although all factors should be considered in making a determination, at different times and in different situations, some factors weigh more heavily than others. The last factor, the effect of the use on the potential market of the item, is frequently the most heavily weighed.

What Does This Mean for Me as a Cybrarian?

The key points we as cybrarians are concerned with are (1) the inarguable intent that copyright law—which includes both protection for the copyright owner and exceptions for fair use—applies to information in any format, and (2) the application of fair use exceptions in the cyberworld. Two questions of definition that leap out from the law cited earlier are: What does "tangible medium" mean in cyberspace? and What constitutes a "copy" in cyberspace? Indeed, these are excellent examples of issues our legislators and courts are still grappling with.

Let's take two illustrations of these examples. First, is electronic mail protected by copyright law? Is it "fixed in [a] tangible medium"? To those of us who use e-mail daily, not only for personal communications but increasingly for formal business purposes, it would seem obvious that e-mail should be considered equivalent to a letter. Yet there has been no ruling on this issue—the law has not addressed this question.

Second, what constitutes a "copy"? This question has much broader implications. As all cybrarians understand, transmitting information across the Internet requires making copies, whether sending e-mail, sending documents by ARIEL, or simply surfing the Web. "So what?" you say. "That's just the way the technology works." Unfortunately, not everyone sees it that way. For example, one court found a computer service in violation of copyright law because, by turning on the computers it used to provide services, "copies" of the operating program were made to the RAM.[6] Similarly, legislation proposed in Congress in 1994 would have defined the RAM copy made when viewing web pages as a "copy" subject to copyright protection.

Barbara Bintliff provides an excellent and readable discussion of this issue, noting that this interpretation of law would lead to "almost all uses of electronic information [being] based on licensing agreements, which would involve fees. Browsing, reading, lending, and printing would be severely restricted."[7] She also notes that Carol Risher of the Association of American Publishers has specifically stated that "browsing electronically is not a right, it is a privilege subject to being licensed."[8]

Another broad issue that emphasizes why copyright law isn't sufficient in its current state to accommodate cyberspace is that cyberspace knows no geographic boundaries, and yet copyright law differs, sometimes drastically, from country to country. In general, European copyright laws tend to be more restrictive of individual uses of copyrighted materials than is U.S. law. In addition, authors' rights are only fully protected in those countries in which the author has complied with the copyright law of that country. Thus, authors must rely on international agreements to protect their rights around the world.

In December 1996, the World Intellectual Property Organization (WIPO), a United Nations agency, met to discuss international protection of copyright in the age of cyberspace. Representatives from over 150 countries participated in the conference, which resulted in three treaties, including the WIPO Copyright Treaty. Although the preamble to the treaty includes the statement that "contracting parties . . . [recognize] the need to maintain a balance between the rights of authors and the larger public interest, particularly education, research and access to information," the American Library Association (ALA), the Digital Future Coalition (DFC), and others are concerned that the treaties are too general in nature.

The United States must pass implementation legislation to bring American copyright law into line with the provisions in the WIPO Copyright Treaty. Because those provisions are so general, a definite possibility exists that such legislation could severely threaten fair use standards and public access to information. Even at this writing, contentious debate is taking place on Capitol Hill over several pieces of such legislation.

The now infamous White Paper produced by the Working Group on Intellectual Property of the Information Infrastructure Task Force, appointed by President Clinton, is the target of tremendous criticism from information rights groups, such as ALA and DFC. The White Paper purports to maintain the balance between copyright owners and information users that is clearly the focus of the Copyright Act of 1976. However, Laura Gasaway, copyright expert and director of the Law Library and professor of law at the University of North Carolina–Chapel Hill, believes as do many others that the recommendations made in the White Paper strongly favor the copyright owner to the detriment of the public good: "The report's balance is distorted by an apparent view that the owner is entitled to all returns that the copyright holder would have received if there were no fair use privilege."[9] Gasaway goes on to charge that "powerful and wealthy interests such as the movie industry, publishers groups, and the like lobbied hard to affect the outcome of the White Paper, and clearly they were successful."[10]

What Are My Responsibilites as a Cybrarian?

The last sentence in the preceding paragraph should give you a good start. Without question, there is a war of sorts going on between those whose primary interest is the economic benefit of copyright holders and those whose primary interest is protecting the public's right to access copyrighted information. Unfortunately, the former side has the money to fund this battle, as Gasaway notes, while the latter side, composed of librarians, educational organizations, and such, is not so lucky. This lack of financial resources means that other resources—like human resources—become ever more important. Gasaway mentions the hard (and successful) lobbying of industry groups; although lobbying may involve some money outlay, letters are cheap—successful lobbying sometimes requires only time, energy, and concern.

Pamela Samuelson, professor at the University of California–Berkeley in both the School of Information Management and Systems and the School of Law and co-director of the Berkeley Center for Law and Technology, also points to the need for cybrarians and other information rights supporters to stay aware of what's going on in the world of legislation and to take a stand: "[Authors of the White Paper] and the copyright maximalists are relying on several factors to get this legislation through Congress *before the public realizes what is happening and rouses itself to action*" [emphasis added].[11] The impact of public awareness and action, however, could make all the difference.

The preceding discussion would seem to imply that cybrarians need to know a lot about copyright law. In fact, you do not have to be a legal expert, a copyright expert, or a professional lobbyist to be heard and to make a difference. Whether you realize it or not, you are a member of a very valuable group of experts from whom Congress people (and state legislators) do not hear all they should: You are an expert in how the public uses information and, thus, why it is an absolute necessity for our society to protect public access to information. As cybrarians and librarians, we are in a far better position to speak to this issue than anyone else.

There are several ways to keep informed about what's going on in Congress that may affect information rights, cyberspace, and libraries. Many resources are listed at the end of this chapter. One of the most valuable is *ALAWON*, the ALA Washington Office Online Newsletter, which can be delivered directly to your e-mail address. Some state library associations provide a similar service. ALA and other public interest groups also provide several opportunities for lobbying efforts. However, the single most important thing you as a cybrarian can do is to get to know your state and federal legislators and keep them informed about information issues. You can do this by writing letters, sending e-mail, and meeting with your legislators at their home offices—or even by participating in state and national lobbying efforts, such as ALA's annual Legislative Day in Washington, D.C., each spring.

On a daily basis in your own library, be aware of what's going on around you. Get in the habit of questioning everything you and your staff members do in terms of the possibility of copyright infringement. For example, look at your library's web pages. Where did your graphics come from? If they were taken from another web page (or any other existing source), do you know for certain that you do not need copyright permissions to use them?

Set some basic ground rules for yourself and your staff. Under current copyright law, a copyright notice does not have to be attached to a copyrighted work to protect it. Therefore, assume that everything you see in cyberspace is copyrighted unless otherwise stated. In any case, if in doubt, don't use it or copy it.

Take a critical look at what you, your staff, and your users are doing in and with cyberspace. Can you make an analogy to a print situation? If so, are you applying to the cyberspace situation the same copyright guidelines and processes you would apply to the print? Jensen and Scott both very strongly advise librarians to post copyright notices on all publicly accessible equipment, the same statements all libraries post near photocopiers.[12] If you are using electronic reserve services, are you certain you are complying with copyright law? For example, how many copies, in any format, vis-

COPYRIGHT IN CYBERSPACE 109

ible or not, are actually being made when you provide this service? Is this covered by fair use guidelines? Are you following required procedures?

Conclusion

The bottom line is that there are way too many unanswered questions and murky answers out there for any cybrarian to feel confident that she or he is always obeying copyright law . . . or to feel confident that if a slipup occurs here or there, no one will care. The Digital Millennium Copyright Act, passed in the latter part of 1998, raises more questions than it answers, and continued change can be counted on in the digital copyright arena (see *http://www.arl.org/info/frn/copy/dmca.html* for more information).

Wendy M. Grossman, author of *net.wars*, sums up the situation nicely: "In part, what it comes down to is that the Internet scares people, particularly copyright owners whose wealth is tied up in intellectual property."[13] Not only does the Internet scare people, but by its very nature, cyberspace is a totally different animal than any we've seen before. It will take us quite a while to figure out how to deal with it.

Resources

Introductions and Overviews

Bielefield, Arlene, and Lawrence Cheeseman. *Libraries and Copyright Law*. New York: Neal-Schuman, 1993.
> *The* place to start. An excellent and readable guide to American copyright law, with specific applications for libraries. Addendums include excerpts of copyright laws and guidelines pertinent to librarians.

Bruwelheide, Janis H. *The Copyright Primer for Librarians and Educators*. 2d ed. Chicago: ALA, 1995.
> A thorough guide for librarians and teachers of all levels; format for each chapter is discussion of the topic followed by many specific questions and answers. Excellent addenda include guidelines for requesting permission and developing policies, selected court cases with very brief explanations, and further resources.

Fishman, Stephen. *The Copyright Handbook: How to Protect and Use Written Works*. 2d ed. Berkeley: Nolo Press, 1994.
> Aimed more toward the copyright owner, but gives a great understanding of the processes.

Gasaway, Laura N., and Sarah K. Wiant. *Libraries and Copyright: A Guide to Copyright Law in the 1990s*. Washington, D.C.: SLA, 1994.
> Very thorough discussions of applications of specific sections of the law to specific uses and various formats (for example, "Loaning Computer Software"). Includes discussion of international copyright law.

Institute for Learning Technologies. *CREDO: Copyright Resources for Education Online.* (1995). *http://www.ilt.columbia.edu/projects/copyright/ILTcopy0.html.*

Intellectual Property Reference Library. *http://www.servtech.com/~mbobb/.*

Stanford University Libraries. *Copyright and Fair Use. http://fairuse.stanford.edu/.*

United States Copyright Act. *http://www.law.cornell.edu/uscode/17/*

United States Copyright Office. *http://lcweb.loc.gov/copyright/*

Guidelines for Cybrarians

Anderson, Steve J. D. "Copyright and Digital Reproduction in Cyberspace." Copyright Corner. *Information Outlook* (June 1997): 14.

Bintliff, Barbara. "copyright@help! Copyright and Library Internet Use." *Colorado Libraries* (fall 1995): 20–24.

Brinson, J. Dianne, and Mark F. Radcliffe. *An Intellectual Property Law Primer for Multimedia and Web Developers.* Cyberspace and New Media Law Center. (1998). *http://www2.viaweb.com/lib/laderapress/primer.html.*

Build a Safer Web Site (legal considerations in creating web pages). *http://www.netlaw.com/safer.htm*

CONFU: The Conference on Fair Use. *http://www.utsystem.edu/ogc/intellectualproperty/confu.htm*

Copyright Clearance Center, Inc. *http://www.copyright.com/*

Cyberlaw Encyclopedia. *http://gahtan.com/techlaw/home.htm*

Cyberspace Law Center. *http://www.cybersquirrel.com/clc/*

Gasaway, Laura N. "Libraries, Educational Institutions, and Copyright Proprietors: The First Collision on the Information Highway." *Journal of Academic Librarianship* (September 1996): 337–344.

Jensen, Mary Brandt. "Electronic Reserve and Copyright." *Computers in Libraries* 13, no. 3 (March 1993): 40–45.

———. "Legal Matters." *Computers in Libraries* 12, no. 8 (September 1992): 17–19.

Oakley, Robert L. "Copyright Issues for the Creators and Users of Information in the Electronic Environment." *Electronic Networking* 1, no. 1 (fall 1991): 23–30.

Risher, Carol A. "The Great Copyright Debate." *Library Journal* (September 15, 1994): 34–37.

Scott, Ralph Lee. "Wired to the World." *North Carolina Libraries* (summer 1994): 74–75.

What Reference Practitioners Should Know about Copyright and the Web. *http://www.library.sos.state.il.us/isl/training/v980204c.html*

Ongoing Issues and Debates

Caruso, Denise. "Should Copyright Law Apply to Internet?" *CyberTimes.* New York Times Online. *http://www.cybertimes.com* (requires registration).

Gassie, Lillian Woon. "Copyright Law in the Electronic Information Age." *LLA Bulletin* (spring 1995): 208–214.

Information Infrastructure Task Force. The Report of the Working Group on Intellectual Property Rights [the "White Paper"]. *http://www.uspto. gov/web/offices/com/doc/ipnii/*
   President Clinton's task force "to articulate and implement the Administration's vision for the National Information Infrastructure."

Lee, Ya-Ching. "Toward a More Balanced Online Copyright Policy." *Communications and the Law* 20, no. 1 (March 1998): 37–59.

Samson, Martin H. *Internet Library of Law and Court Decisions. http://www.phillipsnizer.com/internetlib.htm*
   Provides brief "summaries of court decisions shaping the law of the Web."

Samuelson, Pamela. "The Copyright Grab." *http://www.wired.com/wired/ archive/4.01/white.paper.html*

Skier, Jason. "The End of Fair Use? Or the IITF White Paper as a Mechanism to Protect the Fair Use of Copyrighted Materials." *http://viper.law. miami.edu/~froomkin/seminar/papers/skier.htm*

Union for the Public Domain's Page on the December 1996 Diplomatic Conference of WIPO. *http://www.public-domain.org/wipo/dec96/dec96.html*

Keeping Up to Date

American Library Association: Advocacy. *http://www.ala.org/advocacy/*

American Library Association Washington Office Newsline (ALAWON). http://www.ala.org/washoff/alawon/index.html
   Can also subscribe for free to receive by e-mail.

Cybertimes: Copyright Issues http://www.nytimes.com/library/cyber/week/ index-copyright.html (requires registration).
   From the *New York Times* on the Web.

IP: The Magazine of Law and Policy for High Technology. http://www. ipmag.com

Digital Future Coalition. *http://www.dfc.org*

Electronic Frontier Foundation. *http://www.eff.org*

Notes

1. Laura N. Gasaway and Sarah K. Wiant, *Libraries and Copyright: A Guide to Copyright Law in the 1990s* (Washington, D.C.: SLA, 1994), 225–229; Janis H. Bruwelheide, *The Copyright Primer for Libraries and Educators*, 2d ed. (Chicago: ALA, 1995), 22, 28, 29, 64; and Marilu Goodyear, "Surviving the Internet: Legal and Policy Considerations" (paper

presented at a workshop of the same title at the University of Houston Libraries, Houston, Tex., August 15, 1997).

2. Arlene Bielefield and Lawrence Cheeseman, *Libraries and Copyright Law* (New York: Neal-Schuman, 1993).

3. James Madison, "The Federalist: A Commentary on the Constitution of the United States," No. 43 in the *Federalist Papers* (New York: Modern Library, 1960).

4. *Copyright Act of 1976, U.S. Code,* vol. 17, sec. 102 (1976).

5. *Copyright Act of 1976, U.S. Code,* vol. 17, sec. 107 (1976).

6. Jessica Litman, "Copyright Law and Electronic Access to Information," *First Monday* (September 2, 1996): note 13 (*http://www. firstmonday.dk/issues/issue3/litman/index. htm/#13*).

7. Barbara Bintliff, "copyright@help! Copyright and Library Internet Use," *Colorado Libraries* (fall 1995): 22.

8. Ibid.

9. Laura N. Gasaway, "Libraries, Educational Institutions, and Copyright Proprietors: The First Collision on the Information Highway," *Journal of Academic Librarianship* (September 1996): 338.

10. Ibid.

11. Pamela Samuelson, "The Copyright Grab," *http://www.wired.com/wired/archive/4.01/ white.paper.html.*

12. Mary Brandt Jensen, "Legal Matters," *Computers in Libraries* 12, no. 8 (September 1992): 17; and Ralph Lee Scott, "Wired to the World," *North Carolina Libraries* (summer 1994): 74.

13. Wendy M. Grossman, "Downloading as a Crime," *Scientific American* (March 1998): 37.

Cyber-Citing: Citing Electronic Sources

Kristin Vogel

Kristin Vogel (*kvogel@titan.iwu.edu*) is access librarian and associate professor at Illinois Wesleyan University. For the past seven years she has worked on information technology issues and implementation for liberal arts colleges.

As the helpful voice responding over the phone to a desperate researcher at the end of the day, I field such questions as "What page does this article end on? I forgot to write it down," or "My photocopy cut off the journal name. I know the author and title. Can you help me?" Now I am getting a brand-new question: "I forgot to write down the URL and my paper's due tomorrow! Can you help me?" As reference librarians know, this is another version of the dreaded "How do I cite this?" question. We must be ready to answer this, and we can be.

Reminding ourselves of the purpose of the citation helps keep things in perspective and provides direction in the search for the "documented answer" to the question. Scholarship has one primary use for the citation: Readers require a citation to successfully locate the original source. The reader may need clarification or may have doubts about the content. The reader may wish to reconstruct the argument and need each individual part, or the reader may simply have an insatiable hunger for knowledge.

Citations to electronic sources have the dubious honor of aiming at a moving target. Potential problems arise because of the constant state of flux in technology and the relative impermanence of electronic documents. A nightmare begins when the source has been

- deleted and may never be found again,
- edited and may never be the same again,

114   THE DOCUMENT AS OBJECT AND COMMODITY

- moved and may never be found again, or
- corrupted and may never be the same again.

Currently, scholars and librarians are discussing and hotly debating how to handle all this. Is it okay for the original source to change? Should an archival copy be kept and not be allowed to change or disappear? What are the necessary parts of the citation?

Looking at the question from the point of view of the practicing reference librarian, this chapter will provide an up-to-date guide to citing electronic resources, using a variety of standards and style manuals.

Print Style Manuals

Meanwhile, my phone rings, and in response to my enthusiastic "How may I help you?" the desperate voice on the other end asks, "How do I cite this?" I ask what style manual the caller is using, and in reply I hear, "Style? I don't know. Aren't they all the same?" I head to my well-stocked reference collection and begin to peruse the style manuals. In the reference collection there are a few existing style manuals that may help answer this question. With each revision of the major style manuals, additions and changes are made to guide authors in the creation of bibliographies that must incorporate electronic sources.

Publication Manual of the American Psychological Association

First I examine the *Publication Manual of the American Psychological Association* (APA), which contains an appendix on the "Elements and Examples of References in APA Style" and incorporates a subsection on electronic media. Before opening the book, I feel encouraged by the notation that this is the fourth edition, 1994, and must certainly contain everything I need. I read the section on page 175 on creating a reference list and anticipate what is included. I find:

> Because one purpose of listing references is to enable readers to retrieve and use the sources, reference data must be correct and complete. Each entry usually contains the following elements: authors, year of publication, title, and publishing data—all the information necessary for unique identification and library search.

I even see an admonishment by Brunner dating back to 1942 that indicates that "an inaccurate or incomplete reference 'will stand in print as an annoyance to future investigators and a monument to the writer's carelessness.'"

In my continuing effort to determine the APA style, the following information jumps off pages 175–176:

> Because a reference list includes only references that document the article and provide recoverable data, do not include personal communi-

cations, such as letters, memoranda, and informal electronic communication. Instead, cite personal communication only in text.

My skin begins to crawl. What does this mean? What is the APA saying about electronic mail? Quickly, very quickly, I flip back to pages 173–174 to the section defining personal communications and find the following:

> Personal communications may be letters, memos, some electronic communications (e.g., e-mail, discussion groups, messages from electronic bulletin boards), telephone conversations, and the like. Because they do not provide recoverable data, personal communications are not included in the reference list. Cite personal communications in text only. . . . Use your judgment in citing other forms of personal communications; networks currently provide a casual forum for communicating, and what you cite should have scholarly relevance.

Indeed, now my skin has jumped off and done a few laps around the building, gone upstairs to share the news with colleagues, e-mailed my brother-in-law, and returned feeling particularly prickly. I take note of the fact that the personal communications definition may include discussion lists that therefore would be in the text of the paper but would not be included in the reference list and would not be considered to have scholarly relevance. That may be true, but, oh, what a can of worms this opens!

It is as though a fork in the road has appeared, and I begin gazing through a fog to try to determine which way to go. What's up the road to the north? It looks somewhat like a gravel road, with electronic communications relegated to the status of an "invisible college." To the south, I see a barely discernible trail blazing the way through a jungle of electronic communications and that points to a radical change in scholarship and research. You can tell that someone has gone in that direction, but the road is merely a trail with few directional signs.

Pull back! Pull back! My caller is still on hold, and even if I feel I am on the edge of a new frontier, the metaphysical discussion must wait a while longer. I need more information! In the APA's appendix on electronic sources, I take note of the examples of online journals, online journal abstracts, abstracts on CD-ROM, software, and data files. I also note the included parts of the citation: author, date, title, and an availability statement that includes protocol, directory, and file name.

Chicago Manual of Style

The 1993 *Chicago Manual of Style* is the next manual I investigate. Encouraged, I remember that, although it is establishing rules, "the renunciation . . . of an authoritarian position in favor of common sense and flexibility has always been a fundamental and abiding principle." I also know from browsing the book when it was still on the new-book shelf that "computer programs are given more attention and are augmented with more examples, and guidelines for the citation of electronic documents have been added." I flip to the sections on documentation and discover guides to materials obtained through "loose-leaf, computer, or information services" as well as "computer programs and electronic documents." The examples contained here include two for electronic bulletin boards and imply the inclusion of discussion lists.

To confirm or refute this, I move to the section on personal communications. Although this section does not mention electronic sources, I do notice statements dictating the citation of personal communications within the text, as opposed to in the bibliography, implying that the sources are unobtainable. I note that this manual indicates that the parts of this citation include author, title, description of source, citation date, and an availability statement that includes the address for obtaining the item.

The inclusion of addresses in this citation appears somewhat vague as there are no examples that illustrate a file obtained using FTP. I write down information on how to contact the International Standards Organization, which is the guiding entity for electronic source citations for the *Chicago Manual of Style.* ISO may be helpful in determining how to handle my questions about addresses.

MLA Handbook for Writers of Research Papers

The Modern Language Association of America's *MLA Handbook for Writers of Research Papers* (1995) states in its foreword that

> the rules for citing electronic material that the MLA committee established are not presented as definitive, and they will surely change as the technology and practices governing electronic communication evolve.

Turning to the sections on electronic sources, I am first interested to find how MLA handles "personal communication" and so read with interest on page 165 that citations for an "electronic journal, electronic newsletter, or electronic conference document should be similar to one for an article in a print periodical, though there are a few necessary differences." Elements of the citation include author, title, publication date, pages or paragraphs or no pagination indication, medium, name of computer network, and access date. The three final elements are where the primary differences lie.

Reading further on the page, I note that following the examples is a direct statement about addresses: "At the end of the entry, you may add as supplementary information the electronic address you used to access the document. . . . Your instructor may require this information."

Another important section that I peruse is 4.10.7, titled "A letter, a memo, an e-mail communication, or a public online posting." This indicates that, according to MLA, my caller would need to treat a personal e-mail message similarly to a memo and would include it in the works-cited list.

Electronic Style: A Guide to Citing Electronic Information

The final book that I examine is *Electronic Style: A Guide to Citing Electronic Information.* Li and Crane published this manual in 1993, intending to provide concrete examples of how to cite electronic sources in APA format. APA's fourth edition cites it as the guide for APA-style manuscripts. The parts of the citation included here are author, date, title, type of medium, and availability statement, which includes the information on accessing the source again.

I notice that there are subtle differences between this style manual and the current version of the APA style manual. It will be important for my caller to evaluate the importance of using the most recent style manual versus the extent of the examples in Li and Crane's manual. From my professional reading, I am aware that a new edition of this book came out in 1996 and that it includes a section following MLA style as well as revising the section following APA style.

Internet-Obtained Style Manuals

Ten years ago I would be able to stop and provide my caller with the information that I've found. On the other hand, ten years ago I might not have gotten this question at all! Now, I can't stop with the print reference collection. I must also check the Internet to see what may be available to guide the caller.

Several guides to citation styles exist, and I am almost overwhelmed by discovering that nearly everyone has an opinion on citation of electronic sources. Not only does everyone have an opinion, but also everyone is now able to electronically publish his or her version of a chosen style manual. After browsing through a number of these, I narrow them down to just a few more-general sites and save the others for later. (For URLs of these sites, see the references at the end of this chapter.)

Columbia Guide to Online Style

The first site I visit virtually is Janice Walker and Todd Taylor's 1998 *Columbia Guide to Online Style*. Walker created the original version to handle the information she found in her research and to answer her students' "How do I cite this?" questions. I note the suggestion to adapt the punctuation of the MLA style when necessary to eliminate confusion with Internet addresses. The parts of the citation include author, title, title of complete work, protocol and address, and the date of posting or date of citing.

Walker and Taylor's treatment of electronic personal communication, such as e-mail and discussion lists, is equivalent to their treatment of other electronic sources. These would all appear in a citation list. E-mail and discussion lists do have unique citation styles. For e-mail the authors recommend "Omit the e-mail address." Apparently originally written shortly before the publication of the fourth edition of the *MLA Handbook for Writers of Research Papers*, this guide contains some conflicts with the current

MLA rules. Along with Todd Taylor, Walker has expanded the original ideas and now includes information on scientific citation style.

ISO International Standard 690-2

During 1997, the International Organization for Standardization (ISO) published a new standard for citing electronic sources. Because the existing bibliographic citation standard 690 was renamed to 690-1, the new standard is called 690-2. The ISO Technical Committee 46, Subcommittee 9 wrote the standard.[1] The citation parts include primary responsibility (author), title, type of medium, place of publication, publication date, citation date, availability and access, and, if available, standard number (for example, ISSN, ISBN). In addition, rules for capitalization, abbreviation, and punctuation are explicitly delineated.

Other Electronic Sources

In the characteristic manner of our times, it is possible to find information about a book on the Internet even before print publication. I find two style sheets online titled Electronic Sources that illustrate the methods for citing electronic sources used by Li and Crane to update their 1993 book. One style sheet illustrates the revised APA format. The second illustrates MLA-style citations.

Answering the Original Question

When I return the patron's call, I indicate that I have information to help answer the question. I have in front of me a variety of style manuals, and I prepare myself with documentation to back up my answer. I navigate through the call with ease and am able to give the caller confidence that the citation is accurate and that the library is indeed the place to go with these questions!

Future Citation Guides

So, I've answered the question. I've gotten what I needed to provide resources for the caller. Unfortunately, the question doesn't end there. It will come back tomorrow, next week, next month, and next year. Things will continue to change. I've mastered the Gopher citation and the online information service citation. I've learned to think about the analogies between paper and electronic sources to make my way through the style manuals. I've learned that the personal communications sections of the style manuals are just as important as the electronic sources sections.

Today I'm working on the WWW citation. What citations will I need tomorrow? Are the basic rules of citations enough to make the transition? What about scholarly relevance? Will it be up to cybrarians, editors, peer reviewers, or serendipity?

Examples

The following is a guide to the resources I've identified and examined, and includes some examples of citations.

Publication Manual of the American Psychological Association

Schonfeld, M. (1995, Spring). Introduction to justifying value in nature [18 paragraphs]. *Electronic Journal of Analytical Philosophy* [On-line serial], (3). Available WWW: Hostname: www.phil.indiana.edu Directory: ejap/1995.spring File: schonfeld.1995.spring.html

The Chicago Manual of Style

Documentation 1

Schonfeld, Martin. Introduction to Justifying Value in Nature. In *Electronic Journal of Analytical Philosophy* [journal online], (spring) no. 3. (1995) [cited 11 February 1996]. Available from WWW www.phil. indiana.edu/ejap/1995.spring/schonfeld.1995.spring.html

Documentation 2

Schonfeld, Martin. 1995. Introduction to justifying value in nature. In *Electronic Journal of Analytical Philosophy* [journal online], (spring) no. 3. [cited 11 February 1996]. Available from WWW www.phil.indiana.edu/ejap/1995.spring/schonfeld.1995.spring.html

The MLA Handbook for Writers of Research Papers

Schonfeld, Martin. "Introduction to Justifying Value in Nature." *Electronic Journal of Analytical Philosophy* 3 (1995) : n. pag. Online. Internet. 11 February 1996.

Optional

Schonfeld, Martin. "Introduction to Justifying Value in Nature." *Electronic Journal of Analytical Philosophy* 3 (1995) : n. pag. Online. Internet. 11 February 1996. Available WWW: www.phil.indiana.edu/ejap/1995.spring/schonfeld.1995.spring.html

Electronic Style: A Guide to Citing Electronic Information

Schonfeld, M. (1995, Spring). Introduction to justifying value in nature. *Electronic Journal of Analytical Philosophy* [On-line], (3). Available WWW: www.phil.indiana.edu Directory: ejap/1995.spring File: schoneld.1995.spring.html

Columbia Guide to Online Style

Humanities style

Schonfeld, Martin. "Introduction to Justifying Value in Nature." *Electronic Journal of Analytical Philosophy* http://www.phil.indiana.edu/ejap/1995.spring/schonfeld.1995.spring.html [11 February 1996].

Scientific style

Schonfeld, M. (1995). Introduction to justifying value in nature. *Electronic journal of analytical philosophy* http://www.phil.indiana.edu/ejap/1995.spring/schonfeld.1995.spring.html [11 February 1996].

ISO International Standard 690-2

Schonfeld, Martin. Introduction to justifying value in nature. *Electronic Journal of Analytical Philosophy* [online]. 1995. No. 3 [cited 1996-02-11]. Available from Internet: URL:http://www.phil.indiana.edu/ejap/1995.spring/schonfeld.1995.spring.html. ISSN 1071-5800.

Other Electronic Sources

APA style

Schonfeld, M. (1995, Spring). Introduction to justifying value in nature. *Electronic Journal of Analytical Philosophy* [Online], (3), 18 paragraphs. Available: HTTP: http://www.phil.indiana.edu/ejap/1995.spring/schonfeld.1995.spring.html [1996, February 11].

MLA style

Schonfeld, Martin. "Introduction to Justifying Value in Nature." *Electronic Journal of Analytical Philosophy* 3 (1995) 18 pars. Online. Available HTTP: http://www.phil.indiana.edu/ejap/1995.spring/schonfeld.1995.spring.html. 11 February 1996.

Resources

American Psychological Association. *Publication Manual of the American Psychological Association*. 4th ed. Washington, D.C.: APA, 1994.

Chicago Manual of Style. 14th ed. Chicago: University of Chicago Pr., 1993.

Gibaldi, J. *MLA Handbook for Writers of Research Papers*. 4th ed. New York: Modern Language Association of America, 1995.

International Organization for Standardization. *ISO TC 46/SC 9: Standards for the Presentation, Identification, and Description of Documents (excerpts)*. (1996). Available: *http://www.nlc-bnc.ca/iso/tc46sc9/standard/690-2e.htm*.

Li, X., and N. B. Crane. *Electronic Style: A Guide to Citing Electronic Information*. 2d ed. Medford, N.J.: Information Today, 1996.

———. *Electronic Sources: APA Style of Citation.* (1995). Available: *http://www.uvm.edu/~xli/reference/apa.html.*

———. *Electronic Sources: MLA Style of Citation.* (1995). Available: *http://www.uvm.edu/~xli/reference/mla.html.*

Walker, J. R., and Todd Taylor. *The Columbia Guide to Online Style.* (1998). Available: *http://www.columbia.edu/cu/cup/cgos/idx_basic.html.*

Walker, J. R., and Todd Taylor. *The Columbia Guide to Online Style.* New York: Columbia University Pr., 1998.

Note

1. J. Thacker, personal communication, January 1, 1996.

5

Puttin' It Out over the Net: Sources and Services

Collecting Electronic Resources: What You Don't Know, You Can Learn

Kimberly J. Parker

Kimberly J. Parker (*kimberly.parker@yale.edu*) has been the electronic publishing and collections librarian for the Yale University Library since November 1997 when the position was created. Before then, she was the chemistry librarian and science bibliographer at the Sterling Chemistry and Kline Science Libraries of Yale University. Kimberly began her career as a National Library of Medicine Associate. Among her many past projects have been efforts to create a virtual desktop environment for chemists, exploration of electronic seminar options for the discussion of articles, and experimentation with digitizing classic science articles. At present she is wrestling with issues of appropriate standards for archiving electronic resources, and achieving comparable usage statistics for networked products.

There is no single approach to collecting electronic resources. Every institution is evolving different policies and procedures. Some are asking their librarians to "do it yourself," while others are choosing to handle everything centrally. Different models work better at different institutions.

No matter where your institution falls on the continuum, there are issues in common that will need to be examined and reviewed. Much of this chapter assumes the librarian facing these issues has little central support. If this is not the case in your situation, don't tune out. Even though the administration may be handling the acquisition process, that doesn't mean you shouldn't offer your expertise.

Broken down into parts and examined as an extension of selection and acquisition practices in the non-electronic world, the process of "collecting" electronic resources becomes easier. This chapter will consider a variety of factors that are, however, unique to electronic media collection development.

Use Your Experience

If you have been applying selection criteria to purchase decisions for other formats, you have many of the tools you need to judge electronic resources. Issues of content, overlap with other resources, usefulness, and so forth apply in both the print and electronic worlds.

Keeping these skills in mind, and realizing that they are more than half the battle, let's take a look at the other issues you face: communicating and cooperating with colleagues; evaluating interfaces; looking at licenses; understanding technical issues; arranging trials; and communicating with acquisitions and cataloging departments.

Tom Nisonger makes a good distinction between evaluation and selection. A product may be the best thing since sliced bread, but if it isn't compatible with your technical capabilities or your ability to teach something completely different to your patrons, it may not be worth selecting.[1]

Don't Go It Alone

Most librarians have colleagues within their institutions with whom they can collaborate on electronic products. These could be colleagues in a branch library, who just happen to have patrons who have been pestering them for years to duplicate something in your library.

With electronic resources, location becomes much less of a factor in ownership, and you not only have the opportunity to share costs, you also are in a position to coordinate purchases with your colleagues. If you have never thought of your colleagues in other branches as allies, now is the time to do so.

Evaluating Interfaces

Electronic resources come in multiple flavors. (Don't we all wish the flavors were chocolate chunk, peppermint stick, or cookie-dough!) Deciding if you want your electronic resources from Ovid or OCLC or SilverPlatter or Ebsco or Blackwell's can be as heartrending as being told you are only allowed to get one scoop of ice cream. On the other hand, think about having thirty-one different journal publishers producing electronic journals in thirty-one different ways, requiring you and your users to remember thirty-one different browse modes, thirty-one different search structures, and so on. Suddenly, only one scoop of ice cream starts to look appealing.

But the choice of an interface is far more costly than picking a new flavor of ice cream. What if you find out that a resource you are interested in is not available through the interface your library is using? You might want to encourage the publisher of that resource to make it available to the vendor who is providing your library's interface.

COLLECTING ELECTRONIC RESOURCES: WHAT YOU DON'T KNOW, YOU CAN LEARN   127

If that's not possible, is your library willing to pay more to get the conformity? What if your online system loses a little functionality with your chosen interface? Will your library now pay a little more to get more functionality? What if your institution's consortium decides to go with a different interface provider?

But this is nothing, right? Librarians have been facing tough choices since the early days of the printing press. Remember to breathe, and you can manage this obstacle course.

Licensing, Contracts, and Legalese

Learning to understand licensing language, identify problems, and negotiate changes to a licensing agreement can consume daylong seminars. If you are given complete responsibility for license negotiations, I highly recommend attending an appropriate workshop, or at least educating yourself by examining a useful resource, such as the LibLicense website (*http://www.library.yale.edu/~llicense/index.shtml*). Even if you are not given responsibility for final license negotiations, or if your institution chooses to handle the review and negotiation of licenses centrally, you still need to understand certain details of the license agreement.

Most licenses will specify what authorized users are allowed or not allowed to do. Often they will outline the institution's responsibilities in enforcing the terms of the license. Some licenses get very specific about contact channels for technical issues. The frontline librarian needs to know what is in the license, and what can and cannot be supported in implementation. In negotiating a licensing agreement, certain features are inherently important to a library's online system. The following scenario, although fictitious, could happen to anyone.

Picture a well-intended lawyer taking every care to make sure a contract's license terms reflect proper indemnification for your institution, and the proper adjudication venue, and all other legal verbiage that means a lot to administrators. Now picture this same lawyer passing right over the terms that say end users are not permitted to download or print, and signing the license with a sense of accomplishment.

The purpose of this example is not to malign attorneys, but to offer a warning about checking for unacceptable provisions in a contract. Obviously most lawyers will obtain expert advice about issues unfamiliar to them. The point is that frontline librarians are often the ones with the expertise, such as knowing about a unique subject resource. Will the vendor make that resource available? Therefore, you should read the licenses for your materials carefully, preferably before they are reviewed by the group or person responsible for final license negotiation. Provide comments on issues of concern to you.

Legalese and MARC are alike because reading licenses is a bit like learning the MARC field tag codes. The more you look at the codes, the more you are surprised that you understand what you are looking at. The same is true of legal terminology. Soon you will reach the point where terms and clauses that will give you problems stand out as if they were highlighted on the page.

Working through Technical Needs

If your library has a well-organized and integrated technical systems group, you're at an advantage. If the group has already created a list of technical issues that need to be considered with any electronic resource purchase, thank them with all your heart. Then make sure they haven't been concentrating so hard on technical problems that they've forgotten the patrons' needs.

The problem with considering technical needs when purchasing an electronic resource is that the issues change—almost daily. Take, for example, authentication. Many large sites like to use IP authentication because they do not have to manage passwords and user IDs for vast numbers of authorized users. Other sites prefer password authentication because their users move around a lot.

Let's make the example more specific. On March 1, a large-site systems staff recommends IP authentication. On March 2, they hear from colleagues at another library about a password scripting program that will allow them to filter out users by IP address and supply a password behind the scenes to the vendor. They test it out on March 3. On March 4, the recommendation has changed: "We prefer IP authentication, but use of passwords is acceptable." Moral: Stay in touch, and don't assume yesterday's recommendations apply today.

You will probably need to stay on top of the following items with your systems team:

- Are team members willing or able to do local customization if needed for a resource?
- Are they willing or able to load a resource locally on a server at your library? If so, how often are they willing or able to load updates to the data or the server software?
- What are your institution's chosen network clients, and does a desired resource work properly with them? (If it doesn't work properly, how much effort are they willing or able to expend to fix it?)
- Is your systems team willing to support unique pieces of client software if needed by a particular resource, even if that piece of software won't run smoothly with your institution's workstation setups? Or even if the software does work well with the current default setup, can you rely on the systems team for support?
- What authentication modes are they prepared to deal with? Can they arrange for authorized users to get access when not on campus?
- Are they willing or able to acquire usage statistics for locally loaded or remotely accessed resources?

Taking Advantage of Trials

Most major vendors will enable your system to run a free trial of their service. Many small vendors will at least provide a short period of free access as they bring a product online for the first time. There is almost no way to properly evaluate a product without at least several weeks to wander through all its idiosyncrasies.

Having a vendor demo the product for you, or testing it once yourself, is not the same as using it for days or weeks, as well as having patrons use it. It's amazing how many annoying little quirks will show up once you've purchased a product, even if you have taken it for a trial spin.

Completing Acquisition and Cataloging Processes

Don't forget in the midst of all your sales conference calls—and license negotiations—that you need to ensure the product goes through a formal acquisitions procedure. This could simply mean creating an order/pay/receipt record on your acquisitions system, but believe me, you need that record in place when the invoice arrives!

Alternatively, many institutions have a very detailed acquisitions process for electronic resources, such as running down an elaborate checklist and review process. Whatever your institution does, it isn't always easy to remember when there's no physical object to shepherd through a receiving process. Make twice the effort to communicate with acquisitions staff and you should be all right.

Also, don't forget that you want the resource cataloged! You have been telling your patrons for years to look in the catalog to find things. Don't confuse them now. The key once again is to have good communication lines to the cataloging staff. If you have an internal website for staff, you can use a Web form that will send e-mail with relevant information to the appropriate cataloger. This ensures that the correct information gets into the cataloger's hands.

The Bigger Picture

The issues presented so far have addressed the short-range goal of obtaining and maintaining an electronic resource system. However, there is a bigger picture, which involves long-term as well as philosophical concerns. Many discussion lists that explore these subjects in depth are available online. Some of the relevant discussion lists you might want to join are: *liblicense-l@lists.yale.edu*, archived at *http://www.library.yale.edu/~llicense/ListArchives/*; *diglibns@sunsite.berkeley.edu*, archived at *http://sunsite.berkeley.edu/DigLibns/archive.html*; or *arl-ejournal@arl.org*, archived at *http://www.cni.org/Hforums/arl-ejournal/*. The "Statement of Current Perspective and Preferred Practices for the Selection and Purchase of Electronic Information" of the International Coalition of Library Consortia (*http://www.library.yale.edu/consortia/statement.html*) is also a good place to immerse yourself in some of the bigger issues of electronic collecting. The following sections deal with a few of these issues.

Long-Term Access

Long-term access and control involve such questions as: What is the true importance of a resource? What are the implications of buying it, loading it locally, or licensing it short-term? Are you considering archiving this resource, or buying perpetual access to it? Do you just want to link to a resource or mirror it at your own site?

In other words, the ownership versus access issue is muddied by all the technical possibilities of a digital environment. No one else can really answer questions like this for a specific subject product except the subject librarian.

Long-term access can mean continued access after cancellation or just that you plan to continue leasing this resource for at least five years. When you buy a resource, you need to think about how long you want to have it available. There is no need to panic. Most institutions have already made this decision. You have your "discard after two years" titles. You have your "keep older years in microform only" titles, and you have your "keep forever and buy replacements if you have to" titles. For an example of decision factors used by one library for e-resources, see the digital collecting levels of the Berkeley Digital Library SunSITE Collection and Preservation Policy (*http://sunsite.berkeley.edu/Admin/collection.html*).

Ultimately, the access and archive methods used impact the amount of control a library has over its electronic resources. The following questions highlight some of the problems:

- Does your institution want to be the party in control of a journal's archive, or are you willing to have someone else do it for you? (A vendor? Another library? A publisher?)
- How do you want to differentiate between local loading (control) and remote access? Are you making those choices based on convenience and costs instead of archiving and preservation considerations?
- If libraries opt too often for remote access, are we abdicating our archival responsibilities?
- Does having an archive even matter for all e-resources?
- Are there technical capabilities for creating archives of some of these resources?

Price

Pricing of electronic resources is vastly different from that of print. Part of the problem is the large number of pricing models. Those of you already digging into the electronic collecting world will recognize that the marketplace for electronic journals is still defining itself. There are as many pricing models being tested as there are creative people to come up with them.

Prices can be based on user populations, print equivalents, packages, historical purchasing patterns, budgets, and those ever-confusing consortial deals. Let's hope there's never pricing based on square footage of the library times the square root of the departmental FTE plus the salary of the top five institution officers divided by pi.

Things will get better: The marketplace for electronic abstracting and indexing tools has become relatively stable. The balance of print and e-purchases for abstracts and indexes has calmed down, with a slow but steady decrease in print subscriptions in favor of their electronic equivalents. This has happened over roughly ten years, if we count from the beginning of stand-alone CD-ROM databases. It will happen faster for the journal world, partly because the indexing tools already exist, and the capability of linking directly to articles will encourage use of e-journals.

But there is a current problem: While the market is stabilizing, there will be a demand for both print and electronic journals. Unless you have an enormous and flexible budget (and who does?), you are going to have unhappy patrons who are either forced to move into the digital world faster than they want to (if you switch to electronic only) or are held back from using all the capabilities of the new digital world (if you move cautiously into electronic only).

Then there are the hybrid digital collections that are available for purchase. These pull together an assortment of electronic resources, index them minimally, and sell them at "discount" prices. Are you willing to give up selection control to acquire these at a lesser price? Walters et al. mention three good criteria to consider when purchasing aggregations of electronic materials: content, coherence, and functionality.[2]

Consortial pricing can confuse the picture even more. Often publishers will provide consortial advantages based on the number of institutions involved, or on the number of FTE enrolled in academic institutions. From the standpoint of the frontline librarian, consortia bring advantages and disadvantages (just like any other cooperative venture). Price advantages can sometimes be offset by the necessity of following a larger group's priority in negotiating for a resource, and, sometimes, of participating in acquisition of a less-desired resource ahead of a more-desired resource. Even with those consortia that allow flexible membership participation for each resource, there is still some loss of control to gain price advantages.

Are you willing to try a transaction-based pricing scheme? It will work well for less-used titles. Will you know which titles to subscribe to and which to buy articles from as needed? Do you have contingency plans in place if the transactions are much higher than you anticipate?

Scholarly Communication

Libraries face the task of providing information in both print and electronic media. Consider how the world of electronic resources impacts users. For instance, how will your patrons react to a world where browsing means tables of contents delivered to their electronic mailboxes, or where searching means choosing between the full-text search capabilities provided across your journal collection by an aggregator and going into a subject-based abstract/index resource that has a controlled subject vocabulary?

How fast will patrons move into a world of information units instead of journals, a world of knowledge environments instead of books? How will scholars integrate all these electronic resources into the other tools they are using on their own desktops, and what difference will that make in their demands for new features on the products we acquire? The way libraries answer these questions will ultimately define the breadth of service offered.

Reviewing and Weeding

Subscriptions to print resources are quite reliable. Journals and magazines arrive on a regular basis. And libraries have established policies to review and refine their print collections. But what about the electronic collection? Consider the following questions.

Are you prepared to review your resources after one year, or two years, or five years? The world changes pretty quickly these days. Are you (and your users) willing to switch interfaces if the features are better in a different interface, or the license use terms are better, or a different interface or vendor offers more appealing archiving options?

How will libraries keep tabs on whether a publisher is publishing articles as soon as possible? Can you claim late issues when there is no print equivalent to let you know an issue is "late"? Will you want to instead keep track of submission-to-publication timing? If "issues" are no longer published, will you choose to build into your license the number of articles to be produced a year, so that you know you're getting your money's worth?

And what about measuring use? How will you know to switch from subscription access to transaction access for a particular journal? Admittedly, our current methods for tracking print usage are very crude. But some useful information can be extracted and assessed by people who are used to considering all the implications of differences in time of year, impacts of intense research projects, different use patterns in different disciplines, and all the other caveats that usually accompany statistical analyses.

Will you have anything that tells you an electronic resource is no longer worth buying? Do you want to depend on what the publisher or vendor supplies you, or will you try to capture information at your local site? A helpful resource that deals with usage statistics was issued November 9, 1998, by the ICOLC. "Guidelines for Statistical Measures of Usage of Web-based Indexed, Abstracted, and Full-Text Resources" is available at *http://www.library.yale.edu/consortia/webstats.html*.

Conclusion

Every library is struggling with the same questions and issues. Have you noticed how many library conference sessions are devoted to some aspect of dealing with digital materials? Colleagues around the world are building policies and procedures, laying the groundwork for those who will follow.

Although some libraries don't post their policies and procedures, others have placed versions on the Web that can be found with a little digging. I've collected some of these at *http://www.library.yale.edu/ecollections/ infolist.html*. You may find them useful as you continue on your way to treating e-resources as just another format to collect.

Notes

1. Tom Nisonger, "Collection Management Issues for Electronic Journals," *IFLA Journal* 22, no. 3 (1996): 233–239.
2. William H. Walters, Samuel G. Demas, Linda Stewart, and Jennifer Weintraub, "Guidelines for Collecting Aggregations of Web Resources," *Information Technology and Libraries* 17, no. 3 (September 1998): 157–160.

Let's Put It All on the Web: Practical Information for Digital Imaging

Andrea Bean Hough

Andrea Bean Hough (*ahough@statelib.lib.in.us*) is the senior subject specialist of the Indiana Division, Indiana State Library, where she is involved in a number of imaging and electronic conversion projects. Previously, she served as the university archivist at the University of Houston.

> To digitize is one thing. To develop useful collections over the long haul is another.[1]
>
> —Nancy Zussy, State Librarian of Washington

Digitization has become more than a buzzword in the special collections and archives arena. To survive and thrive in this technological age, it is almost a necessity. Patrons, who expect to find everything on the Web, are hungry for primary sources—photographs, letters, diaries, maps. And archivists and special collections librarians, who too often must fight the perception that their materials are accessible and relevant only to a select few, have grasped digitization as a way to make themselves and their collections seem more relevant to those who control the funding. Repositories throughout the world have begun scanning their collections and putting them on the Web as fast as possible.

But why are they doing it, you may wonder? Imaging projects have been introduced for three reasons, the most common of which is access. Traditionally, scholars have had to travel to special collections and archives to use one-of-a-kind materials. Imaging, and placing those images on the Internet for worldwide access, offers a way to overcome that problem. The second most commonly stated reason for beginning a digital imaging project is preservation. Although many conservators and preservation officers still do not accept digitization as a way to "preserve" the original, you can argue that by making high-resolution images available, the wear and tear on the original item is reduced.

The third reason, alluded to earlier, is the appealing nature of digital imaging. Some repositories and their staff want to be seen as on the cutting edge. Digital imaging can be a way to flush potential donors and funding agencies out into the open. Whatever the reason, hundreds, if not thousands, of repositories have started digitizing projects.

Let's say that your repository has decided to "do" digitization. Who has the time to digitize the materials? How hard can it be, anyway, to find some neat stuff, scan it, and throw it out on the Web for the masses? After all, anyone can use a scanner, right?

Before you rush out to buy your scanner, before you write a grant for funding that digitization project, before you turn your repository upside down in order to get on the digitization bandwagon—there are some subjects you should study, so that your imaging project doesn't become an example of a project gone wrong. Instead, it will become a useful digital collection for the long haul.

This chapter addresses the issues involved in a digital imaging project. Included are descriptions of the evolving best practices and standards in imaging, an overview of the planning process, and basic information on intellectual control and copyright. This paper is based on a presentation given at the Society of Indiana Archivists 1998 Annual Meeting.

The Planning Process

Until recently, many articles on the topic of digitization glossed over the planning process. It was hard to find basic information in one place about the issues that should be considered before beginning a digitization project, including selecting collections, creating work flow, identifying file formats and storage media to use, and planning for the obsolescence of that media. Imaging projects already mounted on the Internet tended to provide varied background information as to why a particular collection was selected or how the images were created. As a casual user could tell, these projects' coordinators put varying amounts of time and effort into planning and thinking about digital imaging issues.

By now, many digital imaging projects on the Internet have passed the one- and two-year mark (and, in some cases, the five-year mark). You can find examples of projects that weren't well planned, as well as projects that appear to be withstanding the test of time. Libraries have discovered that without proper planning, a project can very quickly become a burden—hard to maintain, hard to use, and nearly impossible to migrate when technological changes come along. And they will come along!

You should answer a number of questions before beginning a project:

What is your repository's mission?

How does digital imaging fit into that mission?

Who are your patrons?

What do your patrons want?

How does digital imaging meet their needs?

What collections would benefit the most from increased access through digital imaging?

What collections could most easily be digitized?

How will you select the collections to be digitized?

Will you digitize entire collections of materials, or select particular items for digitization?

Are you attempting to create comprehensive digital collections, or are you following more of a "treasures" approach?

How will you staff a digital imaging project?

How will you fund a digital imaging project?

What is your institution's commitment to continual support of the project (including maintenance and migration of the data into the future)?

Where will you physically put the digital imaging project?

Do you have the necessary technical expertise on staff or available in the area?

What type of image capture device will you use?

What are the legal implications of digitizing the materials you select?

What types of metadata are necessary for administrative control over the images and for intellectual access to their content?

How will patrons use the digital images?

Will you scan from original material or from an intermediary, such as microfilm or photographic copies?

What, if any, type of digital manipulation will you do to the images before making them available?

How will you make the digital collections accessible? Will you use the Internet, CD-ROM, or in-house workstations?

These are the big questions that must be tackled long before you make decisions on file formats, on what to name the image files, and at what resolution you will scan. Until you have answers to these questions, your projects will not be as good as they might have been. Do you have the resources to redo the project if it fails in some way? Most repositories don't. You can't afford not to do the job right the first time.

Resources are available that can guide you through the planning process. One of the best is Howard Besser and Jennifer Trant's *Introduction to Imaging: Issues in Constructing an Image Database*. This online manual, produced by the Getty Information Institute, is an excellent overview of the imaging process and covers all the basic issues. Included is a glossary, which defines such terms as *pixels* and *resolution* in language that beginners can understand. The manual is available at *http://www.ahip.getty.edu/intro_imaging/index.html*.

In 1998, the Council on Library and Information Resources published a book specifically geared toward selecting collections for digital imaging.

LET'S PUT IT ALL ON THE WEB: PRACTICAL INFORMATION FOR DIGITAL IMAGING   137

Digital Imaging for Libraries and Archives, written by Anne R. Kenney and Stephen Chapman and originally published by Cornell University in 1996, is considered to be the Bible of digital imaging by a number of librarians and archivists.

Once you have decided what collections will best serve your patrons' needs through imaging, verified that your repository has the resources to execute and support the project, and determined that the collections will be made more useful through imaging, you are ready to move on to the next stage: planning for your particular project. The Library of Congress' National Digital Library Program Project Planning Checklist is the best resource available for working through an imaging project. The checklist is available at *http://memory.loc.gov/ammem/prjplan.html*. Adapt that checklist to the needs of your project and you should be able to avoid any number of pitfalls.

Legal Issues in Imaging

I have attended a number of workshops and talks on digital imaging over the past few years. In nearly all of them, the speakers have glossed over the issue of copyright in the digital environment. One said that copyright was too complicated to explain to the audience. Another said that his repository didn't worry about it, because so far they hadn't had any problems. Even if these speakers are ignoring the issue of copyright, you should not. Copyright applies in the digital age just as it does to printed materials. The chapter titled "Copyright in Cyberspace" in this manual deals directly with copyright in the digital environment. However, the basic information as I (a nonlawyer) understand it, is:

If the materials you are digitizing are not in the public domain, if you do not own the copyright to the items, and if you do not have the copyright owner's permission to digitize the materials and make them available over the Internet, you are in violation of the federal copyright law.

The federal copyright law reserves to the copyright holder several exclusive rights. Among those are the right to reproduce the work and the right to exhibit that work. Digitization could be considered to both reproduce and exhibit the work. Just because the letter, photograph, or diary is in your collection does not give you the copyright. The creator of the item—or the heirs or executor—holds the copyright. Because of the changes made to the copyright law over the years, this can vary, so it is very important to do your homework. You must talk to a lawyer to get answers to your specific questions.

Make sure that you are up to date on the current federal copyright laws by using the resources cited in the chapter "Copyright in Cyberspace." There is also a wonderful site on the Internet compiled by Georgia Harper, an attorney with the University of Texas at Austin, that provides answers to many of the copyright questions you will have in creating a digital collection of materials. The site is available at *http://www.utsystem.edu/OGC/IntellectualProperty/cprtindx.htm*.

138 PUTTIN' IT OUT OVER THE NET: SOURCES AND SERVICES

Best Practices in Imaging

As of this writing, no standards are available for digital imaging projects. In September 1998, the Research Libraries Group and the National Preservation Office of the United Kingdom and Ireland began working toward standards for digital imaging, but no conclusive guidelines were issued at that time. There are, however, *best practices* that you can emulate to provide a good beginning. These best practices have been evolving for almost a decade in some instances, allowing a modicum of stability in an ever-changing digital world.

There are a number of ways to learn about the current best practices in digital imaging. Many of the major academic and research libraries have already paved the way through their projects, and there is no sense reinventing the wheel. Libraries in such institutions as the University of Virginia, Columbia University, Cornell University, the University of Michigan, Yale University, the University of California–Berkeley, and the University of California–Los Angeles have all undertaken massive digitization projects using a variety of material formats. Most have posted their technical information on imaging as well, often including information on file type, compression, and resolution as well as what metadata they are using.

One of the most comprehensive resources available on the Internet for best practices are the technical guidelines produced by the Ameritech/Library of Congress competition, a national competition that awards money to libraries for digital imaging projects that support or complement the collections on the American Memory site at the Library of Congress. These guidelines include "Technical Formats for Digital Reproductions" (*http://lcweb2.loc.gov/ammem/award/html/technical_notes1.html*) and "Technical Notes on Interoperability and Access Aids" (*http://lcweb2.loc.gov/ammem/award/html/technical_notes2.html*).

The Library of Congress' American Memory project provides additional information on both formats for digital images and database construction at "Digital Formats for Content Reproductions" (*http://memory.loc.gov/ammem/formats.html*) and "Digital Historical Collections: Types, Elements, and Construction" (*http://memory.loc.gov/ammem/elements.html*). In October 1998 the Library of Congress released its final report on the Manuscript Digitization Demonstration Project (*http://memory.loc.gov/ammem/pictel/index.html*).

Hardware

There are advantages and disadvantages for almost any hardware or software package. Right now, nothing is perfect, and that will probably continue. Decide what you need in order to make the best possible use of your materials with the resources you have available (staff, space, and money). Then buy what you can afford.

The first questions you need to address regarding hardware are: What material formats will you be scanning? and What is the best way to capture the information on those items? Your options for access are creating images or creating text, or using a combination of the two. Both images and text can be captured from a scanner; if you want to create text files, you perform additional work using those image files. The options for image creation as of this writing are scanners (which come in different forms) and digital cameras. Each works best with a particular type of material.

Scanners. The first product that made image files possible was the scanner. The flatbed scanner resembles and is used much like a photocopier. It works well for flat objects, such as standard-sized photographs, documents, and letters. If you are going to scan materials larger than eight by fourteen inches, you may have to learn how to "tile" or digitally combine several scans of the same image to create a composite image of the original. There are open book scanners that scan from above the book, adjusting for the curvature of the pages. These cause much less damage than a standard flatbed scanner does, but are fairly expensive. Drum scanners, used in such industries as banking and insurance for high-speed information capture, do not work well with fragile items.

Digital Cameras. The second option, the digital camera, tends to work well with three-dimensional objects and oversized images, such as maps. Digital cameras look and work like regular cameras, and can be hooked into your personal computer to download the files of the images you captured. To use a digital camera to its fullest, you will need a photo copystand with lights. This can take up a great deal of room, which must be considered if your repository is already squeezed for space. When shopping for a digital camera, remember that what you pay for is what you get. Trying to use a camera made for use at home on oversize, detailed maps won't work. Bite the bullet and invest in the best possible camera that you can afford, knowing that within months the price will have dropped.

Software

There are two types of software for digital imaging projects. Usually your scanner will come bundled with some type of scanning software that may have some image manipulation abilities (rotating and cropping images, etc.).

Adobe Photoshop. For all practical purposes, Adobe Photoshop has become the most widely used image processing software in use in digital imaging projects. It is a powerful software package, providing more options for image manipulation than you will use.

OCR (Optical Character Recognition). The other type of software that you may use is a package that performs OCR (optical character recognition). This is used to convert images with words into text files. OCR can be useful, but for older materials with inconsistent type, it often doesn't work well. If you are going to invest in an OCR package, make sure that its accuracy is at least 99.5 percent. The accuracy rate usually applies to clean, modern-day typefaces, so your 1864 book with stains and irregular type darkness won't scan as well.

Some institutions have reverted from using OCR to convert their text-based documents into a machine-readable form and are now relying on the art of data entry. In some cases, it can be faster to rekey the information than to scan it, convert it through OCR, and proofread it. For more information on OCR and scanning text, see the University of Virginia's Electronic Text Center "Text Scanning Helpsheet" (*http://etext.lib. virginia.edu/helpsheets/scantext.html*).

You will also need some sort of software to organize your digital images, whether you are setting up the database within your library's online catalog system or creating a stand-alone database that will be served over the Web. Again, there are no firm rules or places to go for information. Look around the Web and see what you like about different projects and the way they are organized and provided to the public. Then contact the repository and see what software they are using.

Storage Media—Present and Future

One of the most important choices is the medium used to store both your archival TIFF (Tagged Image Format File) files and to serve your JPEG (Joint Photographic Experts Group) files to the public (see below for more information about file formats). Because the type and cost of storage changes, it is best to do your research at the time that you will need it. For example, CD-ROM costs have dropped dramatically over the past five years. DVD (Digital Video Disk) may become the storage choice of the future, but at the present time, that is unclear.

File Formats. At present, it is standard practice to produce three (if not four) images from each scanned item. The breakdown is as follows:

1. A thumbnail image (measuring one to two inches) for quick retrieval and use. Usually a JPEG file. JPEG files can be compressed to create smaller file sizes, although it is a "lossy" technology, meaning that some information from the original scan is lost.
2. A larger image to provide patrons with useful information. Also a JPEG file.
3. An "archival" image (TIFF file), stored off-line, to be used to generate future images. TIFF files are "lossless" and let you retain the information from your high-resolution scan. However, TIFF files tend to be very large, and at present, most Web browsers do not support TIFF-file viewing without a separate plug-in.
4. Some projects also include a "fetchable" image at a high enough resolution to be used in publications, but this is not universal. This is usually a higher-resolution JPEG with minimal compression.

Of these files, the archival TIFF file is the most important for future use. The TIFF format allows the file to be saved with no loss of information. The TIFF file, which experts are now recommending be scanned at 400 dpi or higher, is saved for the future. From this file, you can generate JPEG, GIF, and other files for use by patrons. Many repositories are now saving their TIFF files on CD-ROM, although others are

LET'S PUT IT ALL ON THE WEB: PRACTICAL INFORMATION FOR DIGITAL IMAGING   141

using tape. DVD, not currently in common use by archival repositories, may become a standard storage format in the future. For more information on creating digital images, the University of Virginia's Electronic Text Center provides helpsheets on digital image creation (*http://etext. lib.virginia.edu/helpsheets/specscan.html*) and on image scanning (*http:// etext.lib.virginia.edu/helpsheets/scanimage.html*).

File Migration. One of the most common concerns of archivists and librarians is what will happen when their digital image files (or more important, the hardware to read those files) become obsolete. Vendors make claims that their compact discs will last for one hundred years—but who will have the equipment to read them? And do we even care, since we won't be alive by then? Just kidding. This is a gray area for now, with no clear answers and no standards. Libraries with digital imaging projects are saving their files on a variety of formats and planning to migrate those files to the most-developed storage medium on a regular basis. For example, the Denver Public Library, which has digitized over 55,000 photographs, plans to migrate its files ten years after the creation of the file. Other repositories may set up a five-year plan.

The important thing is to realize that you will have to migrate your files and to plan accordingly. This is why you should get the best scan you can the first time and save it to the best of your ability. You also must build into your budget the costs (both equipment and staff time) that will be required to transfer files from the old format to whatever new format you have chosen.

Metadata

The term *metadata* has permeated archivists' discussions of imaging and electronic records. Basically, metadata is data about data, which falls into three categories for scanned material (with brief examples):

Administrative metadata collects the information you need to preserve the image down the road. What software was used to capture the image? What kind of scanner was used?

Descriptive metadata provides the information about the resource. Is it a photograph? What subject headings describe it?

Structural metadata provides the system with the information it needs to deliver the right thing to the patron. What is the page number of the item, if it is from a book?

You should be aware of both current and future needs when deciding what metadata you will collect and attach to each image or entry. Some institutions compile into their metadata structure information on the person scanning, the type of scanner used, and the time of day scanned. This may be useful down the road if you discover that one of your staff members was color blind, or that the afternoon sunlight streaming through the window affected the image capture when using your digital camera. See the chapter "Metadata 101: A Primer" earlier in this book for more information on metadata.

Encoded Archival Description

It would be wrong to not mention Encoded Archival Description (EAD) in a discussion of digital imaging. EAD, a document type definition of SGML (Standard Generalized Markup Language), has been developed by the archival community as a standard way to mark up inventories to their collections. It was developed at UC–Berkeley and has been tested and used by a number of repositories, including the Library of Congress and Duke University.

One of the benefits of EAD is that you can place images of individual items within the finding aid structure. The Society of American Archivists devoted the 1997 summer and fall issues of the *American Archivist* to exploring the history and development of EAD and its use by repositories. For additional information, see the Library of Congress site on EAD at *http://lcweb.loc.gov/ead/*.

Other Issues

File naming, creating a database, and protecting the authenticity of the images are all issues that have to be addressed. Fortunately, sources are available for in-depth study and practical advice. The important thing to remember is to plan ahead so that midway through the scanning of 50,000 images you don't have to rename each one.

A major issue that does not receive a great deal of attention is image manipulation.You have just scanned a lovely photograph of a woman in a black dress, but there is a large scratch running through her skirt. Will you remove the scratch, so that the digital image is no longer a true representation of the original item, or will you leave it?

Now that "the thrill is gone" from many digital imaging projects, more and more repositories are not performing major image manipulation. They may bump up the contrast on the images or sharpen the edges, but they do not erase scratches or crop out unsightly buildings. If our intention is to produce digital surrogates for the originals and allow the originals to be removed from day-to-day use, then the digital image must match the original. Scholars need to be able to feel confident that the image they are using is authentic, not a creative work of art by a bored staff member at a scanner.

Conclusion

Nothing is certain except death and taxes, the saying goes. In digital imaging, you can add one more certainty: Things will change. Technology will change, forcing you to migrate your database and images onto new platforms and new hardware. Your patrons' tastes will change, as they demand higher-resolution and faster-downloading images. Your day-to-day activities in the repository will change too, as imaging projects become more ingrained.

Be sure to think through your entire project before beginning. Digital imaging projects of special collections materials involve people, and people's time costs money. Select collections for which you have permission to scan the images, or begin with materials in the public domain while you track down the copyright holders for materials you would like to add in the future. To avoid having to rescan items down the road, and to save time and hassle when the inevitable migrations come along, make sure that you have planned ahead. Scan at the highest resolution that you can handle with your equipment and storage space. Use as much metadata as you think you may ever need. In the end, you and your patrons will have a project that you can be proud of over the long haul.

Resources

Arms, Caroline R. "Historical Collections for the National Digital Library: Lessons and Challenges at the Library of Congress." *D-Lib Magazine* (April 1996).

> *http://www.dlib.org/dlib/april96/loc/04c-arms.html* (Part 1)
> *http://www.dlib.org/dlib/may96/loc/05c-arms.html* (Part 2)
> Excellent overview of the planning process, challenges, and successes occurring at the Library of Congress during its digital imaging projects. Part two addresses patrons' use of the collections as well as plans for maintaining the digital files.

Bearman, David, and Jennifer Trant. "Authenticity of Digital Resources: Towards a Statement of Requirements in the Research Process." *D-Lib Magazine* (June 1998). *http://www.dlib.org/dlib/june98/06bearman.html.*

> Discusses the importance of authenticity for scholars working with digital images. Looks at the issues of protecting images against misuse as well as providing scholars with the information necessary to have confidence in the digital images they use.

Ester, Michael. *Digital Image Collections: Issues and Practice.* Washington, D.C.: Commission on Preservation and Access, 1996.

> A good overview of the issues involved in digital imaging, with information on various projects under way at the time.

Mintzer, Fred, Jeffrey Lotspiech, and Norishige Morimoto. "Safeguarding Digital Library Contents and Users: Digital Watermarking." *D-Lib Magazine* (December 1997). *http://www.dlib.org/dlib/december97/ibm/12lotspiech.html.*

> Thorough explanation of watermarks and their applicability to the digital environment. The article is graphics-intensive.

Ostrow, Stephen E. *Digitizing Historical Pictorial Collections for the Internet.* Washington, D.C.: Council on Library and Information Resources, 1998.

Ostrow provides an excellent overview on digitizing photographs and other pictorial images. He lists questions that should be answered before beginning, offers advice on selecting collections for scanning, gives necessary technical information, and doesn't omit copyright issues.

Waters, Donald. "Planning for Digitization: Overview of Major Issues." Presented at *Planning for Digitization: Bringing Down Another Barrier to Access,* a conference sponsored by the Western Council of State Librarians, Denver, Colorado, September 18, 1998. *http://www.clir.org/diglib/presentations/wcsl/sld001.htm.*

Slide presentation highlighting key points from Waters' presentation. Addresses many of the issues involved in planning a good digital imaging project.

Note

1. Opening remarks at the Western Council of State Libraries' conference, "Planning for Digitization: Bringing Down Another Barrier to Access," Denver Public Library, September 18–19, 1998. Quoted with permission.

DIGITAL LIBRARIES

Paul Jones

Paul Jones is director of MetaLab (*http://metalab.unc.edu*), a collaborative project in applied digital library and multimedia publishing research at the University of North Carolina (UNC). He is on the faculties of the School of Information and Library Science and the School of Journalism and Mass Communication at UNC. He is coauthor of *The UNIX Web Server Book* (Ventana, 1997) and coeditor of *Internet Issues and Advanced Applications 1997–1998* (Scarecrow, 1998). He may be reached at *paul_jones@unc.edu*.

What Are Digital Libraries?

One thing we can learn from the past is that we rarely understand or give meaningful names to new technologies and their uses. The "wireless telegraph" was a very poor name for the radio. The term "iron horse" was at least poetic and may have helped soften the impact of such a large, loud, and initially ugly intrusion on people's lives, as the steam engine spewed its acidic smoke through pristine valleys. I've often wondered if the name "horseless carriage" didn't impede the development of a decent steering mechanism for the automobile.

The name "digital libraries" carries with it not only a collection of misinterpretations and high aspirations, but also a kind of cultural conservatism that at once masks the possibilities of the new technologies and mistakenly attempts to protect certain cultural resources and practices from a scary technological interloper. The famous Middle Eastern story of the blind men and the elephant is especially applicable to digital libraries: Six blind men encounter an elephant for the first time. Each man grasps a different part of the animal: One holds the tail, one a leg, another the side, another an ear, still another the trunk, and the last the tusk. Each man then describes the elephant to the others: It is much like a rope. No, like a sturdy tree. No, a rough wall. You're wrong, it's like a fan. Fools, it's like a great snake. Oh, it is smooth and cold; it's dead and we are feeling its bones.

Our digital library "blind men" (and women) come from computer science, libraries, book publishing, bookstores, the magazine and newspaper industries, broadcasting, recording companies, advertising, library automation companies, cataloging, indexing, the research community, learned societies, and multimedia companies. They are teachers, writers, students, and everyone who reads, listens to recordings or radio, or watches television. I surely have left more than a few out of the list, but as you can see, the number is great, and each is attempting to form a definition of our digital library that most suits his or her own interests and experiences. And, of course, all are fighting over their interpretations with the kind of conviction that only those with this kind of blindness can summon. Suffice it to say that this brief introduction to digital libraries will likely offend, in some way, each of our "blind people."

What, can we say, is a digital library? One very broad definition is this: software implemented in such a way that computer systems can emulate and possibly extend at least some of the functions performed by a traditional library.

The controversy begins when the exact functions of a traditional library are defined and emulated. Does digital library software aid in ordering books? Does it keep track of patron records? Does it assist in cataloging? Does it help the librarian or the patron or both? Is it a virtual card catalog? A complete collection of related text? A multimedia archive? A sophisticated search-and-retrieval program? A reference service? A community discussion area?

One alternative definition might be this: any software, proposal, project, or great idea seeking funding from any of the many agencies, foundations, or organizations that fund projects, initiatives, or conferences with the words "digital library" in their titles. This definition, however waggish and jaded, reflects the current politics and vagueness of the digital library area. Further, it is not new. In his 1965 book *The Libraries of the Future*, J. C. R. Licklider spends a great deal of his famous energy describing various projects to perform primitive syntactic analysis of natural language, to perform inadequate and now completely antique measures of content of books, and to minutely describe certain programming techniques for the PDP-1 computer.[1] Although some of this research did bear fruit, it is obvious looking back thirty-five years that the work was not aimed at the problems of libraries and the desires of their patrons.

Even the Association of Research Libraries has found it difficult to choose a single definition of digital library:

There are many definitions of a "digital library." Terms such as "electronic library" and "virtual library" are often used synonymously. The elements that have been identified as common to these definitions are:

The digital library is not a single entity;

The digital library requires technology to link the resources of many;

The linkages between the many digital libraries and information services are transparent to the end users;

Universal access to digital libraries and information services is a goal;

Digital library collections are not limited to document surrogates: they extend to digital artifacts that cannot be represented or distributed in printed formats.[2]

Donald Waters reports that the Digital Library Federation takes a different tack by focusing on the organization rather than the elements of the library:

Digital libraries are organizations that provide the resources, including the specialized staff, to select, structure, offer intellectual access to, interpret, distribute, preserve the integrity of, and ensure the persistence over time of collections of digital works so that they are readily and economically available for use by a defined community or set of communities.[3]

Perhaps the digital library is best defined by how one encounters it. And so we return to the elephant by noting some examples of outstanding digital library work.

Some Recent Digital Library Initiatives

As the newer technologies are better understood and as a stronger link to libraries and their patrons is insisted upon, digital libraries have flourished and have begun to take a recognizable form.

The National Science Foundation (NSF), along with the Department of Defense Advanced Research Projects Agency (DARPA) and the National Aeronautics and Space Administration (NASA), has funded six major projects under the Digital Library Initiative program. These projects—at the University of Michigan, the University of Illinois, the University of California-Berkeley, Carnegie-Mellon University, Stanford University, and the University of California-Santa Barbara—have in common their promise to work with multimedia collections and with distributed collections. See the list of Online Resources at the end of this chapter for each project's website.

The NSF-funded projects are focused first on technology development and research. Other agencies, however, have focused more strongly on the quality and depth of content in digital collections. For example, the American Memory project of the Library of Congress has thus far made available over forty-four major digital collection projects, varying from baseball cards, personal papers of important persons, general African American history, and dance instruction manuals to music of all types, American regional information, maps of railroads, maps of Liberia, and recordings of all types.

Since 1996, the American Memory project, with funding from Ameritech, has provided support for major digital collection projects at over fifteen university libraries, museums, and historical societies around the United States. Chosen on a competitive basis, these projects reflect the need to create digital collections of important primary sources in areas complementary to those at the Library of Congress, especially with a regional and historical interest. These awards are given every other year and are now in their third round. More information is available online at *http://lcweb2.loc.gov/ammem/award/*.

Some other notable library collections are listed in the Online Resources section at the end of this chapter.

Beyond the Technical: Problems for Digital Libraries

The problems of digital libraries are the same as those of physical libraries, bookstores, and museums, only magnified and enhanced. They involve access, authority, copyright and payment, preservation, and locating materials.

Access

Who can have access to online materials has become a very sticky issue. In some areas, for example, children are restricted from using certain materials. The question is how to provide adults the information that they desire while limiting children to appropriate online resources. To further complicate matters, the definition of "adult" is not uniform, and opinions on what is or is not suitable for children vary widely from city to city and from state to state. In addition, some materials are restricted to U.S. citizens, to qualified physicians, to members of certain organizations, and so on.

Authority

Which materials are to be trusted more than others? Is the text you are reading actually the text written by the author as listed? Are the photographs or maps to be trusted? What writers might be able to challenge established authorities? Can new voices emerge in the new medium and in new collections?

Copyright

The claims of copyright owners over the use of their work have been extended and made stronger by recent laws and by the promise of digital watermarks. With attention both to these rights and to the library tradition of providing free access to all citizens, how can a digital library function fairly and ethically? How can copyright owners be compensated? How will payment be collected?

Preservation

Several studies have noted that digital materials tend to experience "format rot" at a very fast pace. In fact, although in theory digital materials might be copied clearly and cleanly many times, it is more often the case that the computers on which these materials were created, the physical devices on which they are stored, and the way in which the material was encoded have a life expectancy of less than five years. How can preservation work in such a world? How often will these wonderful archives noted earlier need to be refreshed and redigitized? What will be culled from our heritage at each step?

Search Issues

"Over a million images in our database" reads one digital library's web page. But how do you find the image you want? How do you compare that image to one in another collection? Is there enough metadata available to fully and accurately describe each text, image, or sound? How long will it take to find what you want?

Resources for digital library research and practice aim to address these issues and more. Among the most useful are those listed in the Online Resources section at the end of this chapter.

What Next for Digital Libraries?

Coming from a vague but evolving definition, driven in very different directions by funding sources with vastly different goals, and up against an array of new problems—what does the future hold for digital libraries?

In the best of all possible worlds, all the treasures of humankind would be available at a moment's notice regardless of the physical location. What we want and what we need will be delivered to us in the form we most prefer at an instant's notice. Served by H. G. Wells's WorldMind or Vannevar Bush's Memex, we would all be happier, healthier people.[4]

In another world, there would be no libraries, only distributed information stores. Information would be squirted directly into our short-term memory—after the proper access privilege check and the deduction of a small payment from our accounts. Except for a few members of the elite and even fewer primitives, no one will have any long-term memory.

We all have some influence over what scenario becomes reality.

Online Resources

Digital Library Initiative Participants

http://www.cise.nsf.gov/iis/dli_home.html
NSF's Digital Library Initiative site

http://www.si.umich.edu/UMDL/
The University of Michigan Digital Libraries Research Project

http://dli.grainger.uiuc.edu/
"Building the Interspace: Digital Library Infrastructure for a University Engineering Community," led by the University of Illinois

http://elib.cs.berkeley.edu/
"The Environmental Electronic Library: A Prototype of a Scalable, Intelligent, Distributed Electronic Library," led by the University of California-Berkeley

http://informedia.cs.cmu.edu/
"Informedia: Integrated Speech, Image and Language Understanding for Creation and Exploration of Digital Video Libraries," led by Carnegie-Mellon University

http://www-diglib.stanford.edu/
The Stanford Integrated Digital Library Project

http://alexandria.sdc.ucsb.edu/
"The Alexandria Project: Towards a Distributed Digital Library with Comprehensive Services for Images and Spatially Referenced Information," led by the University of California-Santa Barbara.

Digital Library Collections

http://digital.nypl.org
New York Public Library's selections from various collections

http://www.ndltd.org/
Networked Digital Library of Theses and Dissertations at Virginia Tech

http://www.dlib.indiana.edu/
The Indiana University Digital Library Program, home of the Variations Digital Music project

http://sunsite.berkeley.edu/
Berkeley's Digital Collection project (not to be confused with the NSF-funded research project noted earlier in this chapter); contains collections and resources for those building digital library content

http://www.iath.virginia.edu/blake/
The William Blake Archive, one of several far-reaching projects at the University of Virginia's Institute for Advanced Technology in the Humanities; different editions of William Blake's prints are made available, many for the first time, with careful color correction and scholarly annotation by leading Blake scholars in searchable formats

http://www.perseus.tufts.edu/
The Perseus Project, Greek and Roman Classical materials on the WWW, with additional collections in the offing

http://www.thinker.org/imagebase/
The Fine Arts Museums of San Francisco's searchable image database; one of the finest and most complete collections of fine arts images

http://memory.loc.gov/ammem/
The American Memory Project at the Library of Congress

Digital Library Research and Practice

http://www.dlib.org/
> *D-Lib Magazine*, the monthly publication of the Corporation for National Research Initiatives, providing articles, news, and views

http://sunsite.berkeley.edu/DigLibns/
> DigLibns, an electronic discussion list for practical issues relating to digital librarianship

http://www.vrd.org/Dig_Ref/drb.html
> Dig_Ref, an electronic discussion list for digital reference issues and answers

http://sunsite.berkeley.edu/Web4Lib/archive.html
> Web4Lib, an electronic discussion list for library-based WWW server and content managers

http://www.cni.org/
> Coalition for Networked Information

http://www.ukoln.ac.uk/services/elib/
> eLib: The Electronic Libraries Programme in the United Kingdom

http://www.bookwire.com/LJDigital/diglibs.articles
> Digital Libraries, Roy Tennant's practical series of articles on digital libraries from *Library Journal*

Notes

1. J. C. R. Licklider, *The Libraries of the Future* (Cambridge, Mass.: MIT Pr., 1965).
2. Association of Research Libraries, "Definition and Purposes of a Digital Library," October 23, 1995, *http://sunsite.berkeley.edu/ARL/definition.html*.
3. Donald Waters, "What Are Digital Libraries?" CLIR Issues 4 (July/August), *http://www.clir.org/pubs/issues/issues04.html#dlf*.
4. H. G. Wells, *Science and the World-Mind* (London: New-Europe, 1942); and Vannevar Bush, "As We May Think," *Atlantic Monthly* 176, no. 1 (July 1945), 101–8.

In Search of the Elusive E-Journal

Marilyn Geller

Marilyn Geller (*marilyn.geller@mindspring.com*) has worked as advisor to the Electronic Services Department of Blackwell's Information Services. In 1994, she joined Readmore, Inc., part of the Blackwell's Group, as manager of Internet Services. She is the coauthor, with Birdie MacLennan, of *NASIGNET and Beyond: Electronic Networking Resources for Serialists*.

If it can be said that dealing with serials is like "nailing Jell-O to the wall," then dealing with e-journals is like nailing Jell-O to the wall when it hasn't quite yet gelled. Since the early 1990s, libraries have been grappling with issues related to integrating e-journals into their collections. First on the list of tasks is finding electronic journals appropriate to a specific library collection. It is not enough, however, to simply order these titles as we did in the past for printed journals. These days, librarians must also understand the variety of pricing options that accompany these titles. And we need to find, read, understand, and negotiate the related licensing. Libraries must then provide access to these materials through an aggregated collection or through a gateway collection, or by individual links on a web page, or by using a hypertext link from our OPACs.

If it all seems more trouble than it's worth, librarians should remember that these electronic journals will bring deeper indexing access, broader interactive features, and farther-reaching distribution, pushing the library collection and its services beyond the walls of our buildings.

Definitions

So what is this Jell-O that hasn't quite gelled yet? The term *electronic journal*, or *e-journal*, generally refers to an entity that is issued successively with some kind of numeric or chronological coding system that uniquely identifies each part. Like its print counterpart, it is an ongoing endeavor, but unlike its print counterpart, it is accessible electronically.

Implicit in this element of electronic accessibility is the use of the Internet. Strictly speaking, an electronically accessible journal could be delivered on a CD-ROM or floppy disk, but the use of the Internet as a delivery mechanism has become a de facto part of the definition of e-journal. Early in their history, individual e-journal issues were delivered to subscribers by e-mail or made available through FTP or gopher sites. More commonly in the late 1990s, e-journals are mounted on websites. Some of them appear only in electronic form, but the explosion of interest in e-journals within libraries has come primarily with the development of electronic versions of print journals.

E-journals can be electronic twins of their print counterparts; they can include all the elements of their print versions with exactly the same layout. We usually refer to these electronic twins as full-text e-journals, but a more accurate term might be "full-featured," connoting the electronic replication not just of text, but also of graphics.

Alternatively, e-journals can vary from their print counterparts in the embellishment of layout or content. Although printed materials can include photographs, tables, charts, and bibliographies, e-journals can theoretically include movies, audio files, data manipulation tools, and hypertext links from bibliographical references to the actual articles. On the other hand, pseudo e-journals can vary from their print relatives by delivering less-than-full-featured versions. This category includes electronic delivery of tables of contents or selected articles from a print journal; it is the gastronomic equivalent of an appetizer, not a full-course meal.

Selecting Electronic Journals

Librarians use a variety of tools to identify and evaluate resources that might be added to existing collections. Existing print journals can be evaluated by citation counts and user recommendations. Existing serial collections can be compared to collections from comparable organizations. Resources for reviewing journals are a standard part of the selection tool kit. In many cases, librarians just "know" about printed journals within specific disciplinary areas based on professional experience and subject expertise. Publishers and subscription agents are also worthy sources of information about printed materials.

The preliminary source of information about any journal, print or electronic, is always the publisher. Publishers distribute their catalogs of offerings using many avenues. Early in the e-journal development period, publishers made the mistake of alerting only individual scholars in appropriate disciplines about the availability of electronic versions of their titles. These researchers would come to the library with electronic access information and would expect that the library could support their access to these titles. It was not uncommon for librarians to feel the frustration of being "out of the loop," and they often turned to their subscription agents for help. Equally, it was not uncommon for subscription agents to feel the same frustration. At that time, some of us in the scholarly communications chain didn't even know that others were making the Jell-O!

Fortunately for librarians, standard resources and procedures are beginning to emerge for reviewing and selecting appropriate electronic journals. A variety of websites and printed directories have come into existence to fill this need for locating information about e-journals:

The *Colorado Alliance of Research Libraries Electronic Journal Access* (*http://www.coalliance.org/ejournal/*) is organized as an alphabetical e-journal listing that is both browsable and searchable. It is also searchable and browsable by Library of Congress subject heading. An individual title record for an e-journal includes an active link to archival sites, a brief abstract, and bibliographic information.

The *Full-Text Electronic Journals Project* (*http://www.lib.uwaterloo. ca/Ejournals/*) is arranged in both alphabetical and broad subject lists, but there is no searching capability. Each reference lists publisher information and has an active link to the archival site.

The *Directory of Electronic Journals, Newsletters, and Academic Discussion Lists* (*http://arl.cni.org/scomm/edir/index.html*), published by the Association of Research Libraries, is now in its seventh edition and is available both in comforting print and in electronic format.

The *Full-Text Archives of Scholarly Society Serial Publications* (*http:// www.lib.uwaterloo.ca/society/full-text_soc.html*) is arranged alphabetically by scholarly society and includes active links to archival sites.

NewJour (*http://gort.ucsd.edu/newjour/*) includes alphabetical access and a searching mechanism for all e-journals that have been announced on the NewJour electronic mailing list since 1993. Individual files have the original announcement and an active link to the archival site.

The World Wide Web Virtual Library: Electronic Journals (*http://www. edoc.com/ejournal*) breaks down e-journal listings into categories (academic, etc.) but also has searching capability across all categories and includes active links to archival sites.

The *Electronic Journals Resource Directory* (*http://library.usask.ca/ ~scottp/links/*), a new resource from Peter Scott of the University of Saskatchewan Libraries, includes categories for e-journal directories, library indexes, library-related journals, mailing lists, major electronic journal publishers, software, and vendors of related e-journal services, among others. This new website could become one of our greatest assets for discovering where to go to find out about e-journals.

Pricing Options

Let's suppose that you have figured out who's making the Jell-O. Do you know in what flavors this Jell-O might be available? Publishers are now producing e-journals that are freely available with a print subscription, or separately priced, or priced as a combined package, or priced in a tiered package based on number of sites or number of users or number of workstations.

Not only do these pricing policies vary among publishers, they also vary from year to year. A publisher who formerly offered e-journals free with print subscriptions might begin to charge in the next subscription year. Publishers are currently struggling to find a pricing model that will continue to generate revenue, allow them to experiment with potential products, and give their traditional audiences an opportunity to learn how to use e-journals successfully.

Pricing information is less elusive than it used to be. Most subscription agents can now generate lists of titles for which individual clients are entitled to free electronic versions or have the option of purchasing electronic versions. Publishers are also mailing out informational letters to librarians about their electronic products and pricing. Our biggest problem with regard to pricing is remembering to look for it and then remembering to look for it again in ensuing years.

Licensing

When librarians are finally armed with the tools to identify appropriate titles and pricing options, the road ahead gets a bit more difficult. Finding title and pricing information for electronic journals has parallels in the print universe; this is a traditional library skill that has been translated to the electronic environment. The next step in the process, licensing, is far less traditional and certainly less normalized. In the print environment, librarians applied the copyright laws and the embedded principle of fair use to guide user access to materials. Simply stated, copyright laws basically allow that under certain circumstances, you can make a copy of an article if you don't do it too often, if you acknowledge that it is a copyrighted work, and if you don't cheat the copyright owner out of money by doing it.

Distribution

The element of the electronic environment that is vastly different from the print environment is the mechanism for distribution. It is both the technological beauty and the economic nightmare of electronic publishing, and it has ramifications for the way we think about copyright and fair use. In the print environment, articles are packaged in issues, duplicated in large enough numbers to fill all the subscriptions, addressed to all subscribers, and sent through the postal system to their destinations. Once at a destination, they are processed by library staff and made physically available to users who present themselves at the library. This is a time-consuming and expensive process, and, for those of us who have had to deal with claiming missing issues, not a foolproof one.

In the electronic environment, articles need not necessarily be bundled into issues to be made available. Individual copies do not need to be printed for each subscriber, nor do they need to be individually addressed or sent through the postal system. Instead, the original article can be mounted on an Internet accessible server, and users can be allowed to access it at will. In this scenario, there is no longer a physical entity, nor is there the need to be present in the same place as the article in order to retrieve it. Additionally, though librarians are still important contributors to the collection and organization of information, they are no longer physically present, reminding users to acknowledge the copyright laws.

Elements of Site Licensing

The use of a site license by most publishers is an effort to define the legal uses of copyrighted materials in ways that the current law may not address. It is bold new territory—not one with which we have much familiarity. However, several basic elements of a site license appear to be emerging. The first element is the *definition of users*—in other words, who will be allowed to access the material in question? Publishers may choose to restrict access to users who are in one physical location, or, alternatively, for a larger fee, to a broader geographical group.

The second element of a site license is the *definition of use*, or what the user is allowed to do with this material. This is the section of the site license that will define who is allowed to create copies of articles, in what formats, and with what manner of distribution or delivery.

The third element of the site license is the *definition of access*. By this the publisher means to fix the limits of how users will get to this material. Publishers may choose to restrict access to a single workstation located within the physical confines of the library building, may allow access from several workstations, may restrict access to a given number of simultaneous users, or may define the number of times a given piece of material may be viewed.

License Agreements

Many electronic journals have associated licensing agreements or terms and conditions. Finding the license agreement in our current environment is very labor-intensive. And once found, librarians must identify the appropriate people within the organization who can read, understand, negotiate, and sign on behalf of the agreeing parties.

It is not unusual, however, to discover that a publisher has no licensing agreement in place. This alone is significant information to have, but proving the absence of a licensing agreement may take longer than proving its existence. Currently, librarians may expect to spend a great deal of time and energy finding licenses or proving the absence of these licenses. It's quite possible, however, that services will become available to find and interpret licenses more readily.

IN SEARCH OF THE ELUSIVE E-JOURNAL   157

Third-party aggregators are beginning to collect and provide access to licenses related to titles offered through their services. In addition, there are movements afoot to create standard licenses and standards for licenses. Notably, in North America, the American Library Association in collaboration with many other professional organizations has produced the "Principles for Licensing Electronic Resources" (*http://www.arl.org/scomm/licensing/principles.html*). This document is an attempt to identify the elements that ought to be included in a license; however, it does not attempt to suggest specific policies in the license. In the United Kingdom, libraries, library associations, and publishers have come together under the National Electronic Site License Initiative to create a standard license (*http://www.nesli.ac.uk/nesli8.html*), moving the entire licensing process in a more streamlined and scalable direction.

Access

Assuming that you've found the electronic journals you want, that you've sorted out your pricing options, and that you've actually found, read, negotiated, and signed the license, the next step is to create access for your end users. In the print environment, this is as simple (or as complex) as cataloging, labeling, and shelving the first volume. Where you shelve a journal in the electronic environment is not quite so straightforward.

Many, but certainly not all, e-journals are available through aggregated collections offered by third parties. The beauty of using an aggregated collection is that you can provide one user interface in one Internet location with one security checkpoint for many e-journals. The problem is that your library's e-journal holdings are presented within the aggregator's collection. Creating a generic link to an aggregated collection will not integrate e-journals into a library's collection of resources.

Librarians have two good options for achieving integration by using a *gateway mechanism*. One gateway mechanism or front door to collected resources is the trusty OPAC. Catalogers can embed a hypertext link in the MARC record for an e-journal, and that link can be activated. This essentially allows end users to access the catalog, find an electronic resource from the total universe of all library resources, and click to get to the title they want. Alternately, librarians can choose to create lists of available electronic resources within the library's website and have active hyperlinks embedded here. Librarians can use either or both methods, and the best way to decide may be to ask yourself, "Where is the front door to my library?"

Why E-Journals?

Although there are many similarities and parallels between print and electronic journals, e-journals are still problematic and more labor-intensive than their print counterparts. Why bother? The existence of scholarly communication in an electronic format will allow researchers to search through millions of bytes of information in ways that printed indexing and printed articles could never allow. The use of natural-language processing will give users opportunities to sift through data in ways that keyword searching overlooks.

Autonomous intelligent agents will allow users to keep current with far less effort. Researchers will have access not only to the results of other scholars' research but also to the raw data and data modeling tools that will allow an entire professional community to replicate and build on existing research in the network environment. Traditional library services and electronic resources will be immediately accessible to end users in off-site locations, and this will allow scholars to obtain and use resources when and where they need them, eliminating the restrictions of the physical world.

It's a very good idea to think about the process of bringing the elusive e-journal into the library collection, so that you'll be ready when the Jell-O actually gels!

Developing an Internet-Based Reference Service

Blythe Bennett

Blythe Bennett (*blytheb@vrd.org*) is the KidsConnect Q&A coordinator. KidsConnect is a component of ICONnect, a technology initiative of the American Association of School Librarians, a division of the American Library Association. Bennett works on the Virtual Reference Desk at the Information Institute of Syracuse (New York).

Thinking of building and managing an Internet-based question and answer (Q&A) service? In 1992, the Information Institute of Syracuse did just that, launching AskERIC, one of the first and most reliable Q&A services on the Internet. Four years later, in 1996, KidsConnect, a service much like AskERIC but for K–12 students, grew out of the partnership between the Information Institute and AASL (the American Association of School Librarians), a division of the American Library Association. This chapter presents developmental issues, budgeting considerations, technology and staffing concerns, common or recurring problems, and evaluation methods for an Internet-based Q&A service.

First, however, let's look at another Information Institute project, the Virtual Reference Desk, a project creating the foundations for a national cooperative digital reference service. The Virtual Reference Desk has compiled a set of quality indicators in its "Facets of Quality for K–12 Digital Reference Services." The quality indicators fall into two main categories: user transactions and service development and management. If you plan to build an Internet-based Q&A service, consider the following twelve quality indicators:

User Transactions
- Accessible
- Prompt turnaround

- Set user expectations
- Interactive
- Instructive

Service Development and Management
- Authoritative
- Trained information specialists
- Private
- Reviewed
- Unbiased
- Provides access to related information
- Publicized

The Virtual Reference Desk defines these indicators and presents strategies for achieving them on its website at *http://www.vrd.org/training/facets.html*. The Virtual Reference Desk also provides an electronic discussion group called Dig_Ref. For further information, check *http://www.vrd.org/Dig_Ref/dig_ref.html*.

Mission

One of the first things you will want to decide is your mission and some supporting goals. Since this is your guiding philosophy, make sure you are clear about what you want your service to provide for your users.

Some topics to consider are your audience, the scope of the service, a response (answer) policy, and whether the service will be fee-based or free.

1. Who will be your audience? Will you serve all age groups, all geographic groups, or, if you limit these, how will you do so? If you are serving only a specific group (for example, local community patrons), how will you enforce that limit? Will users need a password or some other means of identification to use your service?
2. What is your scope area? Will the service cover a variety of subjects or only one? Who will be responsible for deciding whether a question is in scope? Do you have a policy for denying a question that is not in scope?
3. What kind of response do you intend to offer? Do you plan to offer instruction on how to use a particular resource (such as your own organization's database, the World Wide Web, an almanac)? Will you give specific answers or just paths to follow and pointers to answers the patron can find? Will you include a variety of resources or just Internet-based resources? Is user education one of your goals?
4. Will you charge a fee for this service? How will you determine the cost of answers? Will you have a different fee scale depending on the amount of information given in an answer, the amount of time it takes to find an answer, or other factors? How will you collect or charge that fee?

KidsConnect's audience is the K–12 community of students and the adults who work with them for curricular support. The majority of the questions come from K–12 public school students in the United States, but also from students in private schools, home schoolers, and students in many other countries. We assist parents, teachers, and librarians who are working with students and need our guidance in finding resources for curricular-related topics.

Our scope is any school-related topic and, if appropriate, special interests (hobbies, and so on). KidsConnect strives to educate the students and the adults who work with them on how to find their own resources. We provide a path and keywords, often with an explanation of how to compose a search string, and pointers to resources where students will find their own answer. We are not a homework helper in that we do not usually offer specific answers. We serve much as a school librarian in his or her own school library, guiding students in the use of resources. The KidsConnect service is free to the public.

Policy

Before launching any service to the public, you must establish some guiding policies. They must be in written form and should be composed by individuals in your profession. They should be approved by the governing board of your service. Once you begin with a set of policies, add to them as you find topics you neglected to include. Situations are sure to arise during actual service that were unforeseen in the preliminary stages.

Here are some specific questions to consider:

1. What is your policy on confidentiality of users and staff? Will you make the questions and responses public? What is your policy concerning liability? Where will you display a disclaimer?
2. Will you respond to questions asking for advice? If so, how will you respond?
3. What is your policy for denying service to people who are not in your defined audience or who ask a question not within your scope?
4. How do you deal with specific problems, such as suicide, controversial topics, inappropriate comments, or abuse from a patron? Will you respond to all questions that are in scope or just a portion of those questions?

KidsConnect has policies written by the project manager and approved by the AASL KidsConnect governing committee. Topics include: abuse, advice, controversial topics, copyright, liability, privacy, and inappropriate questions and comments.

Governance

You will need to decide who will be responsible for establishing policy, daily operations, and overall management of the service. Most Q&A services are sponsored by a governmental, educational, or professional organization that has a governing board. For example, AskERIC is a service of the U.S. Department of Education, KidsConnect is governed by the American Association of School Librarians, and Ask Shamu is part of the educational service from Busch Gardens.

Questions to consider are:

1. Is your service sponsored by a reputable organization? Does this organization carry authority in the field?
2. Do you have a partnership with "sister services" with which you can share questions not in your scope? Does your service fill a gap in existing Q&A services?
3. Who has access to the materials and data? What copyrights exist for training materials, data collected, and question/response pairs?
4. Who is responsible for policy making and quality control?

Funding/Budget

When planning for start-up or future funding, consider how much of your organization's resources are already available and how much you will need to provide yourself. You have a head start if you already have the workstations, phone lines, or other necessary wiring.

If you need to hire a staff person to manage the project, you will need to consider the salary, cost of benefits, and so on. Perhaps you can move a current staff person from one position to another. Remember to include the additional cost of people who provide administrative, secretarial, and technical support to the project.

Regarding the software you choose to use when operating your service, you might plan to use preexisting software or you might decide to have software customized for your particular service. Publicity can be costly depending on the products you produce, but it can also be free if you publicize on your own website and through electronic discussion groups.

When you plan for the future, presume that your question load will increase over time or at least remain stable. Consider carefully the need and desire for publicizing your service. You may get more business than you bargained for!

The following are questions to consider for funding issues:

1. Will you buy, borrow, or build your own software? This could include an e-mail package, Web development tools, automation and tracking software, and databases.
2. Will you need to purchase new hardware, such as workstations, wiring, and servers? If your service is funded by a company, are you compelled to point to products made by your sponsor?
3. Will you need to hire, or at least supplement the pay for, administrative, secretarial, and technical staff?

Because of the partnership between the Information Institute of Syracuse and AASL, KidsConnect is managed as part of the Information Insti-

DEVELOPING AN INTERNET-BASED REFERENCE SERVICE   163

tute, where support staff is already in place. Although initial donations of workstations were given by the underwriter, Microsoft Corporation, the wiring, utilities, and other "housing costs" are provided by the Information Institute. Software is also provided by the Information Institute.

Technology

You will want to think about how technology can enhance your service. You will need to consider the question of "delivery method," such as e-mail and Web-based messages. You might also decide to incorporate a real-time reference interview in a chat room or through a MOO client (a real-time computer connection connecting multiple users). Keep your options open for incorporating new technologies if they can enhance your service or assist your staff members.

Questions to consider regarding technology are:

1. Does your method of question delivery exclude any users? Do you have alternative methods for sending questions and receiving responses that will allow "lower-end" users to access and use your service?
2. Do you have a way to archive a knowledge base, and is it kept for private purposes or is it open to the public?
3. What accommodations have been made to provide for assistive technologies?

Because KidsConnect is a service for children, we maintain a private knowledge base for confidentiality reasons set forth in our policies. Although that means fewer people can take advantage of the core of knowledge we have developed, our patrons and volunteer staff maintain their privacy. KidsConnect is accessible to users with e-mail and Web access.

Web Presence

You will almost certainly have a website to provide access to the question and answer service, but you may also have some content on your site that will benefit your service, your staff, and your patrons.

Questions regarding the Web content are:

1. Who will be responsible for writing and maintaining the collection of resources? Will you have links to other websites, and, if so, what are your selection criteria? How frequently will you update your public site?
2. Will you provide access to Frequently Asked Questions (FAQs)? Will you allow access to your knowledge base of question/response pairs?
3. Will your entire site be public or will you maintain some password-protected sections?

KidsConnect maintains a private website for training at the Information Institute of Syracuse. The public website is housed at the American Library Association. The public site includes a set of "Favorite Web Sites" categorized by curricular topics that were selected by school librarians. There is also a growing collection of Frequently Asked Questions that are developed by school librarians. These follow the format of the usual question/response pairs but are enhanced with a greater number of websites as resources for information. There is also a Web form where students can send their questions.

Personnel

You will need at least one manager of the service, but more may become necessary depending on how large you plan to grow and how much you intend to offer your users. You might find the need for different managers in charge of daily question and answer maintenance, training, and content development. You will need to consider personnel for technical support, secretarial support, and fund-raising. Depending on your scale of service, you might have a team of paid professionals who respond to questions, as is the case with AskERIC, or you may have a team of trained volunteers, as does the KidsConnect project.

Some questions to consider regarding personnel are:

1. How will you organize your volunteers or staff? Will it be by areas of expertise, by age levels of patrons, or by random assignment? Will you have team leaders or mentors, or will each staff person be on his or her own? Will the personnel be on-site or distributed?
2. Will there be one manager and what are the duties of that position? How will you provide backup if that person is unavailable?
3. If you are relying on volunteer power, what are the benefits of service for those people? If your system is distributed, is there a way to build community among the participants? Whether they are paid staff or volunteers, how will you provide feedback for them? What are the criteria for selection as a volunteer or paid professional?

The KidsConnect service is staffed with one manager and a large distributed network of volunteer librarians. The manager receives support at the Information Institute from a director who assists with fund-raising and collaboration with AASL, the secretarial staff, the systems staff, and the Web developer. AASL provides assistance with Web development, fund-raising, and policy guidance. The volunteer corps is a group of more than two hundred dedicated librarians, mostly school librarians, who have undertaken a training process before becoming members of the volunteer team and offer their free time and expertise to assist with questions every other month.

DEVELOPING AN INTERNET-BASED REFERENCE SERVICE   165

KidsConnect volunteers are organized in teams of approximately ten people, each working with different age groups of students. There are teams for elementary, middle, and high school as well as some special groups of K–12, vocational school, and other specialized student groups. These small teams often have a leader who has experience with the Kids-Connect project and who serves as a mentor. Each team has a discussion list so members can ask for assistance from colleagues if necessary. The entire volunteer group is also on one large discussion list, which helps to build community, provide updates on the service, and discuss topics related to KidsConnect.

Training

Training is essential for all members of the Q&A organization. Often this means self-training for the manager of the service. Take advantage of other organizations who have created a similar service, and borrow and adapt from their training, if possible. Different procedures will work for different organizations and missions, but there is no need to begin from scratch. The *AskA Starter Kit*, written by R. David Lankes and Abby S. Kasowitz, is an excellent resource for any organization starting an "AskA" service on the Internet. The kit is available from ERIC.

Some organizations have an extensive training session before a staff person or volunteer takes real questions. In other organizations, the person takes real questions, but the responses are screened by a mentor before they go out to the patron. You will need to decide what method is best for your organization.

The following are questions to consider regarding training:

1. What do you want your staff and volunteers to know and do? What is the level of competence you wish each staff member and volunteer to reach before she or he begins handling questions?
2. How do you plan to deliver the training materials? Will they be in print, presented face-to-face, through the Web, or by e-mail? Will you use a combination of media? What job aids will you create and provide? Will there be a series of practice questions with feedback from the trainer?
3. What do you want your staff members to know before beginning the training? Do they need to be familiar with e-mail, chat clients, or how to search the Web effectively? Do you have a system for retraining after some of your "veteran" staff members or volunteers have been answering questions for an extended period?

KidsConnect uses e-mail and the Web for training delivery. In-person training at conferences proved to be insufficient for such a lengthy process. Currently, training begins with a person reading materials online and then undergoing a series of practice questions through e-mail.

Procedures

Depending on your mission, you might simply assist patrons by providing the answer that was requested, or you might educate them so they become comfortable using the tools and resources you used to find the answer.

The following are questions to consider when planning the answering procedure:

1. What will be the path a question takes from start to finish? How much or how little information will you give a patron? For example, will you give an answer or just point to a set of resources?
2. What will be the format of your responses? What will be the tone of your responses?
3. Will you test each e-mail address before working on a response? If you choose not to test, do you have a phone number option on the Web form so that you can call if a response bounces back to you?

KidsConnect generally provides the path taken in print or online or both to find suggested resources. On occasion, we do provide a direct answer. Sometimes the path is too complicated for the capability of the student, sometimes the path produces inappropriate websites, and sometimes the answer is in a place most students would not be able to access, such as a print item in a special collection, a phone interview with an expert, or another less-accessible location.

At KidsConnect, a question first comes to the main account, where it is read and then "pinged" to test for a valid e-mail address. Only the questions coming in through the Web form are tested; rarely will a direct e-mail question have an invalid address. We do not ask for phone numbers on the Web form because we do not have a budget to allow for long-distance calling nor do we want to encourage students to divulge that kind of personal information.

After it is determined that the e-mail address is valid, the question is sent to a KidsConnect volunteer who works with students in the appropriate age group (elementary, middle, or high school). If a student does not fill in the grade level on the Web form, or if we cannot determine the age from the question, the question is usually sent to a volunteer who works with all ages. The volunteer has two school days, not counting weekends or holidays, to send a response to the student. If the volunteer is delayed, he or she should send a "busy" signal to the student indicating that the message is being worked on.

The KidsConnect volunteer will find resources to suggest, usually websites or basic reference materials, and will compose a response suggesting those resources to the student. Supplying the pathway, such as the search engine's URL and the keywords or search string used, provides an opportunity for the student to learn how to use that particular search engine. Often, the volunteer indicates why different terms or Boolean operators were used and how they work. We often provide two or three specific URLs where the student can find the answer or other relevant information. When the response is ready, one copy is sent directly to the student and a second copy goes to KidsConnect for archival purposes.

Problems

Every digital reference service encounters problems. You can be forewarned about some, but you will encounter others of your own. This is a new field, and many of us are learning as we go. You will need to establish procedures for handling common or recurring problems, and you might need to consider teaming with "sister organizations."

Topics to consider are:

1. What do you do with stumpers (questions for which you cannot find an answer)? How will you clean up the "sludge" or unanswered questions in a timely fashion?
2. Can you team with other organizations so they take your out-of-scope questions while you assist them with ones that fit your area?
3. How do you manage growth that you cannot control? How can you automate processes to save time? How will you manage when the number of questions becomes overwhelming? How will you handle staff members who are late in responding to their questions?

KidsConnect has encountered all these problems, and more! We try hard to respond to all appropriate questions within our two-school-day turnaround criterion, but sometimes that does not happen. On occasion we do run into stumpers, and we need to notify the student that we could not find any helpful resources. In such cases, we also tell the student what was tried. The manager must maintain housecleaning operations to make sure old questions do receive a response, even when late.

KidsConnect works with AskERIC daily by sending questions about educational research from parents, teachers, and librarians. AskERIC reciprocates by sending all K–12 student questions they receive to KidsConnect. When appropriate, KidsConnect refers students to specific services, such as the Mad Scientist Network, Ask Shamu, the Math Forum (Ask Dr. Math), and other subject-specific services.

Managing growth is more difficult. We attempt to stay one jump ahead of demand, but sometimes training lags behind incoming questions. We also have peak periods where incoming questions are overwhelming. During those periods, we often let students know we are running behind schedule, and they may experience delays. For this reason, publicity has been light for KidsConnect, lest we damage the reputation of the service by being so overwhelmed that we must shut down.

Evaluation

You will want to evaluate many aspects of your service on a regular basis. Training materials must be evaluated and updated. There might be continuous evaluation of new trainees. Veteran staff members will need refresher work and debriefing. Along with the training aspect, the service as a whole should be reviewed periodically. Web-based resources should also be updated, using quality criteria.

Questions to consider are:

1. How do you know your service is of benefit to your users? Are your users satisfied? Will you send out surveys or questionnaires to your users?
2. How will you know your staff members are continuing to produce quality responses? Are your staff members satisfied? How will you evaluate trainees as they go through the training process?
3. How will you maintain quality services and resources? Is your service cost effective? What statistics will you gather and interpret regarding Web hits, numbers of questions, and so on?

KidsConnect conducts occasional surveys of its patrons and also of its volunteer base. Most answers are reviewed by the manager, and, if problems are found, the student and volunteer receive a note with the corrections. Further studies need to be conducted to evaluate the benefit of the service to its patrons. A refresher course for veteran volunteers will be developed to assist with continuous improvement of the service.

There is a great deal more to learn about the impact of KidsConnect on the students, teachers, librarians, and parents who send in questions. A number of benefits for volunteers have been ascertained already. There is the constant need to enhance the mechanics of the service related to automating, routing, and tracking the question and response pairs. We are continually adding to and editing the material on the website for the benefit of our users.

Digital reference is an exciting aspect of librarianship; there is much to learn and we welcome newcomers to the field!

Resources

Bennett, Blythe. "Handling the Quirky Questions: A Model for Reference Service." *Knowledge Quest* 26 (January/February 1998).

Bennett, Blythe. "KidsConnect: Teacher–Librarians Helping Kids Solve Their Information Problems on the Internet." *The Teaching Librarian* 4 (winter 1997): 14–17.

Lankes, R. David, and Abby S. Kasowitz. *AskA Starter Kit: How to Build and Maintain Digital Reference Services.* IR-107. Syracuse, N.Y.: ERIC Clearinghouse on Information and Technology, November 1998.

Lankes, R. David. *Building and Maintaining Internet Information Services: K–12 Digital Reference Services.* IR-106. Syracuse, N.Y.: ERIC Clearinghouse on Information and Technology, June 1998.

Online Resources

AskERIC
http://askeric.org/

KidsConnect
http://www.ala.org/ICONN/kidsconn.html

Internet Public Library
http://ipl.org/

Math Forum
http://forum.swarthmore.edu/

Virtual Reference Desk
http://vrd.org/

Ask A Scientist Archives
http://newton.dep.anl.gov/newton/askasci/askasci.html

Ask A Mad Scientist
http://www.madsci.org/

Ask Shamu
http://www.seaworld.org/ask_shamu/asindex.html

Chicago Public Library Archive
http://www.chipublib.org/008subject/005genref/gisques11.html

Electronic Reserves: Concepts and Models

Jeff Rosedale

Jeff Rosedale (*rosedale@columbia.edu*) is a systems librarian at Columbia University. He has previously worked in Access Services functions at Columbia's Butler and Lehman Libraries. He maintains the Electronic Reserves Clearinghouse website at *http://www.columbia.edu/~rosedale*.

Course reserves are a staple on the menu of academic library services. Familiar features of this service include:

- High visibility
- Faculty selection of materials
- Time-sensitivity of processing and availability of materials
- Cyclical demand by students for readings, with intense peaks
- Limitations on the number of copies made available
- A designated area in the library for storage and retrieval
- Short loan periods and high overdue fines

The paper environment imposes natural limitations and restraints on the freedom with which students can consult the course-related materials placed on reserve. Library location and hours, competition for a limited number of copies—especially during exam times—and loan and fine policies can conspire to make reserves access complicated and frustrating. Given this context, it is not difficult to understand how some have looked to the reserves function as a high-impact area to improve library service and to simultaneously show off academic information technology.

Two major factors have contributed to the growth of electronic reserves services: the increasing orientation of academic libraries toward improving customer service, and an escalating expectation on the part of students and faculty that technological solutions will advance their educational pursuits. (For background, general information, and links to course reserves websites, see my home page at *http://www.columbia.edu/~rosedale*.)

A Bit of History

Some reserves managers, myself included, once hoped that a large vendor might be willing to supply articles in digital form and allow libraries to store and use them in their reserves operations. However, studies of reserves lists in similar courses and disciplines across a number of institutions revealed so little overlap in assigned readings that undertaking such an endeavor would not bring adequate returns on investment. To bring course reserves into the digital age, libraries were going to have to pick up the ball themselves.

The technologies and processes necessary to convert course reserves from a paper to a digital library service have existed for more than a decade: reformatting materials from paper to electronic form; compressing and storing the large resulting files; delivering them to one or more workstations by way of network protocols; and displaying and printing the digital objects across a variety of hardware platforms. Indeed, the first experimentation with electronic reserves at San Diego State University (on a local area network within the library) took place in the early 1990s.

Toward the mid-1990s, a sizable number of pilot projects sprang up at institutions around the United States and Canada. The advent of the World Wide Web as a simple, common, and flexible delivery system combined with plummeting costs of storing large databases were the primary catalysts for broader experimentation. Viewers like Adobe Acrobat served the function of delivering page images across various platforms at acceptable rates of speed.

Contents and Copyright

Dozens of production systems are currently in operation in North and Central America and in Europe; Northwestern University, San Diego State University, and the University of Michigan, for example, are operating highly evolved electronic reserves services. The variety in systems applications parallels the idiosyncratic nature of faculty selection and the individualized environment of each institution and library.

Science and technology libraries may have reserves databases filled with scanned problem and solution sets, lecture notes, and student projects; social sciences and humanities libraries may have journal articles and other commercially published materials. Many sites have some combination of locally and commercially produced materials. Although image-based services delivered over the Web are the premier form of delivery, there are still some ASCII text sites out there.

Similarly, there are a variety of interpretations regarding when and whether electronic reserves uses of materials can be considered fair use as defined in the Copyright Act. As a result, the policies and practices regarding payment of copyright permission fees vary from service to service. The Copyright Clearance Center (CCC) offers an electronic reserves permissions service, but an institution using the service must accept CCC's definition of fair use. Some libraries, therefore, prefer to seek permissions—where they are warranted—independently.

Another reason for the lack of a "Good Housekeeping Seal of Approval" model of electronic reserves is the variability in publishers' and authors' approaches to copyright. A single article may contain graphics and photographs that are subject to different copyright conditions than the text. Although some publishers are including clauses in database license agreements for use of materials in electronic reserves databases, others are so fearful of unbridled reproduction or malicious alteration of anything electronic that they reject out of hand any request for such uses.

Underlying the numerous copyright interpretations of electronic reserves are the types of uses that materials undergo in the process of being reformatted and networked. Publishers have often argued that the process of assembling an electronic reserves database resembles custom publishing (that is, electronic course packs) and that the "copying" of a work during scanning, storage, and viewing on a screen is comparable to republication, distribution, and public display or performance!

The wide divergence of mainstream publishers' views from mainstream librarians' views resulted in an impasse when the Conference on Fair Use (CONFU) attempted to hammer out a set of Electronic Reserves Fair Use Guidelines in 1996. Although the last draft of these proposed guidelines represents the nearest thing to "official" instructions on how to proceed, more recent discussion of the document has revealed that it contained too many compromises to be truly acceptable to either side. Though this lack of a broadly accepted outcome was disappointing, it did not inhibit the development of new systems or the expansion of those already in existence.

Many libraries do not seek permissions to place paper items on reserve, so the degree to which copyright considerations have been perceived as make-or-break in determining whether to launch an electronic reserves service has generally been overemphasized. Local copyright policies and practices will affect how a system is designed—and an electronic reserves service should not be launched without some detailed discussion and local consensus on the role of fair use and permissions requests.

To the surprise of some in the publishing community, to whom librarians can appear to be cavalier advocates of free access to information, the advent of electronic reserves has sparked a vigorous and diverse dialogue in libraries and on campuses about copyright compliance, permissions, and responsibilities in addition to fair use rights. Librarians designing electronic reserves systems have done so in the context of a drive to become fully informed about copyright; the Association of Research Libraries has committed significant resources toward copyright education for this purpose.

How Much Does It Cost?

One major concern of those interested in establishing an electronic reserves system is that this is a relatively labor-intensive service, in a time when academic library budgets have not necessarily been generous enough to support expansions in staffing and equipment. This is highlighted all the more when one considers that most electronic reserves systems have been envisioned as operating in parallel with a continuing paper-based reserves service for the same courses!

Cost Considerations

Costs will vary significantly according to underpinnings and assumptions on which systems are based. A few examples are:

1. *Will you optimize for display or printing?*

   Most agree that students will simply print out reserves materials, rarely reading them on the screen. The cost implication here is that optimizing for display may involve more extensive editing of scanned images or higher resolutions in the scanning and display processes or both.

2. *Will you assume some degree of fair use rights?*

   Most copyright experts agree that at least some types of electronic-reserves use of commercially published materials will require seeking permission from the copyright holder. This means it would be wise to establish a budget for permissions fees.

3. *Will you offer free printing?*

   Charging a modest fee for printing may be an effective way to recover some costs, but this must be carefully weighed against the degree to which fees may deter some from using the service.

4. *Will you need additional staff to establish your service?*

   Student labor has often been used in the actual reformatting process, and small operations have been able to mount pilot projects without adding staff.

Unfortunately, one weakness in the electronic reserves community is ineffective sharing of information. There is virtually no published research on the topic, and many institutions keep cost, staffing, usage, and evaluation data close to the chest. This leaves unanswered important questions about scalability, student and faculty satisfaction, comparative costs of different approaches to copyright permissions, and more.

Individual questions are often answered on the Electronic Reserves Discussion List (*http://www.cni.org/Hforums/arl-ereserve@arl.org*) and through the ACRL Electronic Reserves Discussion Group, which meets regularly at

ALA Annual and Midwinter conferences. I also hope to have an electronic reserves FAQ mounted on my Clearinghouse page (*http://www.columbia.edu/~rosedale/*) before the end of the century! These resources notwithstanding, this is an area crying out for some good research and analysis.

Implementation Checklist

Here is a short list of issues to consider when contemplating the establishment of an electronic reserves system. In addition to thinking and talking about these issues locally, institutional sponsors should talk with their peers about ideas, plans, and experiences.

- Which faculty members and courses should be involved in this project?
- Are there other strategic partnering opportunities here (for example, with computing specialists, the bookstore, specific publishers)?
- How can users' input be solicited to ensure that the system meets their needs?
- How much content is already locally available in digital form?
- What is the extent of current infrastructure to support delivery of digital materials to end users? If an expansion of this infrastructure is needed to support the new service, how will this be paid for?
- What is the projected scope of the electronic reserves project, both initially and in the longer term? Will it include commercially published materials?
- What is the local copyright policy with regard to reserves uses, both in paper and electronic form?
- If permissions are warranted at any stage, how will the required fees be paid?
- What hardware and software components will be used for scanning?
- What is the projected size of the database, in both the near and long term?
- Will this activity create temporary or permanent staffing needs?
- How will the success of the project be measured?
- How can this program be marketed to faculty, students, administrators, alumni, friends groups, and others?

A Look toward the Future

Several factors indicate a continued viability for the development and maintenance of electronic reserves systems, at least for the foreseeable future. Among the most important are:

- The inability of publishers to coordinate on digital delivery
- The rapid pace of digital library development
- The expansion of academic technology infrastructure
- Technological competition among academic institutions

- The eagerness of faculty to integrate the Web into instruction
- The idiosyncratic nature of faculty selection of course material
- Libraries' willingness and ability to assume leadership roles

Even with the advent of full-text article databases from major vendors, which some said would sound the death knell for electronic reserves, new systems continue to proliferate and diversify. Vendors are slowly responding to the notion that e-reserves will be around for a while; UMI recently introduced a product called SiteBuilder (*http://www. umi.com/sitebuilder-demo/demo*), designed to organize links to its full-text resources and present them in the context of a class syllabus. Innovative Interfaces has an electronic reserves module, and Phil Kesten's low-cost E-Res product (*http://www.docutek.com*) is attracting a widening circle of academic customers. Pilot projects have been launched in co-operation with big names like IBM and Xerox.

Although electronic reserves will probably never fuel an economic engine of any appreciable size for publishers, vendors, or academia, it has caught the imagination of faculty and students in a way that demands our attention. Once written off by publishers as illegal and by administrators as too expensive, electronic reserves is firmly establishing itself as a deservedly popular service that emphasizes the interconnectedness of faculty, students, and the libraries that serve them.

6

The Library'd Be Fine If It Wasn't for All Those People!

Providing Web Access in Libraries: A Practical Guide

Alicia Abramson

Alicia Abramson (*abramson@csus.edu*) is director of Library Information Systems at California State University, Sacramento. She recently completed a study of the use of the World Wide Web by patrons of American University Library entitled "Monitoring and Evaluating the Use of the World Wide Web in an Academic Library: An Exploratory Study" (*Proceedings of the American Society for Information Science Annual Meeting* 35, 1998).

Welcome to the Web-enhanced library, with access to hundreds of databases, online journals, and reference sources, some of which your library actually owns! Not to mention thousands of unidentified, unclassified, and possibly useful sites waiting to be discovered. And, of course, each Web-based resource has its own unique interface to navigate.

Here we observe a day in the life of you, the average cybrarian:

9:00 A.M. Coffee

9:30 A.M. A student wants to know why she can't find a description of the habitat and mating habits of the Sarcastic Fringehead fish on the Web. You take her to the Aquatic Sciences and Fisheries Abstracts CD-ROM station.

10:15 A.M. Professor Smith just called to say that he couldn't access the library's Web proxy server because it kept telling him "you are not an authorized user." He really needs to do a Lexis-Nexis search before noon.

11:30 A.M. You discover that none of the URLs in the MARC 856 field is active in your library's Web OPAC.

12:10 P.M. Lunch!

180   THE LIBRARY'D BE FINE IF IT WASN'T FOR ALL THOSE PEOPLE!

1:15 P.M.   The server of "the most reliable, information-filled Web database in the universe" goes down for fifteen minutes. Four people complain that they lost their searches.

2:30 P.M.   You discover that the security on OPAC workstation 9 has been hacked, and the Netscape Web browser has been deleted and replaced with the Microsoft Internet Explorer browser.

3:05 P.M.   A 1986 model dot-matrix printer is spewing out 1,000 pages of garbage after someone tried to print a highly graphical, JavaScript-enhanced web page with frames.

3:30 P.M.   Everyone in the library (staff, patrons, and the maintenance crew) is asking "Why is the Web so slow today?"

4:00 P.M.   A line is forming for use of the Web computers, and you note that several people have been camped out for hours doing e-mail and chatting on the Web. What's a cybrarian to do?

Thanks largely to the World Wide Web, libraries are able to offer their users unprecedented access to a vastly expanded information universe. This chapter will explore some of the key technological, computer-user, and policy issues that come with the territory when providing Web access in libraries. First, we'll look at the basic nuts and bolts of providing Web access—the technological setup. Then we'll spend some time discussing computer-user issues and how cybrarians can facilitate the information seeking and gathering process at public Web computers. Last, we'll explore some of the policy questions being debated in libraries everywhere.

Public Web-Access Computer Setup

The technological aspect of managing Web access in libraries can make some cybrarians reminisce, misty-eyed, about the old days of mainframes and dumb terminals—days when upgrading and adding on (software, hardware, and firmware) were not daily facts of life, security was relatively simple, and response time seemed fast for a dumb system. Managing public access computers in the age of client/server computing, the Graphical User Interface (GUI), and the Web requires considerably more attention to public-access systems in terms of networking, workstation setup and maintenance, security, and application management.

In addition to basic technical knowledge in all these areas, the well-equipped cybrarian must also constantly keep her ear to the ground to stay informed about the latest technological developments that might save the library money in either equipment cost or personnel time or enhance the information-seeking and retrieval capabilities of the computer-user.

A good starting point for current information and problem solving in the Web computer management game is *The Library Web Manager's Ref-*

erence Center, hosted by librarians at the Berkeley Digital Library SunSITE at *http://sunsite.berkeley.edu/Web4Lib/faq.html*. The site is an archive of cybrarian-created how-to guides, reference sources, and technical information covering a variety of public Web computer management topics, including "Bombproofing Win95 User PCs," "Public Access Computer Security," and "Exploiting and Abusing Netscape Navigator (for those trying to prevent such)."

There is also a good "Current Awareness Resources" section with links to online publications covering a host of Web-related topics, including technical and design issues. It also includes Web resource evaluation and discovery guides, such as *BrowserWatch*, the excellent librarian-produced *Current Cites* newsletter, and the *Scout Report*. The Web4Lib electronic discussion, hosted at the same site (*http://sunsite.berkeley.edu/Web4Lib*), is also a great forum for issues related to providing Web access in libraries.

Hardware

By the time you read this, Intel could have come out with the 64-bit Momentium V©, 2.6-gigahertz CPU chip with built-in artificial intelligence. Should your library move up to the latest model? Not necessarily—it depends on the state of your current equipment, the demands of the applications you are running, and whether there will be any real performance benefit (and, of course, the availability of funds).

With those thoughts in mind, let's just say that the rule of thumb when purchasing computer equipment for serving up the Web seems to be: "bigger, better, faster, more!" This applies to almost everything: RAM, cache memory, CPU speed, hard-drive capacity, video card speed, and monitor size. And don't forget expandability: Expansion slots to which new (video, audio, etc.) cards, devices, and hard drives can be added are key to extending the life and utility of the computers you buy. Another rule of thumb is that you will probably be replacing or at least upgrading your equipment every three to five years. Unfortunately, no magic bullet will ease the strain that constant upgrading and procurement of new equipment places on library budgets.

Getting the best value means getting the word from the street before committing thousands of dollars to new equipment. Two sources that should be checked for reviews and recommendations of the latest generation of hardware are *ZDNET*—which publishes most of the reviews that appear in *PC Magazine*, *PC Week*, and *PC Computing*—at *http://www.zdnet.com*, and *Computers in Libraries* online, which publishes an annual buyers' guide at *http://www.infotoday.com/cilmag/ciltop.htm*.

Under the right conditions, upgrading, as opposed to replacing computers, may help the bottom line a little. Upgrading should be considered when it is possible to either add RAM or replace the CPU chip on the motherboard to improve speed and performance. Complete replacement of the motherboard is time-consuming, is more expensive than upgrading RAM and CPU chips, and can be fraught with configuration headaches, all of which add up to resources better spent elsewhere.

If the much-hyped but little-seen "Network Computer" (think "dumb terminal that runs Windows") ever blooms into a viable product in the marketplace, this may well be one solution to the problem of technology cost containment in the digital library environment. Purported features of the Network Computer include a slimmer, trimmer box less expensive than a PC and capable of running the latest GUI operating system with easier upgrading and administration.

PC Setup and Security

Without Network Computers, it is up to the cybrarian to individually configure PCs for Web access. A typical setup for public-access Web stations might look like this: Client computers run Windows 95/98/NT and connect to either a Windows NT or a Novell NetWare server. The clients are set up to log in to a server automatically (as a public user with minimal permissions) where each station's start-up settings reside. Security software, such as Fortres or WinU, protects each computer's local hardware and software settings by blocking unauthorized access to programs, files, and control panels, and by disabling the ability to boot from the A drive. Virus protection software is installed; it is updated with new virus identification data regularly. On start-up, a program such as a Web browser or a menu system is launched to provide users with a starting point.

For more information about PC setup and security, consult the previously mentioned *Library Web Manager's Reference Center*, which has links to numerous step-by-step guides, or read Allen C. Benson's "Building a Secure Library System" (*http://www.infotoday.com/cilmag/mar/story2.htm*).[1]

It is also possible to accomplish much of what is described here without a server or special security software. The Schenectady County Public Library in New York set up a secure, peer-to-peer Windows NT public network without either; they describe their methods at *http://www.scpl.org/publicnt/index.html*.

To publicly install more than a couple of computers at a time, a drive-cloning program like ImageCast (*http://www.imagecast.com*) or Norton Ghost (*http://www.symantec.com/sabu/ghost/index.html*) comes in handy. Drive-cloning software allows you to clone an entire computer's setup, software and all, and copy it to another computer in minutes—as opposed to the hours it takes to install and configure each component individually. Drive-cloning software is also useful in the case of a disaster, such as a major hard-drive crash, to restore the computer to working order relatively quickly after repair.

Network Security and Performance

Network security is even more important than workstation security. In order to prevent hackers (in and outside of the library) from wreaking havoc on mission-critical systems, cybrarians need to be informed about security issues, understand the types of network attacks that their systems are vulnerable to, and implement security systems like firewalls and proxy servers to protect their library's network. A good starting point for background on computer and network security issues is the Center for Education and Research in Information Assurance and Security (CERIAS) site at Purdue University (*http://www.cerias.purdue.edu/*)—it's one of the most extensive computer security sites on the Internet, with links to software, documentation, how-to guides, and much more.

Because security is so complex, you should also have a few desktop reference sources to consult, such as these titles from O'Reilly & Associates (my favorite computer book publisher): *Building Internet Firewalls* by D. Brent Chapman and Elizabeth D. Zwicky (1995), and *Practical UNIX and Internet Security*, 2d ed., by Simson Garfinkel and Gene Spafford (1996).

Firewalls. *Firewalls* are the heart of network security in the age of the Internet. A firewall is software that runs on a computer stationed at the entryway to your network (usually a router) and that allows users to access only an administrator-defined set of network resources and services, such as requesting pages from a Web server. For a general overview of firewalls, read "Avoid Disaster: Use Firewalls for Inter-Intranet Security" (*http://www.infotoday.com/cilmag/oct/story2.htm*) by J. R. Charnetski.[2] One highly regarded Unix-based fire wall product mentioned in the article is the Trusted Information Systems Internet Firewall Toolkit, freely available on the Web at *http://www.tis.com/prodserv/fwtk/readme.html.*

Proxy Servers. Another option related to security is the *proxy server.* The primary purpose of a proxy server is to provide a way to allow off-site access to library Web resources that use IP address authentication, but it also has additional security and network performance benefits. Some proxy servers can be configured to act as firewalls and prevent unauthorized access to the library's network from computers on the Internet. There are numerous proxy server software packages available, including a number of free proxy server packages for the Unix platform, such as the Apache Web server (which has a proxy module), available at *http://www. apache.org*, and Squid, available at *http://squid.nlanr.net/Squid.*

For libraries on Windows machines or libraries with a limited number of dial-up connections to the Internet, a relatively inexpensive proxy solution is WinProxy at *http://www.winproxy.com.* This product allows you to funnel multiple users through a single dial-up connection, thereby increasing the number of simultaneous users you can support. WinProxy also has built-in firewall support.

Another benefit of many proxy servers is the ability to cache frequently accessed web pages on a local server, thereby reducing the amount of network traffic in your library, increasing the speed at which users can download web pages, and improving overall network performance. For a treatise on proxy caching of Web documents, and why it's a good practice, check out *Cache Now!* at *http://vancouver-webpages.com/CacheNow.*

One problem with implementing proxy servers is that users who wish to obtain off-site access to library resources must be taught how to configure their home PCs to work with a library proxy server. Another problem with proxy servers is authenticating external users. First, programs must be created that check user-entered data against databases with user login and password information (or there must be an interface between the proxy server and an existing database). Second, many proxy servers don't encrypt the password information. This sensitive information is vulnerable to hackers who can "sniff" TCP/IP packets and capture unencrypted passwords. A good article that addresses these shortcomings and proposes an alternative to the standard proxy server setup is "Pass-Through Proxying as a Solution to the Off-Campus Web-Access Problem," by Richard Goerwitz at Brown University (*http://www.stg.brown.edu/pub/proxydoc/Proxy.tr98.1.shtml*).

The Public User and the Web Workstation

On the user end of the public Web-access computer, cybrarians have much work to do. In advance of the much-hyped "Digital Library" of the future where the ideal interface will seamlessly guide users to their desired destinations in the information universe, cybrarians must be prepared to help users through the disorganized jumble of resources that is the Web today. This means creating user-friendly, well-organized, reliable portals to Web information. The library's home page, which may be the first page on-site users see when they sit down at a public Web computer, has a role to play in facilitating Web information discovery.

Site Design

Of course, building useful and relevant websites is no simple task. It involves not only providing access to our electronic collections and links to high-quality Internet resources, but also developing user-centered design. Cybrarians take note: Don't underestimate the power of design! Although some complain that it is hard to get a handle on just what our users want, user feedback is a major component in the development of good design. A well-designed website will have repeat users, and a bad one will not. It is that simple.

Usability tests are an excellent way to obtain feedback on websites—and they don't have to be empty exercises or costly, monumental projects. According to Web design guru Jakob Neilsen, "A usability test with 5 users will typically uncover 80% of the site-level usability problems plus about half of the page-level usability problems on those pages that users happen to visit during the test."[3]

With user-centered design as our mantra, cybrarians can provide users with more than a Web browser placeholder on their way to somewhere else. A book that will go well on the user-centered cybrarian's bookshelf is *Web Navigation: Designing the User Experience*, by Web designer and librarian Jennifer Fleming.[4] The entire focus of the book is on designing sites that are easily navigated by users; it was called a "gleaming jewel" by a reviewer at WebDeveloper.com (*http://www.webdeveloper.com/reviews/book32.html*). Another good source of tips on website design is Jakob Neilsen's bi-weekly Web column, Alertbox, at *http://www.useit.com/alertbox.*

Text Editor

Because of the versatility of the Web as an information-seeking and a communication tool, providing Web access also means taking into account all the things users might want to do at a Web-based computer and facilitating those tasks. With ever more full text online and with access to innumerable information resources, people will naturally spend more time at the computer—reading text, compiling data from multiple databases, and trying to analyze and synthesize the information they gather. To facilitate the process of gathering and synthesizing information from multiple Web resources, public Web computers should include access to a basic text editor, into which URLs, citations, and data from various sources can be cut and pasted, then printed, saved to disk, or e-mailed for future reference.

Printers

Another important component of providing access to full-text and page images through the Web is the provision of high-quality printing capabilities. Dot matrix printers, old workhorses in the dumb terminal environment, just don't cut it for the graphics-intensive Web. Options include inkjet and laser printers. For most libraries, higher-capacity laser printers will probably better survive heavy patron use, though they come with a higher price tag and higher maintenance costs.

To contain the cost associated with providing high-quality printing, one option is to charge for printing. One printer-payment system is UnipriNT by PHAROS Systems (*http://www.pharos.com*). This system works in conjunction with a standard vending-card reader (like the ones used for photocopy machines) and tells the user in advance how much his or her print job will cost. Although the system runs on a Windows NT server, it can accept jobs from users on Novell NetWare networks.

Specialized Services

To accommodate visually impaired users, your library should have at least one computer equipped with some combination of the following: a screen reader and screen enlarger, a textual Web browser like Lynx (available at *http://lynx.browser.org*), screen enlargement software, screen text-reading and speech synthesis software, and a speech synthesizer card. Web computer managers should consult the Equal Access to Software and Information (EASI) site at *http://www.rit.edu/~easi/resources.html* for more detailed information about some of the products available to facilitate visually impaired access to the Web. The National Federation of the Blind also has a list of software and hardware vendors that produce products for the blind at *http://www.nfb.org/tech.htm.* Last, a useful service for translating Adobe

Acrobat (PDF) files into plain text can be found at *http://www.pdfzone.com.* The user simply mails the PDF file as an attachment and receives e-mail with the converted text.

Policy

We recognize that the new information and communication environment will influence our societal structure and value systems.[5]

One of the great attractions of the Web as an information and communications tool is its two-way nature. Web users not only can take from the vast electronic information store, but can contribute to it as well—by posting to electronic discussion groups, by participating in online chats and conferences, and by creating their own web pages, to name a few ways. They can also e-mail Aunt Millie in Peoria or book a flight to Europe right from the library. Depending on your point of view, this either poses a problem for libraries because it challenges our traditional idea of what a library is all about and how library resources should be used, or it represents an exciting development where libraries, long mythologized as stodgy book warehouses, are transforming into cutting-edge electronic communications and knowledge centers.

Access to Web Resources

Either way you look at it, today's cybrarians face managerial and policy challenges that will shape the definition of libraries for both library users and librarians in the twenty-first century. One major question confronting libraries everywhere is whether or not to support all the extra capabilities that the Web allows. Some librarians view the use of library Web computers for e-mail, chat, and freestyle Web surfing as a waste of expensive and scarce resources and would rather limit use to those Web resources that the library owns or has selected as part of its electronic resource collection. Other librarians view these activities as legitimate uses of a new medium and as an electronic extension of activities that libraries have long supported in the analog world.

In October 1998, a fascinating debate took place among members of the Web4Lib discussion list over whether or not to allow e-mail access in libraries, with convincing, impassioned statements on both sides of the argument. Those arguing in favor of allowing e-mail use in libraries cited First Amendment rights, the value of e-mail in scholarly communication, and the idea that e-mail is just one component of a changing information paradigm. They also noted that the library may be the only place where some people can access e-mail. Those against supporting e-mail in libraries argued that the cost of providing Web access justified limiting its use to designated information-seeking activities. The fact that many users have alternative access points, such as computer labs or home computers, also seemed to influence the "anti" side.

One observation I couldn't help making is that regardless of whether or not the participants in the debate supported the use of e-mail by patrons in libraries, e-mail was obviously an important tool for advancing the debate, exploring professional issues, and communicating with a respected peer group. It seems to me that these same values should be in force when deciding whether library users should be able to engage in similar electronic discussion from the library. The debate now stands as part of the electronic record of librarianship; it can be found by searching for the Boolean phrase "email and libraries" in the 1998 Web4Lib archive at *http://sunsite.berkeley.edu/Web4Lib/archive.html* and looking at the messages in October.

Because a debate exists regarding what Web services and information resources libraries should provide, it is important for libraries to reexamine their existing policies regarding information access and decide whether limiting or denying access to certain Web services or resources is in line with the library's stated mission, goals, and objectives. If it's been a while since your library visited the issue of information access policy, it may be useful to take a look at ALA's *Access to Electronic Information, Services and Networks: An Interpretation of the Library Bill of Rights* at *http://www.ala.org/alaorg/oif/electacc.html* for recommendations about dealing with some of these questions. For examples of public library policies that address Web use, an archive of 125 policies representing libraries across the United States, large and small, is available at *http://www.ci.oswego.or.us/library/poli.htm*. Revealing my own bias against restricting the Web activities of users, I would direct academic cybrarians to review the materials at the Computers and Academic Freedom archive hosted by the Electronic Frontier Foundation at *http://www.eff.org/CAF/*. This site includes a "Library Policy Archive" at *http://www.eff.org/pub/CAF/library/*.

Strategies for Equitable Web Computer Management

In situations where the demand for Web computers frequently exceeds supply or where a library's primary clientele must compete for Web computers with other users, cybrarians may need to develop strategies that address the issue of equitable access to library Web computers. Following are three strategies for providing equitable access.

Time Limits. Time limits can be enforced by requiring people to sign up for use of a Web computer and allowing each user to be on the system for a specified period. On a web page discussing "Workstation Security" (*http://www.leeric.lsu.edu/lla/1998_conference/workstation/*), librarian Monica King describes two different software programs that can be used to electronically enforce time limits. The big advantage of time limits is that everyone gets a fair chance to use the system when the library is busy. One major disadvantage is that time limits can be set too short, causing frustration or dissatisfaction among users.

Prioritizing Types of Use. Prioritizing types of use—for example, making online catalog searching and use of the library's Web-based databases top priority, general Web surfing second priority, and e-mail and chat third priority—would allow a librarian to request that a user doing e-mail relinquish a Web computer to a user who is waiting to do online catalog searching. The advantage of this approach is that it only needs to be enforced when the library is busy and demand for Web computers exceeds the supply. The main disadvantage is that users' perceptions of the legitimacy and priority of their activities may differ from those of the library, leading to conflicts and unhappy patrons.

Designating Specific Computers for Specific Tasks. In this strategy, the public computers are divided into purpose-specific groups, such as library-resource-only stations (restricted to, for example, the OPAC and library-licensed databases) and e-mail access stations. The advantage of this method is that patrons will use specific stations for specific tasks, and the library can allocate more computers to higher-priority tasks. The disadvantage is the possibility that users might have to stand in line for computers of one type while others are idle.

These strategies for Web computer management can be used in a mix-and-match way as long as the policy is enforced consistently and equitably from case to case.

Conclusion

I have only touched the tip of the iceberg of what is involved in providing Web access to library users. There is much more work to be done beyond building our local technological infrastructures and formulating policy to bring our libraries into the new information age. Further challenges include:

- helping library users successfully navigate the Web and cope with information overload;
- working cooperatively with other libraries to establish standards for identifying reliable, authoritative, and meaningful Web information resources; and
- preserving digital information so that it can be accessed, searched, and retrieved by future generations.

Some of these challenges aren't necessarily new—after all, identifying, selecting, evaluating, and managing information is what our profession is all about. However, just like other information technologies that have been introduced in the past, the Web is having an impact on libraries and library users far beyond what was originally expected. It is affecting how we approach the tasks of building digital libraries, defining the services and limitations of the library in the digital age, and defining the role of the librarian and the library in an increasingly complex and distributed information environment.

Notes

1. Allen C. Benson, "Building a Secure Library System," *Computers in Libraries* 18, no. 3 (March 1998): 24–29.
2. J. R. Charnetski, "Avoid Disaster: Use Firewalls for Inter-Intranet Security," *Computers in Libraries* 18, no. 8 (October 1998): 44–48. Available at *http://www.infotoday.com/cilmag/oct/story2.htm.*
3. Jakob Neilson, *http://www.useit.com/alertbox/980503.html.*
4. Jennifer Fleming, *Web Navigation: Designing the User Experience* (Sebastopol, Calif.: O'Reilly, 1998).
5. Statement of the Second UNESCO INFOethics Congress 1998, *http://www.unesco.org/webworld/infoethics_2/eng/proceedings.htm.*

Kids, the Internet, and All Those Adult Anxieties

Walter Minkel

Walter Minkel (*wmink@teleport.com*) is the new technology editor at *School Library Journal*. Previously he was School Corps Technology Trainer at Multnomah County Library, Portland, Oregon, where he managed several kids- and education-oriented websites. He also created and manages the Newbery Medal, Caldecott Medal, and Coretta Scott King Award pages on the ALA website. He is coauthor of *Delivering Web Reference Services to Young People* (ALA, 1998).

Young people in my experience do not find the Net a particularly scary place. Depending on the particular child or teenager, it may be exciting, or intriguing, or boring. (Despite the popular mythology that says all kids are computer whizzes, I've seen plenty of them who couldn't care less about it.)

On the other hand, the Net is frequently a very scary place for parents, teachers, librarians, and others who work with children. Here, for example, is a list of Internet "Tips for Kids" that were part of a pro-Net-use promotional campaign called America Links Up (this list of tips is available at *http://www.americalinksup.org/*). The sponsors of America Links Up included Microsoft, Disney, the National PTA, and the U.S. Department of Education:

> TIP 1: I won't give out my name, age, school, address, phone number, picture, or any other information about myself or my family without getting permission.
>
> TIP 2: If I see or receive something online that looks weird or bad or that makes me feel uncomfortable, I won't respond. I'll leave that area right away and tell my parents.

KIDS, THE INTERNET, AND ALL THOSE ADULT ANXIETIES   191

TIP 3: I won't get together with anyone I meet online without getting my parents' permission first. I know people sometimes aren't who they say they are online.

TIP 4: I won't open or accept e-mails, files, links, URLs, or other things online from people I don't really know or trust.

TIP 5: I won't give out my password to anyone but my parents or guardian, not even to my best friend.

Stephen Talbott, in an article in *NetFuture*, asks: Isn't the Net as depicted in these "tips" a "strongly anonymous and depersonalized place?" Why, he wonders, are we pushing children "unnecessarily or prematurely into environments where we must ask them to be wary of shadowy, unseen human beings who are vaguely suggested to be capable of dark and unmentionable crimes?"[1] Wouldn't it be better if they read a book or played with their friends?

Whose Anxieties?

Talbott's short article is a clear statement of the quandary of many adults about young people on the Net. Everyone who has spent time on the Net is aware that there are some very dysfunctional people out there. Many seem unable to post messages in newsgroups that don't splatter other posters with volleys of four-letter words, and our mouths hang open sometimes at the thoughtlessness of those who post junk e-mail or spam.

Among those who have an e-mail address and use the Net regularly—including many young people—who hasn't been smacked with spam inviting us to a triple-X page of "hot babes?" Who among us hasn't done a Web search for something we think is innocent, like the librarian who searched for "girls and science," and received hits we never anticipated? Once I saw a student searching for "Asian American women" in AltaVista for a multicultural report and blushing at the results.

The Internet introduces a whole new set of problems for parents—issues that did not exist when they were growing up. And even though the "really bad stuff" is a very small part of the Net, there are no guiding rules about children's exposure to "adult" material, let alone a fixed standard about the Web's place in education.

Those of us who work with young people and the Net also know that there are some incredible resources out there if we know where to look. The Net can answer lots of those questions that kids have been asking librarians since homework was invented. We want young people to know about the good things while keeping the "bad things" at bay. Most of us also want to present the Net in the most positive light possible, offering our community of users an opportunity to learn how to use the Net effectively and wisely.

And—let's be honest here—we also want to avoid negative reactions or liability claims. Any librarian who has kept up with the news about Net access issues in public and school libraries has reason to be leery of releasing an important, but wild and unedited, resource to the public. Having the unfiltered Net in the supposedly "safe" library is disturbing to many adults, parents or not, and has led, in some places, to loud complaints to the governmental bodies that fund libraries.

Parental signatures, "Internet drivers' licenses," and filtered Net stations in children's areas are uncomfortable choices for librarians who espouse intellectual freedom principles and the Library Bill of Rights. Many library directors and frontline librarians feel such protective strategies are necessary, despite intellectual freedom qualms, for continued good relations with their communities. Adults, concerned about children's unfettered access to the Web, may be less inclined to mount complaints against a library with protective measures in place.

How should we think about kids and the Net, and, in particular, how should we think about them as they coexist in libraries? For adults, the Internet presents a shift in the way the world works, not unlike what parents faced in the 1960s when enormous sociopolitical changes were afoot. By the same token, adults may forget that youngsters have never lived in a world without technology. Their view of the Internet may be far different from that of adults who have lived in a less-technological world. Rethinking our ideas may help us deal with the "kids and the Net" issue in a way that's fair and sensible.

Ten Things to Think About

Here, in brief, is what I've learned after training young people and librarians, dealing with Net workstations in libraries, and working on library websites for the past four years. If there is a single principle that binds these thoughts, it might be that change happens, and so do new resources and media. We can learn to play with and enjoy the good parts of the Net, work out strategies to deal with the not-so-good parts, and provide a balanced perspective for our patrons. We know that the Net is affecting the world in incredible ways now, but next year, or ten years from now, something else even more "paradigm-shifting" will appear.

Kids think of the net as part of the landscape. The Internet really isn't the big deal for kids that it is for many of us adults. My own daughter, who is thirteen, uses the Web for homework assignments and to check out the sites of her favorite TV shows, but most of the time she'd rather be playing soccer or reading. Plenty of other young people I know feel much the same way—the Net is fine, in its place. There is a minority of young people whose lives do become extremely technology-focused, but they are a fairly small group.

Kids think they know everything about computers. How many times have you read an article or heard a speaker who makes jokes like this one: "Every time I have computer problems, I call in an expert—my eight-year-old son." Many adults who aren't comfortable with computers believe that kids know it all. Well, kids know some things, like when to press Control-Alt-Delete or how to free a stuck floppy, but just as often they can't spell well enough to do a Web search. They don't know how to tell whether a site is produced by a legitimate organization or whether a commercial offer is believable. Kids are often computer-savvy without being information-savvy. Librarians not only can help kids negotiate the Net, but also can offer interpretive skills that can enhance children's ability to distinguish between legitimate and questionable Web offerings.

The younger students are (and the more male), the more they think they know. A recent study by John Lubans of Duke University compared attitudes toward the Net of seventh to tenth graders and of Duke University freshmen. Lubans discovered that many of the younger male students rated themselves "best" on the scale of expertise, while the Duke freshmen of both sexes, who typically used the Web more often than the younger students, rated themselves less able and more often frustrated.[2] This finding suggests that youngsters, especially boys, may feel more "in control" than is really the case, which challenges librarians, who want to provide a helping hand to kids, and parents, who require enough technological sophistication to monitor their kids' level of Web expertise.

Half of American families don't own Net-capable computers. About 50 percent of youngsters' exposure to computers is in school or at the library. As one might expect, lower-income and minority families are least likely to own Net-capable PCs. Web access at the public library is the only non-school access many young people have.

Young people often feel that many adults (including some librarians) don't trust them or respect their judgment. In some quarters, adults seem to believe that young people are either constantly searching out pornographic sites or are potential victims wandering in chat rooms, totally vulnerable to any pedophile. I have found that the more you treat young people as if you have faith in their good judgment, and the less you come around to see what they've got on their screens, the more likely they are to justify that faith—and vice versa, because young teens, particularly, like to "test." A good rule for librarians when approaching a young person at a workstation is to first look her or him in the eyes before looking at the screen, "asking permission" to look and acknowledging that person as an individual.

Problems in libraries involving the use of public Internet workstations are behavior problems, not "technology problems." All libraries with public Net workstations should have a clear, posted, and enforceable use policy. The key word is *enforceable.* A typical problem involves people who "camp out" on the workstations, not relinquishing them to others. One solution is a sign-up system, a posted time limit, and a staff willing to confront those who don't leave when their time is up. Libraries with workstations for young people often post signs at those workstations advising "all adults must be accompanied by a child," and staff members don't hesitate to direct lone adults to the adult workstations even if no one is waiting. Be clear, be proactive, and be pleasant. Everyone should be treated the same.

All legal uses of the Net are legitimate uses, but libraries have the right to limit use fairly. This point is the hardest for some libraries to deal with. For a sizable minority of younger Net users, e-mail and chat rooms are the most important part of Net use. But given the fact that many young people's chat runs along the lines of "Hi, I'm [insert pseudonym]. How old are you? Where do you go to school? Hey, that's tight," it may not seem very legitimate to many librarians. Some libraries wrestle with the "proper use" of their public Net workstations. My own opinion, after discussing public Net workstations with librarians all over the United States, is that time limits are the best way to convey that everyone's legal use is legitimate. (Standards for what is legal vary from community to community, but often only viewing or reading child pornography is prohibited.) This kind of clarity makes life easier for staff members who must enforce the library's policy.

If the library treats the Net as a legitimate reference resource for young people, Net-savvy users will know how their needs will be treated. Such an attitude also tells adults that the library has acted proactively and identified trustworthy resources, so that young people can find information quickly without wandering all over the Internet. I have looked at a great many libraries' websites for young people, and the ways in which they treat Net resources vary tremendously. Websites are no different from books or any other media we deal with, and they should be organized just as seriously. All collections of websites should be alphabetized, annotated, and updated regularly. All reference staff should be trained in how to identify quality sites, and given time to identify and add them to the library's resources. All of us who have worked in libraries for more than a year or two know that how our users perceive us is as important as what we actually do for them. Our websites are our faces to the online world. Library sites for young people (actually, library sites for everyone) should greet visitors with pleasant, well-chosen graphics that appeal to the target audience (be they middle-school kids or business people) and enough whimsy to make them interesting. They should also include links to the resources that the target audience wants, described in a way that kids or parents or teachers can grasp and use easily. "Features" on library sites for young people, such as articles, crafts, or link lists on summer reading, holidays, or author visits, should be changed regularly and never left on the site after a holiday is over or a program ended. Library sites should also feature links to librarian-generated Web directories like "KidsClick" (*http://sunsite.berkeley. edu/KidsClick!/*) and the ALA 700-plus "Great Sites" (*http://www.ala. org/parentspage/greatsites/*).

Reach out to parents, teachers, and community members. Holding "Family Technology Nights" with brief talks, hands-on sessions, and Internet resource demonstrations can reassure parents and others about what the library is doing with technology and young people.

Having copies of the Net workstation use policy available to anyone who expresses concern and having staff members with active-listening skills can help defuse complaints before they grow huge. Provide a page of links to sites that educate parents about sensible rules for Net safety (two of the best examples are ALA's "Librarian's Guide to Cyberspace" at *http://www.ala.org/parentspage/greatsites/ guide.html* and The Children's Partnership's "Parents' Guide to the Information Superhighway" at *http://www.childrenspartnership.org/ pub/pbpg.html*). Teachers should be invited to "Educator Evenings" before the new school year begins to learn about the library's policies and receive hands-on training in the library's electronic resources.

Be certain everyone on the library's staff knows the basics about technology. Do staff members who serve young people in your library understand the nature of "information literacy" and why it's important? Do they know what, exactly, the Internet is and how it works? Do they know the difference between a Web browser, an Internet service provider (ISP), and a search engine? Do they know where students can find sources that will tell them how to cite Internet resources in research papers? Do they know the difference between a .com site, a .edu site, and a .gov site? The more staff members understand the basics about the Net—particularly the Net as it applies to education and young people—the better they can share their knowledge confidently with the public they serve.

Educate Your Clientele

If you have public Net access in your library, and if you have a library website, how does your public perceive your attitude toward the Net? Are there opportunities at the library to learn more about the Net and the electronic services the library offers? Are youth librarians visiting the schools, and inviting groups of home-school families to the library? Are these groups receiving instruction in how to dial into the catalog, what databases are available in the library, and how to get maximum value from the links and other features of the library's website from home or in the building?

Much of the educating we do as librarians takes place one person at a time as we answer reference questions. Are all reference staff familiar with at least two search tools and comfortable enough with that knowledge to share it? The information literacy skills essential for Web use aren't that different from many of the skills we use in other media. Reading and understanding a search tool's "hits" page requires the same skills as navigating many reference book entries, notably the ability to determine usability from reading a series of sometimes disjointed words and phrases.

Much of the information on the Web requires an ability to navigate visual information, such as charts, graphs, maps, and visually oriented navigation tools like button bars. If you go to the National Football League's site (*http://www.nfl.com*), for example, down the left side is a double bar of team emblems without words. If you click on the emblem, you'll go to the site for that team. Many kids will find this easier to navigate than many librarians will! The learning and sharing can go in both directions.

Some Anxiety Is Inevitable

Have you had relatives or acquaintances say to you, "You're a librarian. What are you going to do now that everyone can get whatever she wants off the Internet and doesn't need to read books?" We know it isn't that simple. We know that books aren't going away any time soon, just as we know that radio didn't disappear when TV arrived and people didn't stop going to movies when videotapes appeared.

But things change all the same, and every change, piled on all the other changes, makes many of us just a little more anxious. When you add children and teenagers—who occupy an insecure place in the world as it is—into the mixture, our anxieties just grow greater. The role of the library and the school is to share as much information as possible on the nature of the Net, the good as well as the bad. Everyone who is a stakeholder—parents, teachers, librarians, and kids—should understand that we all share responsibility for making the Internet experience positive, amusing, and informative.

Notes

1. Stephen Talbott, "America Screws Up," Net-Future, no. 76 (September 15, 1998), at *http://www.ora.com/people/staff/stevet/netfuture/index.html*.

2. John Lubans, "Key Findings on Internet Use among Students," March 5, 1999, at *http://www.lib.duke.edu/staff/orgnztn/lubans/john.html*.

THE IRON TRIANGLE OF PRIVACY, FILTERING, AND INTERNET USE POLICIES

John A. Shuler

John A. Shuler (*alfred@uic.edu*) is department head and documents librarian at the University of Illinois at Chicago. Since receiving his MLS from the University of California-Los Angeles in 1983, Shuler has been a faculty member and documents librarian at universities in Oregon and New York. Writing, teaching, and lecturing extensively on information policy issues and political analyses of the U.S. Government Printing Office and its system of depository libraries, he serves as reviews editor and editorial board member for *Government Information Quarterly* and editor for the American Library Association's Government Documents Roundtable quarterly publication *Documents to the People*. He also wrote the chapter on government information for the first edition of *The Cybrarian's Manual*.

As librarians seek their own places within a multifaceted world of global information networks, many will see cherished beliefs regarding how and why people use information go through several profound shifts. Librarians endeavor to balance very private information needs of individuals with what are very public library resources or facilities. For the most part, librarians (along with their associations) are information libertarians: They do not judge why people seek knowledge, and they do everything they can to help people get it.

Because of this elemental professional belief, few other issues generate such a bundle of paradoxes as those of privacy and proper use of information found on the World Wide Web. As more libraries install workstations with unfiltered connections to the global information network, there is a growing awareness of just how the private/public act of locating and reading a printed library book differs so radically from the private/public act of accessing information over a library's public computer station. This awareness, at least over the past five years, has focused on technology, software, and laws that deal with children, pornography, and "filtering" in an attempt to keep American youth (legally, anyone under the age of eighteen) from "the back alleys of the Internet."[1]

Libraries are accused of either providing too much access or imposing too many limits on Internet use. When libraries monitor their public World Wide Web stations, regulate their use through age limits, or employ commercial software filters that block access to "bad" places on the network, some patrons applaud while other users feel cheated. On the other hand, if libraries provide full web access, unprepared children or easily offended adults may be exposed to "indecent" or inappropriate information.

In this chapter, I use "parables" taken from several legal documents in two separate court cases filed on behalf of an angry mother in California and a grassroots organization in Virginia. Both cases demonstrate that whatever action the library took in regard to accessing the World Wide Web, it was going to be wrong.

The Parable of the Curious Son

The first action, taken from a court case in Livermore, California, was launched by a mother who charged the public library with failing to prevent her son from accessing questionable material through the Livermore public library's workstations (*Kathleen R., et al. v. City of Livermore, et al.,* Superior Court of California, County of Alameda, Eastern Division, 1998). The library had no interest or expressed policy on regulating access to the global information network. The parable, taken largely from the text of the original legal suit filed by the mother's lawyer, goes something like this:

1. The City of Livermore maintains a library system which includes a branch commonly called the Civic Center branch ("library"). At the library, there are a number of public access computers which individuals, without regard or consideration of their age, are free to use.
2. Certain of these computers ("computers") have a data-link connection to what is commonly known as the Internet or the "World Wide Web" ("Web"). Using these computers, users can request text, images, and other computerized information from computers in other locations which themselves have been connected to the Web.
3. These computers are paid for in whole or in part by public funds belonging to the City of Livermore.
4. On or about the early days of summer in the year of our Lord 1997, without the permission or consent of his parents, Brandon P. went to the library and brought along with him a computer floppy disk ("disk").
5. At the library, Brandon P. stationed himself in front of one of the computers with Web access.

6. Using the computer, Brandon P. accessed websites containing color images of seminude and nude women positioned in sexually alluring and/or explicit poses designed to appeal to the viewer's prurient interest. Some of the images depicted one or more women engaging in sexual activity.
7. Using the computer, Brandon P. transferred an exact duplicate of various of the images from the computer screen to the disk using a process called "downloading."
8. These images were and are harmful to minors, and at least some of them were obscene.
9. Brandon P. then left the library and, without any adult's knowledge or permission, proceeded to use a computer at a relative's house to print out the images. Brandon P. then allowed one or more minors to view certain of the images.
10. On or about the next day, Brandon P. again returned to the library and proceeded again to download sexually explicit images to the disk and again later print them out at a relative's house.
11. Brandon P. did this activity approximately ten times. At no time were his parents aware of his activities.
12. The City of Livermore has been made aware that minors and others can and have used their computers with Web access to view and download sexually explicit images and sexually obscene images. In spite of this, the City of Livermore continues to allow minors to use these computers. (*http://www.techlawjournal.com/courts/kathleenr/Default.htm*)

The Parable of the Aggrieved Information Providers

The other parable comes from court documents in Loudoun County, Virginia (*Mainstream Loudoun v. Board of Trustees of the Loudoun County Library,* 1998 U.S. Dist. (E.D. Va. 1998)). This case represents an entirely opposite response to a library's attempt to regulate use of the World Wide Web resources in its collection. In this case, the county library did institute a clear and strong policy on how the public should (and should not) access the global information network on its public computers. The policy placed library staff members in the role of "monitors" (the screens were situated in such a manner that the public service staff could observe what was on them from time to time). As a further measure, the library installed commercially produced filtering software that blocked "harmful" websites.

A form was then developed that members of the public could fill out if they felt that a website was being needlessly blocked. For the most part, the use policy placed sexually explicit websites in the category of harmful workplace practices that create a hostile working environment and that open the library to charges of sexual harassment. The plaintiffs in this case sued the library for implementing the policy.

1. Plaintiffs-Intervenors ("Intervenors"), who provide valuable information for free on the Internet, seek injunctive and declaratory relief against defendants for their enactment and implementation of an Internet access policy that prevents Intervenors from communicating their constitutionally protected speech to patrons in the Loudoun County Library.

2. The Loudoun County Library is a public library in Loudoun County, Virginia, that provides a wide range of books and other information resources to the public for free. The Loudoun County Library now provides access to the vast and valuable information resources of the Internet, which is fast becoming the library of the future as more of the world's information is put online. This case presents important constitutional questions concerning whether the government can prevent Internet speakers from communicating constitutionally protected information on the Internet to persons whose only access to online resources may be their local public library.

3. Intervenors include individuals and organizations who communicate information free of charge on the Internet's World Wide Web ("Web"). Intervenors all provide valuable, constitutionally protected speech on the Internet, including safer sex information, the full text of books that have been subject to censorship attempts throughout history, resources promoting equal educational and career opportunities for women, a list of books of interest to gay and lesbian youth, an online magazine about politics and government, a daily newspaper column, and visual artwork. Intervenors want to reach all interested Internet users worldwide, regardless of age, including patrons in the Loudoun County Library.

4. On October 20, 1997, defendants, through the Board of Supervisors of the Loudoun County Library ("the Board"), passed by a vote of five to four a policy entitled "Policy on Internet Sexual Harassment" ("the Policy"). The Policy requires that "site-blocking software . . . be installed on all computers" for the purpose of limiting access to materials that are "pornographic" or "harmful to juveniles." The Policy's mandate to block all access to such materials, including access by adults, on its face suppresses speech that is unquestionably constitutionally protected for adults and for minors. By using blocking software to implement the Policy, defendants are in effect "removing books from the shelves" of the Internet by blocking many Internet sites with valuable educational, political, literary, artistic, social, and religious speech that would otherwise be available to library patrons.

5. After passing the Policy, defendants purchased X-Stop, a blocking software produced by LogOn Data Corporation, and installed X-Stop on all of the Internet access stations at the library. X-Stop is created by an outside computer software vendor that has developed a list of sites that it blocks on the Internet. Thus, although by using X-Stop defendants are blocking Internet speech that would otherwise be available to library patrons, defendants do not select the sites that X-Stop blocks.

6. Blocking software cannot be "fixed" to block only speech that is unprotected by the Constitution. There is simply no way for a computer software program to make distinctions between protected and unprotected speech. Defendants' mandate that blocking software be used whenever a patron accesses the Internet, no matter what the software, will suppress ideas and viewpoints that are constitutionally protected from reaching willing patrons.

7. On December 22, 1997, plaintiffs Mainstream Loudoun et al. filed this case. Plaintiffs, who include parents, citizens, and other public library users in Loudoun County, seek declaratory and injunctive relief against the Policy enacted by defendants, which severely limits plaintiffs' access to public information that would otherwise be available through the Internet in Loudoun County public libraries.

8. Intervenors are Internet speakers who seek declaratory and injunctive relief against the Policy enacted by defendants which currently blocks or recently blocked them from communicating information on their websites to patrons in the library through the use of the blocking software X-Stop, in violation of the First, Fifth, and Fourteenth Amendments of the United States Constitution.

9. Defendants also block a wide variety of other websites that contain valuable and constitutionally protected speech, such as the entire website of Glide Memorial United Methodist Church, with over 2,000 members located in San Francisco, California, and the entire website of *The San Francisco Chronicle*.

10. Although defendants block intervenors' speech promoting safer sex practices, supporting gay and lesbian youth and transgendered persons, promoting career opportunities for women, opposing censorship of the Internet, and providing access to previously banned books, defendants do not block a variety of sites that express viewpoints contrary to the viewpoints expressed by Intervenors. For example, the Board does not block sites opposing homosexuality and transgender behavior, opposing employment by women outside the home, favoring Internet censorship, and promoting abstinence rather than safer sex practices. (*http://www.techlawjournal.com/courts/loudon/Default.htm*)

The two parables offer an alpha and omega of the ethical complexities libraries must resolve as they decide what to do with their public World Wide Web stations. Through their very architecture (open stacks, various public reading rooms, accessible reference areas) as well as through their bibliographic structures (indexes, abstracts, public service desks, classified collections and catalogs), libraries traditionally seek to link people with information they need. Some of this mediation takes place in full public view (walking through the stacks, discussing your needs with a librarian at a public desk, opening a reference book or an index), but the most meaningful (and personal) aspects of reading and understanding the library's nondigital resources happen alone and without much interaction with others.

Strangely, using computers to access the World Wide Web changes these internal arrangements. Because computers and their screens are "more public" (people walking by or looking over someone's shoulder can clearly see what is displayed on the screen) and provide access to images or texts not selected by local librarians, public Internet computers blur the boundaries between private act and public display—apparently more so than reading a library book (or checking it out to read elsewhere).

These cyber-contradictions are most evident in the case of young Brandon P. A simple reading of his actions would find little amiss or alarming. He finds the computer; he knows how to use it and how to locate information on the World Wide Web; he downloads the information to a disk brought along for that purpose. He then takes the information to a family computer at home and manipulates it, making it more useful to his individual needs. He shares the results with his friends then goes back and does it ten more times without any assistance from an adult. If it weren't for the fact that he was seeking and downloading pornography, young Brandon would be an American Library Association poster child for the youth-oriented information literacy campaign.

In the case of the Loudoun Intervenors, who were faced with a library policy designed to prevent other Brandon P.'s from using library resources to access such questionable information, definite disagreements exist about how much a library and its staff should monitor this kind of information-seeking behavior. The Loudoun County Library board of trustees, confronted with the unknowable, took the shortest route between two points and reduced everyone's access to the Internet to the level of a small child. To be fair about this assessment, it must be noted that the board of trustees decided to implement the policy over the objections of both the library director and other public officials. The substance of the policy can be found at (*http://www.pfaw.org/courts/loudoun_harrass.shtml*).

How the Technology Works

There appear to be four options available to libraries to deal with the problem of Web access, depending on the local politics and library culture. First, do not install filters and do not monitor the computers. Second, ask people under a certain age not to use unfiltered computers or ask for proof of age before they do. Third, install filters or monitoring software in specific areas designated for children and youth under a certain age. (This would follow the clear library tradition of creating separate collections or services that are age-based.) Fourth and most conservative, install the filters on all machines, and force the adults to ask for exceptions on a case-by-case basis.

From the perspective of technology and administration, there are a number of ways to block access to particular information on the World Wide Web in libraries: by using human intervention; by blocking specific sites through their Web addresses; by identifying specific words or images that could appear on a website; or by relying on a system of predesignated labels. Software and hardware technologies can be purchased from vendors that block specific websites by identifying words, phrases, or images, or through consistent use of intelligent Web crawlers that routinely identify suspect sites. Website labeling is similar to the warning notices on films, videos, television programs, and recorded music.

Libraries are not keen on making Web-based pornography available to children, but products designed to filter these sites are often inexact or overly broad and ban legitimate material along with the undesirable. For instance, as previously noted, the commercial software used by the Loudoun County Library blocked the entire website for the *San Francisco Chronicle*.

An interesting perspective on the problems associated with filtering software can be found at *http://www.ifea.net/joint_nclis_statement.html*, which is the official statement given by the Internet Free Expression Alliance before the National Commission on Library and Information Science. Any or all of these techniques may be combined with intensive monitoring and alert systems that inform the library staff that a computer is accessing something on the Web it shouldn't. See Yahoo! at *http://dir.yahoo.com/Business_and_Economy/Companies/Computers/Software/Internet/Blocking_and_Filtering/Titles/* to begin locating filtering software companies and ISPs.

The Legislative/Legal Background

For the past five years, the federal government has sought a consistent, and legal, solution to block two types of pornography from access on the World Wide Web: obscenity and child pornography. As defined by the 1973 Supreme Court decision in *Miller v. California* (413 U.S. 15), obscenity is any text or image that "depict[s] or describe[s] patently offensive 'hard core' sexual conduct." Furthermore, the Court outlined a three-part test to determine if the text or image in question is obscene:

1. whether the "average person applying contemporary community standards" would find that the work, taken as a whole, appeals to the prurient interest;
2. whether the work depicts or describes, in a patently offensive way, sexual conduct specifically defined by the applicable state law; and
3. whether the work, taken as a whole, lacks serious literary, artistic, political, or scientific value.

The first two measures will be determined by local community values; the third will be determined by a measurement of reasonableness. Since the late 1980s, Congress has tried to enact several laws that included within the definition of pornography "indecent" material or material deemed potentially "offensive" to children's sensibilities. For the most part, either the legislation did not pass, or it was successfully challenged in the courts by opponents.

Most recently, Congress enacted the Communications Decency Act (CDA), part of the massive deregulation of the telecommunications industry in early 1996 (Pub. L. 104-104, 110 Stat. 56). As characterized by its supporters, CDA was a lawful and moral attempt to "protect" children from texts, images, and other data that were "indecent" and "patently offensive." However, as the Supreme Court pointed out in its June 1997 decision striking down the law, the terms were ill-defined and the intent of the law placed too many limits on "adult speech." More importantly for free speech advocates, the Supreme Court ruling, and the appeals case that led to the Supreme Court, placed the Internet and its expanding availability of information resources on the same level as printed material in terms of First Amendment protections.

Issues of Privacy

Although the Court has brought "adult speech" on the Internet under First Amendment protection, it has not specifically clarified issues about limiting access. Neither has it dealt with a very close cousin to access—privacy. This electronic environment is a tough one for issues of privacy. Except in circumstances where strong encryption techniques exist, nothing is private in cyberspace. Encryption simply means converting a message into code. Encryption technology can be used to mask everything from credit card numbers to e-mail messages to chat room discussions to newsletters. The questions for libraries as well as the public are: How—if at all—should encryption technology be used? Should any one entity, such as a federal government, control it? As the earlier discussion demonstrates, many of the filtering software and hardware applications offer the administrative ability to track where people are going on the Web and what they are doing when they get there.

On the other hand, the same network technologies and applications allow individuals and companies to collect, store, and manipulate personal information at levels never before possible in the paper world. At the very least, the government is focusing on the creation of "fair information practices." For a fairly detailed discussion of the issue, read the Federal Trade Commission's June 1998 report *Privacy Online: A Report to Congress* (*http://www.ftc.gov/reports/privacy3/priv-23a.pdf*). Although taken from the perspective of an information economy based largely on a consumer market, the report still speaks to some basic practices and protections necessary to assure that comparable levels of privacy prevail in the virtual world as well as the physical sphere.

These include the following principles: notice and awareness, choice and consent, access and participation, integrity and security, and enforcement and redress. The report also discusses the application of comparable principles as they apply to children.

Conclusion

How do libraries deal with this bundle of complexity? Carefully, and with plans that are well supported by their communities and reinforced with clear documentation. Surrendering the choice of who accesses the World

Wide Web to a third-party software vendor appears to be an option with little benefit for the library. Nothing, either technologically or professionally, prevents librarians from creating their own set of filtering methods and encouraging their use. Access to the Internet's wealth of information should be considered a natural extension of traditional library collection development and public services, and be offered with the same degree of fluidity and freedom that has made open, free, and public libraries such a democratic icon in American society.

That said, accessing the global computer network introduces a new set of ambiguities, and choices will be made that will not be universally acceptable. Faced with these challenges, librarians should speak out on behalf of open access and freedom of information choice. At the same time, however, they should recognize that the material on the Internet may have to be monitored and "filtered" according to some kind of age-based criteria.

Public libraries have a long tradition of separate children and youth services and collections within their buildings, and the solutions to the problems of filtering lie in these traditions. The advent of the Web does not lessen librarians' obligation both to serve the public needs of their communities and to respect the private aspects of their patrons' lives. The issue of privacy remains one of the most seriously underestimated and least understood issues facing libraries today. The Internet raises profound questions challenging long-held beliefs about personal versus public information.

Note

1. The reference is to the title "Cyberporn: Protecting Our Children from the Back Alleys of the Internet," a Joint Hearing before the Subcommittee on Basic Research and the Subcommittee on Technology of the Committee on Science, House of Representatives, 104th Congress, First Session.

Licensed to Teach

Ann Thornton

Ann Thornton (*athornton@nypl.org*) is the coordinator for electronic training at the Science, Industry and Business Library of The New York Public Library, where she manages the public training program in using the library's electronic resources and printed materials. She is an associate editor of *Public-Access Computer Systems Review*, an electronic journal, and a contributor to the first edition of *The Cybrarian's Manual*. A former systems librarian at the University of Houston, Thornton has published and spoken on such issues as discussion lists, adult learning styles, and Internet use in libraries.

At least once a week, someone comes into my library and asks, "Which way to the card catalog?" even though we haven't had a card catalog since Richard Nixon was president. Strangely, this lack of knowledge is a good sign: People see libraries as a friendly place to search for and find any information they need. Librarians have always believed access to information is an integral part of citizenship, and, because computers have become a staple of everyday life, libraries are increasingly equipped with public workstations to access the Internet.

This public access can be a powerful tool to satisfy people's information needs. But access involves more than simply clicking a mouse properly. Though the need for Internet training in libraries may be self-evident, the types of training merit exploration. Because features and resources of the Web change frequently, users need both "procedural knowledge"—the ability to use Web browser features—and "conceptual knowledge"—an understanding of how to select and make effective use of Internet resources.

The sophistication of these searches also requires introduction to how information is organized. Library training should provide techniques for doing searches as well as criteria for evaluating and using information obtained electronically. As search engines' capabilities are constantly enhanced, an awareness of users' information needs and an understanding of continually changing technology make librarians valuable sources of Internet training.

Planning for a Successful Training Program

A successful Internet training program will require not only introduction to the World Wide Web but also basic computer skills and information literacy capabilities. To implement this multitiered program, libraries must assess their users' needs, design training techniques around these needs, promote the programs, and evaluate their success.

Assessing Users' Needs

The first step is to identify the specific needs of your library's clientele. A well-designed Internet training program is one that is responsive to user needs. Following are several ways to gauge these needs.

If your library has any suggestion boxes or user comment facilities, examine them for requests for Internet training. Consider placing at information and circulation desks a needs assessment survey form that asks constituents about their Internet-specific needs and interests. Compile this information and present it to library administrators in order to gain financial and other support for a public Internet training program.

Based on this type of research, libraries of various types and sizes offer special classes intended for certain groups. Following are examples of Internet training programs you might find at other libraries:

Beginning Internet for Adults: Learn the basics of Web navigation in a comfortable, friendly environment. Start surfing here!

Kids Online: Learn how to find the best Internet sites for sports, games, entertainment, and, yes, help with homework.

A Parent's Guide to the Net: Get a closer look at what the Internet is all about and learn how your child can use it to help with homework assignments or to find topics of personal interest.

Web for Seniors: Discover the best places for online fellowship, travel, stocks, and health information.

Job Searching on the Web: Find out how to research careers and companies online, search job postings, and place your resume on the Internet.

Your Business on the Web: Learn what it takes for a small business to establish an Internet presence.

Genealogy on the Net: Discover how to use Internet search tools and sites to trace your family history.

Internet for Personal Investors: Review some of the resources available on the Web for researching industries and companies and for stock trading.

For the Newbie, Keep It Simple

It's important to use a simple, nontechnical approach for patrons who have had no experience on the Internet. Here are the four keys for beginner-level programs:

- Introduce new concepts with familiar metaphors.
- Ensure your students learn by doing.
- Help students identify easy starting points.
- Relate to students' interests.

In Internet workshops for beginners, remember to cover a few basics and keep the jargon to a minimum. Explain new vocabulary, and provide a glossary of acronyms and unfamiliar terms. Introduce new concepts slowly by using metaphors and analogies to help beginners create mental images of the Internet. You've heard many of them before:

- Information superhighway
- Grocery store
- Telephone network
- Driving a car
- Yard sale
- Postal service

The key is to begin with something familiar to the participants and proceed to the unfamiliar while carefully emphasizing the connections between the two. Consider using graphics or diagrams with recognizable features to help users "see" what they are learning.

Most importantly, provide substantial amounts of in-class practice on the Internet so participants can learn by doing. In group sessions with multiple computers for participant use, have another librarian or staff member serve as a "rover" who can assist with hands-on exercises. The additional person observes the participants to make sure everyone is keeping up and fixes any problems that arise.

Realize that new users often come to training sessions with fears and misperceptions about the Internet. Help them to identify good starting points, particularly directories of good-quality websites on a variety of subjects. Many beginning Internet sessions in libraries introduce users to Yahoo! (*http://www.yahoo.com*), one of the most popular sites on the Web and a good, general directory.

Another great strategy for Internet workshops is to personalize them. If possible, find out participants' interests beforehand, and be prepared with examples of relevant websites. These will be places for individuals to begin and will entice further online exploration.

Highlighting basic navigational features within Web browsers (back and forward, search history, and bookmarking, if available) will make a big difference to the beginner. Many newbies are afraid of long, cryptic URLs and worry about getting lost. Since you won't be able to cover absolutely everything in a beginner session, be sure to mention or provide a handout of additional sources of information about the Internet.

Designing Internet Training Techniques

Certain strategies work better than others when teaching Internet skills. Experienced educators and librarian trainers prefer active learning methods rather than passive lectures. Active learning involves all training participants in discussion, exercises, and observation. These activities allow participants to better apply what they have learned.

Examples of exercises include games, puzzles, and quizzes. Here are five simple exercises that you can apply in Internet training:

Before and After: Before beginning your Internet training session, ask users to rate their current level of skill and understanding of the objectives to be covered. This can be done on a single large chart displayed in front of the group where individuals are represented by colored stickers or thumbtacks, or ranking charts can be produced on sheets of paper and given to each participant. At the end of the session, ask the users to go back to the grid or chart and rate their performance. They can then see how they have progressed in skills and knowledge.

Monitor Tents: At the beginning of an Internet training session, ask participants at individual workstations to fold a sheet of paper in thirds (like a letter to place in an envelope). Then have them unfold the sheet just enough to balance on top of the monitor like a tent. On one side of the tent, ask the users to write their names. On the other side, ask the users to write one thing they hope to learn during the session.

Lingo Bingo: After defining new Internet terminology with a group, display a large Bingo-type card at the front of the room with the new terms in each of the squares. Call out the definitions and ask participants to respond with the appropriate Internet term. Keep going until you reach Lingo Bingo on the card, or finish every square. If you have the time to prepare individual Bingo cards to pass out, you could award prizes to the winner(s).

Ask Them First: Before demonstrating a new technique or concept in Internet use, ask participants if they know how or why to do something. For example, rather than instructing users how to scroll down within a Web document, ask if anyone knows how to do it. Then ask that person to demonstrate the technique and explain it to the rest of the group. Likewise, when teaching Web evaluation skills, ask the participants what criteria they think are important in selecting Web resources before going on to cover each one point by point.

Sound Off: At the end of an Internet training session with fewer than ten participants, ask each person to think of one new thing he or she learned during the session. Then ask each person to share that item with the rest of the group. As each person contributes his or her item, main points covered during training are reinforced.

Pairing learners in teams for certain exercises and doing in-session problem solving can help students retain material presented. Consider providing search strategy worksheets, initiating Internet treasure hunts, and allowing ample time for discussion during hands-on workshops. Participants will not only pay close attention, but also have fun.

Marirose Coulson suggested several good tips in *Information Outlook*.[1]

1. Don't touch the learners' keyboards. Though it is often frustrating to deal with slow or inaccurate typists, participants learn better by doing it themselves.
2. Avoid going too fast by inserting pauses after each step. One professional trainer calls this the "click-n-pause approach."
3. Let the learners make mistakes. Adults learn well by trial and error.
4. Show simple and easy-to-understand ways of doing things. Save the advanced tricks for intermediate-level sessions.
5. Accept that training is a continuous process. Don't worry about covering all possible material in a single session. After participants have begun to learn, they will come back for more.

Internet Information Retrieval

Sometimes user questions are as much about information literacy as they are about Internet usage. Here are three ways you can offer guideposts to interpreting information:

1. Dispel the misperception that the Internet is the best source for all information.
2. Teach the different uses of subject category listings and search engines on the Web.
3. Help users learn to evaluate information found on the Internet.

Sometimes new users are under the impression that the Internet is the ultimate source for all their information needs and will therefore spend more than ample time searching it in order to find relevant items. This misperception becomes even more emphasized when libraries have online catalogs with Web interfaces and subscribe to Web-accessible databases. The transfer between one type of resource and another is seamless to the user. When information is displayed in a Web browser window, users often assume the information is available for free as long as they have a computer that can access the Internet.

Explain to users the differences between using a subject-oriented category listing and a keyword search engine. Although it is a familiar theme in information science, "precision versus recall" is confusing to the Internet newcomer. With a subject approach, possible search results are limited to a relevant category, so precision seems high. Keyword search engines have larger, less-specific databases, which retrieve larger numbers of results and are more likely to be comprehensive, though sometimes not as precise.

Automated results-ranking methods and "power searching" features of search engines are important facets to include in intermediate-level Internet training sessions. Users will appreciate having skills to reduce the amount of time they must spend sorting through an imposing amount of information.

As users obtain search results from the Web, help them learn to evaluate the information retrieved. Teach them to ask such questions as: Is this current? What gives the publisher authority? Is the author a recognized expert in this field? How did the author get the information? How reliable is the information? Remind users that much of the free information available on the Internet is generated for advertising and persuasion. (For an excellent guide to evaluating Internet resources, see D. Scott Brandt's "Evaluating Information on the Internet" at *http://thorplus.lib.purdue.edu/~techman/eval.html.*)

Use the Internet to Teach the Internet

An effective way to reinforce Internet skills is to use the Internet itself as an instructional tool. Consider creating in-house web pages to use on public workstations. Provide links to good starting places, recommend search engines, and provide helpful tips and a good Internet glossary. Using these web pages during training sessions makes it easier for librarians to teach and for attendees to follow along.

In-house web pages are particularly helpful when practicing the use of specific websites because participants do not have to enter Web addresses and risk typing errors during hands-on sessions. Providing Internet instruction materials on the Web has the added benefit of accessibility after training sessions. Participants can easily return to a single Web address to practice and continue using what was learned during a session.

The ability to interact with Internet training participants allows for successful learning experiences. Librarians can "test" users while teaching by asking them questions about the material covered, encouraging discussions and sharing ideas, and by getting participants' reactions to specific tools and strategies. In addition, those who attend can ask questions of the librarians and get feedback on hands-on exercises.

Training Trainers

Training staff members is similar to training users. However, teaching how to teach is an equally important aspect of staff instruction. Staff training includes identifying candidates, addressing instruction methods, and providing training space.

Who Does the Internet Training?

Many librarians who are expected to provide Internet instruction to the public have little or no formal training in teaching methods. To identify potential trainers, managers should consider conducting surveys or interviews of staff. Experience is not necessary. As Wendy Scott points out, there are other characteristics of good trainers that many people share:

- Desire to teach and share information
- Ability to apply theory to real-life situations and hands-on practice
- Self-confidence
- Openness to various training methods
- Good listening skills
- Ability to increase learners' confidence
- Capacity to establish an encouraging training environment[2]

Librarians with these qualities can become comfortable leading groups by learning how to project their voices and organize their materials. The goal for preparing staff to teach the Internet is not to "mass produce an assembly line of teachers" with exactly the same style, but to encourage "a team of teachers who can successfully offer a variety of teaching and learning methods to a diverse clientele."[3] Those who do not teach in the Internet training program can participate in other valuable ways by preparing handouts and instructional materials and by helping to market the program.

What's the Best Preparation for Those Who Train?

Most staff training occurs on the job, so there is some merit to just "jumping in" and beginning to offer Internet training for the public. In fact, most trainers agree that good instructors learn by doing. However, librarians who have never attended presentation-skills workshops have much to learn about improving instructional techniques. Some training in public speaking skills and pedagogical techniques is recommended for all those who instruct in libraries. An instruction coordinator or other librarian, if experienced and qualified, can present an in-house workshop to colleagues, or consider bringing in a professional actor or trainer to teach staff how to:

- conceptualize and prepare for teaching
- overcome "stage fright"
- speak clearly and energetically
- use effective body language and eye contact

The best in-house training allows librarians to practice what they learn through workshop exercises.

To reinforce staff training, hold regular meetings with other members of the instructional team to discuss successful Internet teaching techniques and offer constructive advice for how best to handle problems. These meetings will give all those who are doing Internet training at the library the chance to share their own teaching skills and knowledge.

Many helpful organizations promote Internet and library instruction and offer training opportunities for improving instructional skills. These include the American Library Association Library Instruction Round Table (*http://diogenes.baylor.edu/Library/LIRT*), the Association of College and Research Libraries Instruction Section (*http://www.lib.utexas.edu/is*), and the LOEX Clearinghouse for Library Instruction (*http://www.emich.edu/~lshirato/loex.html*).

Designating a Place for Training

The ideal space for Internet training is in a separate room designed for this purpose. Valuable tips can be found in "Resources for Designing Library Electronic Classrooms" at *http://wings.buffalo.edu/publications/mcjrnl/v6n1/class.html*. An adequate number of computers and network connections, high-resolution projection onto a large screen, appropriate lighting, and comfortable furniture all contribute to an effective learning environment. Libraries without such luxuries can use the spaces in which public access takes place.

If the training session is held around a single workstation, be sure to provide time for participants to try searches. A good strategy for encouraging involvement and practice is to ask participants to take turns doing the keyboarding and mouse maneuvering while the librarian instructs. If users are paired at workstations, be sure to include frequent switches so that each participant gets some hands-on time.

Promoting Your Program

Even if you've done an assessment and know that a need exists for Internet training, how do you publicize your program effectively? Publicity is one of the most challenging aspects of offering a training program. The key is to reach a target audience and to convince them that attending your library's training session will be worth their time. Many experienced library trainers know that to be successful, it is important to publicize in as many ways and as frequently as possible. Try the following methods:

- Community or campus newspapers
- Organizational newsletters for specific target groups
- Posted announcements
- Public service referrals
- Web pages
- Discussion list announcements
- Announcements at meetings of target groups
- Word of mouth

Of course, not everyone can or will come to the library for Internet training. The most common obstacles to attending sessions are (1) difficulty in finding time, (2) inability or unwillingness to travel, and (3) concerns of novice users about revealing their lack of knowledge.[4] The desire to reach a greater audience has prompted some libraries to develop Web-based tutorials for teaching Internet and research strategies.

A key advantage to online tutorials for learners is flexibility. Online training offers self-paced, anytime, anywhere learning. Web-based tutorials can increase a library's visibility while providing a service to remote learners. As long as users know how to point and click a mouse and use a keyboard to type a Web address, they are able to take advantage of tutorials.

The design possibilities include animation to illustrate concepts, online demonstrations with full-motion video, and sound clips. Certainly, online tutorials are not better than having a live instructor, but they can be effective alternatives, if carefully constructed, for those who cannot or will not attend classes at the library.

Evaluating and Revising Your Program

Essential to the improvement of a public Internet training program is the gathering of data to inform decision making. Obtaining participant reaction after class sessions is crucial to determining if presentation skills, content, and teaching methods are adequate. Participants should have the opportunity to comment on all aspects of the trainer's style through some type of evaluation form.[5]

Additional instruments for measuring learning outcomes and overall effectiveness of instruction include pre- and posttests for participants, which can help determine the appropriateness of content, the ability of participants to apply the Internet skills learned, and the most practical methods of training. As the public provides feedback, librarians can modify the Internet training sessions to better meet user needs. Assessment results can also be used to demonstrate to library administration that the Internet training program is meeting its goals.

Conclusion

The Internet reaffirms that the practices of traditional librarianship are still relevant, even after the demise of the old card catalog. While increased access in libraries allows for greater potential of information sharing, the Internet can be frustrating for those untrained in its use.

Librarians can assist users by helping them build skills for seeking and evaluating information in new ways. By expanding our area of influence to include Internet training programs, we suggest resources, recommend strategies, facilitate the use of technologies, and enhance information-seeking skills among constituents.

Online Resources

Blue Web'n (*http://www.kn.pacbell.com/wired/bluewebn*) is a "searchable database of outstanding Internet learning sites."

NETTRAIN is an e-mail discussion list for Internet trainers. To subscribe, send the message SUBSCRIBE NETTRAIN first-name last-name to *listserv@ubvm.cc.buffalo.edu*.

BI-L is an e-mail discussion list for all aspects of bibliographic instruction, including Internet training in libraries. To subscribe, send the message SUBSCRIBE BI-L first-name last-name to *listserv@bingvmb.cc. binghamton.edu*.

Notes

1. Marirose Coulson, "Great Expectations: Reach to Teach," *Information Outlook* 9 (September 1998): 15.
2. Wendy Scott, "How to Develop Training Skills," *Staff Development: A Practical Guide*, 2d ed. (Chicago: American Library Association, 1992).
3. Cheryl LaGuardia et al., *Teaching the New Library: A How-to-Do-It Manual for Planning and Designing Instructional Programs* (New York: Neal-Schuman, 1996), 67.
4. Rama Vishwanatham, Walter Wilkins, and Thomas Jevec, "The Internet as a Medium for Online Instruction," *College & Research Libraries* 58 (September 1997): 434.
5. See Diana Shonrock, *Evaluating Library Instruction: Sample Questions, Forms, and Strategies for Practical Use* (Chicago: American Library Association, 1996).

You Gotta Go to School for That? Pac-Man in the Information Arcade

Jerry Seay

On my way home from the College of Charleston I had wandered into the local mall video arcade, attracted no doubt by the whirring beeps, flashing lights, the throbbing of competing, repeating musical themes, and by the fact that I am fascinated by games. In this particular instance, I was attracted by a video cabinet that featured two brightly colored dinosaurs duking it out "Bruce Lee style" while tiny humans in caveman outfits scrambled underfoot trying to avoid becoming dino toe jam. The name of this gaming wonder was *Primal Rage!* and it was quite interesting to observe the demo screen sorting through a series of different dinosaur combatants with different backgrounds and weather phenomena (the battle on ice was particularly exciting).

As I was enjoying this primal slugfest, a small boy of about eight years of age stepped abruptly in front of me, obscured my view of the screen, said, "Excuse me, sir," and gripped the control knobs.

Feeling as if I was suddenly the intruder, I muttered, "Sure," and stepped back while the kid dropped two quarters into the machine, chose a dino avatar from a selection of gruesome beasts on the screen, and proceeded to beat the stuffing out of another dinosaur.

The kid was a master. His hands jerked knobs and pushed buttons on that game panel faster than a good typist on a keyboard. He was deep into it too, as evidenced by his moans and unabashed shouts of "oooooo" and "ahhhh" and "way cool" every few seconds. Every now and then, without taking his eyes from the screen, he would shout, "Hey, Mom, come watch this!"

Reprinted from *Against the Grain* 10, no. 3 (June 1998): 84. Used with permission.

Of course I'm sure his mom, who was nowhere in sight, would have been proud to see her little darling's virtual Jurassic beast bashing the stew out of everything in sight. But, the boy was clearly enjoying himself. In fact he was enthralled.

Watching the excitement and pure joy emanating from this child, of course, could bring only one thought to my librarian's mind: "Boy, I sure wish I could get my Library 101 class only half this excited about what I was teaching them."

Of course, I then could hear my students saying back, "Yeah, if you could make it half as exciting as this, we would be."

To which I would wittily reply, "Yeah, if I had a machine like that thing to help me teach Library 101, it would be exciting." (Of course, dinosaurs would not necessarily be involved. Though I certainly would not rule them out.)

In fact, as I wandered ever farther down fantasy lane, I wondered how such magic machines might affect the library. My thoughts careened dangerously deeper. Indeed, why not have such machines in the library? It would give a whole new meaning to the phrase "information arcade." Can't you just see the excitement it would generate? Golly, just think of it. . . .

(slow blurring wavy picture fades to interior of a library full of video arcade machines)

It is a day not unlike any other day. Worldly bored patrons wander into the library thinking somberly that this is just going to be another average day of information gathering. But, wait! A patron approaches a terminal of the online system, picks up a set of headphones to put on her head, and the computer suddenly comes to life with flashy graphics and pulse pounding music. The patron types in her search and whoosh! The number of hits on her subject blinks crazily on the screen, the music rings out, and a message flashes up that "you have hit the jackpot, choose whatever item you wish!"

Next to her a patron groans audibly as a gong sounds and a booming voice from the machine intones into his headphones, "You have failed miserably in your search attempt, Mortal. Choose wisely this day a new search strategy. You now have only two lives left!"

Across the aisle a patron is intently peering at a screen that shows a heavily armed cartoon character weaving in and out of library stacks stalking a journal article. The patron's sweating hands are gripped tightly around a joystick that he jerks viciously whenever an article runs by on the screen. Suddenly, an article on his subject appears. With steely determination he fires off a short burst of fire from his joystick. Direct hit! He has bagged another one. Another shot like that and his research will be done.

Nearby, a patron has chosen a somewhat less violent form of searching the online catalog: *Pac-Librarian*, a more advanced form of *Pac-Man*. With amazing skill toned from many hours of online searching, she deftly maneuvers her pac-librarian through a maze of stacks on the screen, gobbling up call number tidbits (for energy, of course) along the way. Then, in an instant, the prize appears. A golden door opens on screen filling the screen with brilliant light. A multi-item menu appears. Carefully, oblivious to the in-depth research occurring around her, she chooses item number 4. The screen lights up with color. A deep voice speaks through her headphones, "You have chosen wisely, Mortal. The library owns two copies of this book. Choose this day how you would like the book delivered. Press one for manual checkout. Press two for interlibrary loan. Press three for direct brain downlink. Please have your brain adapter ready to plug in if you choose number three. . . ."

(image becomes wavy as view fades out quickly)

Okay, okay. I guess I was doing good until I came up with that direct brain downlink thing. Admittedly, *that* part is still a long way off in the future. But, hey, the "information arcade" thing just might fly, making *the* library the exciting, hip place to be. Throw in a coffee shop, a trinket store or two, and a really upscale snack bar, and voilà—the library is . . . a mall. Hmmmmmmm. Come to think of it the library already *is* the hip and exciting place to be. If only more folks realized that. What if . . . ? Maybe . . . maybe an online terminal with *Info Invaders*.

7

Cutting Edge or Bleeding Edge: You Make the Call

Security and Authentication Issues

Marshall Breeding

Marshall Breeding is the library technology analyst for the Jean and Alexander Heard Library at Vanderbilt University in Nashville, Tennessee. He is editor-in-chief of *Library Software Review* and writes on topics related to network technology, computer security, and library automation. He can be contacted by e-mail at *breeding@library.vanderbilt.edu*. Visit him on the Web at *http://staffweb.library.vanderbilt.edu/breeding*.

Two important issues facing libraries when retrieving information from the Internet are security and authentication. The key problem involves identifying who is and who isn't allowed to gain access to electronic resources—including local resources on the library's network as well as remote resources the library procures for its users. Libraries need to ensure that their local computing environments are safe from unwanted intruders, but that authorized users are able to get to the computer resources they need. In addition, as libraries subscribe to electronic resources on the Internet, they need access that is convenient but that allows service vendors to retain control over their offerings.

A number of business models have emerged between libraries and information resource providers relating to Web-access sources. Few vendors allow free and unlimited access to their products. Rather, access to electronic information resources is generally limited to those who subscribe to and pay for that resource. These business arrangements rely on various technical methods to control access. None of these technical methods is without complications.

In this chapter we will look at the major methods used by information resource vendors and libraries to control access to information products on the Web. We will examine the limitations and benefits of each, and look at some options that might emerge in the future.

The Challenge of Authentication

A central component of controlling access to networked information is authentication. In other words, how do we authoritatively identify computer users on a network? This process of authentication can operate on a number of levels. Authentication can be based on a name, a social security number, or some other official and authoritative identifier. Other cases require a more generalized approach—one need only be sure that the user of the resource is a legitimate member of a particular institution or a member of a particular category of users.

Authentication is separate from, though related to, the process of authorization. Once a user has been authenticated, the various computer systems involved can be programmed to make a selected set of resources available. Authorization is the process of providing controlled access to an authenticated computer user. In a network that offers a multitude of resources, it is important to carefully control access to each resource. Copyright considerations and license agreements may require a library to limit access to information to specific users. Authentication and authorization are control processes to ensure that a library is meeting its obligations under such agreements. A license agreement specifies such conditions as the monetary compensation that the vendor will receive, the specific resources that the library may use, and to whom access is allowed. The technical authentication and authorization process must work consistently with the terms of license agreements and copyright restrictions.

The classic authentication and authorization scenario in the library environment involves site licenses to Web-based electronic resources. In a typical site license, a library purchases access to a specified information resource for use by its entire user community. The challenge for such an arrangement involves identifying the legitimate users of the library in a way that provides them convenient and uncomplicated access and satisfies the provider's requirement for reasonably controlled access.

A site license will usually specify what qualifies an individual as a library user. In an academic library, users typically include the students, faculty, and staff of the organization, as well as anyone who uses the resource in the library building(s). Licenses stipulate whether access is limited to physical presence on the campus, or whether these same users may dial in from off-campus locations or from other institutions.

Defining the users of a public library can be more complicated. Does the arrangement apply only to those who use computers in the library? Can any resident of the area that the library serves gain access to electronic materials? Are only registered users permitted access? As the realm of access expands from local computers in a library to remote computers in homes and offices, the process of authentication and authorization becomes much more complicated.

Local Authentication Systems

Organizations that rely on networked computers must have some means of controlling access to resources within that network. A local authentication system uniquely identifies each user within the organization and provides that user access to a set of customized resources. Such resources might include access to electronic mail with private and shared folders on a file server, the ability to use shared laser printers, and the use of licensed software.

One of the characteristics of a local authentication system involves the level of detailed information maintained for each computer user. A local authentication system will likely store each user's name, address, a unique identifying number, and very specific information about the technical resources allowed to the user. A local authentication system can access this information to very authoritatively identify each user.

Local authentication systems operate with a universe of computers smaller than the global systems we'll consider later. A local authentication system must be scaled to handle the number of individuals associated with the organization. Small organizations may have only a handful of individuals. Large organizations may have thousands or tens of thousands of users. Given the detailed information maintained for each user, management of a local authentication system can become unwieldy when the number of users becomes quite large.

Many different approaches are available for local authentication, including: Kerberos for Unix-oriented organizations, Windows NT domains, Novell Directory Services, and other multiuser systems that maintain user accounts. Each of the major network operating systems or environments relies on an authentication system that can provide a high level of security if implemented and managed effectively.

The type of information managed within a local authentication and authorization environment may be detailed and personal. Each local institution will generally have policies about how this information is managed, especially with regard to how that information can be shared with external organizations. As local authentication systems interact with other systems, measures are usually taken to mask personal details about each computer user from the perspective of the external system.

Cross-Institutional Authentication

When organizations want to share resources in a controlled way, then some process of cross-institutional authentication must come into play. Examples of these arrangements include one library providing access for a set of resources to selected other libraries, or a commercial information provider offering a site license for a database to a group of library users.

In a cross-institutional authentication environment, the number of users can be immense. The universe of cross-institutional authentication can be as large as the Internet itself. The number of potential users of a resource provided to multiple institutions can approach hundreds of thousands, if not millions. The scale and complexity of a cross-institutional authentication environment far exceeds what would be expected in a local authentication system.

Because of the number of individuals involved, cross-institutional authentication systems generally focus on trust relationships among institutions, rather than performing authentication for each individual. In these systems, each institution trusts the others to have an effective local authentication system. A cross-institutional system treats each member institution as a single user, eliminating the need to authenticate each individual in the institution's user community.

How Much Security Is Enough?

Organizations can choose the level of security and the certainty of authentication that they feel appropriate to control access to their network resources. The amount of hardware, software, and personnel resources devoted to security varies according to the severity of the consequences should a breach occur.

Systems that achieve a moderate degree of security can be implemented with relatively low cost and effort. High-security systems require considerably more resources to implement. Few, if any, security systems can achieve complete protection from a highly motivated, clever, and skillful attacker. When compared to some other industries, libraries have modest security requirements. Let's put this in perspective by looking at the range of possibilities.

High Security. Some resources require the highest degree of security possible. Organizations that deal with electronic commerce or classified government information require extremely high security and strong authentication. For these organizations, an authentication failure can lead to a large loss of money or to a critical compromise of classified information. To achieve this level of security, the most sophisticated approach to authentication, access control, and encryption must be implemented.

Moderate Security. Any organization that relies on networked computers must implement a reasonable number of security precautions. Any computer on a network must be safe from unauthorized access, especially at the level of administrative access. Most libraries and universities operate their internal networks at what would be considered moderate-security levels.

Best-Effort Security. Some environments require only a reasonable degree of certainty that the proper users have access. The consequences of unauthorized access may not be great. For these systems, administrators need to take reasonable precautions that only authorized individuals gain access. Although this level of security seems lax, it is entirely appropriate for some applications.

High Security versus Convenient Access

The convenience of access may be an important concern. Highly secure systems impose many obstacles to access. It is very difficult to create a system that offers extremely tight security and yet allows convenient access to authorized users. The most secure systems are those that don't connect to internal networks, much less the Internet.

Secure systems that connect to networks will impose relatively stringent requirements on their users. It is common, for example, to require users to install special software on a remote computer that initiates an encrypted session with an organization's firewall to gain access to protected information within a secure network. Some systems also require hardware encryption devices or other security devices. In other words, highly secure systems are not designed to be convenient for their users.

Spillage: Accidental or Unauthorized Access

Most Internet providers are willing to accept a certain level of unauthorized access, even though it may result in lost revenue. The access scheme used dictates the vendor's cost as well as the charges incurred by the vendor's clients. For instance, IP source address filtering is cheaper to implement but does not offer as much protection as do some other methods. However, the potential loss of revenue from a certain level of unauthorized use is generally less than the cost of implementing a more secure system.

Most vendors will monitor for egregious episodes of unauthorized access, which will no doubt result in a serious discussion with the client. However, as long as financial processes, highly private information, critical proprietary information, and the like are not at stake, most vendors will accept a reasonable amount of tolerance for imperfect systems of authentication and authorization, at least in the short term. In the longer term, both vendors and libraries seek systems that offer a more comprehensive solution.

The Authentication Alternatives

Mechanisms commonly used in libraries for authentication and authorization include IP filters, proxy servers, and account-based systems. We'll also look at the emerging digital certificate arena.

IP Source Address Filtering

Let's begin our examination of the technologies used for authentication by looking at the one that currently dominates the access to library-oriented electronic resources—IP source address filtering. This method determines that a user is associated with an organization through network addresses.

A network consists of several individual computers linked together. The Internet consists of many networks linked together, all using the Transmission Control Protocol/Internet Protocol (TCP/IP) network protocol. In order to participate in the Internet, each computer must be assigned a *unique IP address* and each network must have a *unique network address*. Under the current version of TCP/IP, IP addresses are 32-bit binary numbers, generally represented by four numbers in dotted decimal notation, for example, 192.12.69.248.

Because the general infrastructure of the Internet relies on TCP/IP network principles that require each organization to have unique network addresses, the use of IP addresses is a convenient mechanism for a general kind of authentication. It is fairly convenient for providers of information resources to use IP network addresses to connect all the computers on that network to the Internet. To control access through IP addresses, all that an information provider needs to know is the IP addresses of all the organizational networks of its subscribers.

IP address filters have been in use in Unix systems and TCP/IP networks for a long time. This approach controls access by identifying trusted computers through their IP addresses. A system administrator can set up a table of IP addresses of computers that are allowed to access a given resource. These tables, called Access Control Lists or ACLs, restrict access based on the IP source address. ACLs can include complete IP networks or individual IP addresses, for example (* is a wild-card character):

Deny *.*.*.*
Allow 129.059.*.*
Allow 199.078.112.*
Allow 199.089.113.*

How much can we trust this method of authentication? Although IP source address filtering offers a convenient way of identifying computers on the Internet, it lacks the ability to perform strong authentication.

One can have a high degree of certainty that the IP addresses have both legitimate source and destination addresses. With the right tools and expertise, however, it is possible to forge an IP address so that packets appear to have the source address of one network when they actually originate from another. This technique can be used by hackers to break into systems that restrict access by IP source address. Such an attack is generally called IP spoofing.

Though it is technically possible to forge an IP address in this way, the degree of difficulty is considerable. This type of illegitimate access could only be accomplished by a highly skilled hacker who has also compromised the security of one or more systems on the internal network of the organization whose IP address is spoofed. It is unlikely that anyone would go through the amount of effort involved to gain access to the kind of library resources under consideration here.

Advantages of IP Source Filters. IP source address filters work well for authentication because they are easy to implement, both for the resource provider and for the client library. The resource provider can use an existing and well-known process for controlling access. IP source address filters and Access Control Lists have been available from the earliest days of TCP/IP networks and Unix systems.

This method is easy for libraries and their users—the security mechanisms operate on the vendor's system. Library users gain access by using their standard Web browsers with no additional intervention. As long as the computer user works from a computer that is part of an authorized network, no additional steps are needed to access resources controlled this way. All the library need do is to provide the resource vendor with a list of the IP addresses associated with its clients. This may be a single IP network address or a list of individual IP addresses.

Disadvantages of IP Source Filters. This authentication method does have its limitations. It fails to distinguish among multiple types of users that might share the same computer, and it does not accommodate all the various ways that users might connect to the Internet.

We noted that IP source address filters control access by physical computer and not by computer user. This method lacks the sophistication to selectively provide access to different users that use the same computer. Most library-oriented electronic resources, however, do not require this level of differentiation among users.

One of the major limitations of IP source address filtering involves providing remote access to an organization's users. Libraries often provide access to users who for various reasons are not physically present. You might be a legitimate member of an organization, but you connect to the Internet in a way that does not give your computer an IP address that is part of your institution's network.

The classic example involves library patrons who use a commercial Internet Service Provider (ISP) rather than a computer directly connected to the library's network or the dial-in facilities provided by the library or its parent institution. Most ISPs do not assign the same IP address to a user each time they connect. This makes it quite difficult for a library to have a definitive list of IP addresses for its patrons who use ISPs to connect to the Internet. For an academic library, this would include faculty, staff, and students who connect from their home computers, distance education students, and traveling scholars.

This issue is especially problematic for public libraries that need to provide access to resources for their patrons from their home computers. For public libraries, all their remote users would likely fall into this problematic category.

Proxy Servers

To overcome the limitations of IP source filters, many organizations have implemented proxy servers. A proxy server allows an external computer to take on an IP address from an organization's network. The proxy server intercedes for an external computer, replacing the external computer's source IP address with the proxy server's IP address. To prevent just any external computer from gaining this level of access, the proxy server will use a local authentication system to identify the user of the external computer.

An organization can set up a proxy server, for example, that prompts for a username and password, which it then checks against a local authentication system, such as Kerberos, LDAP, Radius, NDS, or an NT domain. If the user passes the authentication challenge, then the proxy server mediates the computer's network communications, rewriting each network packet.

Proxy servers can be implemented with readily available technology. Several different products are available for setting up the proxy server itself, and support for proxy servers is built into current Web browsers.

The use of a proxy server in a Web environment requires that the external user configure the Web browser accordingly. Both of the major Web browsers—Netscape Navigator and Microsoft Internet Explorer—support the concept of proxy servers and can be configured to use them.

Advantages of Proxy Servers. Proxy servers help very much to negotiate the limitations that otherwise exist in accessing IP-restricted resources. Because the proxy server makes the IP address of an external computer the same as the organization's network, the resource provider is not even aware of users who are physically external to their organization's network but gain access through a proxy server. No additional effort is required from the resource vendor's environment when a library implements a proxy server. The only complication is the contractual one—the vendor must agree that the additional users who access through a proxy server are allowable under the terms of the license agreement between the vendor and the library.

Disadvantages of Proxy Servers. Two major issues arise with proxy servers. First, users must learn how to configure their browsers and to turn off the use of proxies when they are not needed. A user's browser should be configured to pass through a proxy only for use with restricted resources. Otherwise a great deal of unnecessary network traffic would pass through the proxy server and eventually become a major bottleneck. Unfortunately, many users fail to understand the negative impact of routing excessive traffic through a proxy server and leave the proxy setting active even when it isn't needed.

Second, an organization must have a local authentication system in place. Organizations that have local authentication can take advantage of the username and passwords already in use. But if the organization lacks such a local authentication system, the process of creating one just to support a proxy server can be difficult. Creating user accounts and managing passwords requires considerable effort.

User-Account Authentication

Another commonly used process of authentication involves the use of accounts established by the resource provider. The username represents an account that is associated with a specified set of access privileges to network resources. To gain access to the resource that is managed in this way, each user must enter a username and a password. The password is held in confidence by the owner of the account and is not shared with other computer users.

A number of information resources delivered over the Internet rely on user accounts with passwords to control access. The resource provider generally manages the usernames and assigns passwords. Depending on the level of control needed, accounts may be individual or institutional.

Each individual that accesses the resource may be assigned a password, groups within an organization may share a username and password, or the entire organization might use a single username and password. Having large numbers of users share each username and password simplifies the process of managing accounts.

Advantages of User-Account Authentication. The key to the success of this type of authentication lies in having passwords that cannot be known or guessed by any other computer user. As long as passwords are managed carefully and not shared with unauthorized users, this method can provide excellent security. Usernames and passwords prevail in most local authentication systems. The key to circumventing this type of authentication lies in capturing the passwords associated with computer accounts—especially the ones with administrative access. Most computer systems encrypt passwords when they are transmitted over the network to eliminate the possibility that a password will be captured by individuals who are able to eavesdrop on network communications.

Disadvantages of User-Account Authentication. Problems may arise with this type of system as the number of users increases. For example, the more users you have, the more likely that unauthorized users will gain access to the system through compromised passwords. If a password becomes compromised, it must be changed and all the users of that password informed of the new password.

Additionally, the maintenance of usernames and passwords can be a great source of difficulty. If users deal with a number of systems that require usernames and passwords, and if all those usernames and passwords are different, then it becomes an extremely non-user-friendly environment. The process of communicating to each user what username and password to use for various systems can be very time-consuming.

Finally, when the system exceeds 20,000 to 30,000 users, it becomes quite difficult to manage. At that point, an approach that operates through institutional accounts becomes more practical.

A Note about Password Scripting

A number of information resources continue to rely on the account approach where one must know the username and password to gain access. As noted earlier, one of the difficulties with systems that use this approach involves the need for the users to know the username and password. If the library is providing the resource on behalf of its users, it must communicate the username and passwords they need, even if a single account has been established.

In some cases, the vendor is willing to have the library bypass the username and account prompts for their users, if they can be authenticated some other way. Password scripting is a technique that combines IP source filtering with account-based systems. If a library subscribes to a number of resources that use IP source filtering to grant access, it is inconvenient to have a minority of resources that require the user to enter a username and password.

With password scripting, the library will use a program or script that intervenes between the user and an account-based resource. If the user passes the IP source address filter authentication, then the script will send the username and password behind the scenes. This process happens transparently so that the end user remains unaware that the remote system even requires a username and password.

The password script itself must be handled in a secure way so that it cannot be subverted by users who do not pass the IP source address authentication. Ideally, the password script will use encryption to transmit the username and password over the network.

A password script can also be written to accommodate remote users who do not pass the IP source address authentication. If an authorized user attempts to use a resource controlled with a password script from outside the authorized IP address range, the program can prompt the user to enter the username and password. Alternately, the user can use a proxy server so that even the password script perceives the user as one with an authorized IP address.

Digital Certificates

Digital certificates are the best method available for performing authoritative authentication of a computer user. This method takes us into a more sophisticated realm of security and authentication.

Digital certificates rely on Public Key Infrastructure (PKI) as their primary underlying technology and are defined by the X.509 standard. Public key encryption addresses the issue of secure communications as well as authentication.

Encryption is a method of scrambling data in a controlled way so that it can be transmitted over a network without the possibility of it being understood by anyone who might intercept it along the way. Most schemes of encryption use a string of characters called a *key* that is fed into the program that scrambles the data. Once encrypted, the data are safe to be transmitted over a network.

When the encrypted data arrive at the destination, the recipient uses the same key that was used to encrypt the data to perform the decryption so that the data can again be understood. This method is called *secret-key encryption*. Both the sender and the recipient must know the same key, and that key should never be sent over the network. The main problems with this method of encryption involve sharing the key between the sender and the recipient and avoiding any possibility of a third party learning the key.

Public Key Infrastructure uses a pair of keys for each encryption. In this encryption methodology, each computer user owns two keys—a private key that is known only to the user, and a public key that is safe to share with any potential recipient of data. Data encrypted with one's private key can be encoded only with the corresponding public key, and information encrypted with a public key can only be decrypted with that user's private key. In contrast to the secret keys, it is acceptable to send a public key over the network. Consider this scenario.

User A publishes her public key to all network users, including user B. User B then encodes a message with User A's public key and transmits the message over the network. That message can only be decrypted with the private key of person A, and only person A has that key. Not only was the transmission secure, but there is a high degree of confidence that only the intended user can decrypt and read the message.

A digital certificate is an encrypted electronic document issued by a third party that validates that a given public key can be associated with a particular computer user. Digital certificates are issued by agencies called Certificate Authorities (CA) that perform a reasonable amount of verification of each user before granting a certificate. Digital certificates are signed with the private key of the CA, signifying that the CA vouches for the authenticity of the certificate and the identity of its owner.

Any recipient of information signed with that digital certificate can trust the identity information presented in that certificate to the degree that they mutually trust the Certificate Authority that issued it. Depending on the level of authentication, a Certificate Authority will require various items of documentation from a computer user before issuing a digital certificate. In some cases, an organization will become its own certificate authority for the purpose of issuing certificates among the users within its own community to access resources within that local environment.

Digital certificates are created with the private key of the Certificate Authority and the public key of the certificate owner, contain identification information for the certificate owner, are valid for a limited interval, and can be revoked. In order to guarantee the validity of a certificate, applications that use digital certificates should check the certificate revocation lists maintained by the issuing CA. This need to check certificate revocation lists has proven to be one of the major weaknesses in the use of digital certificates.

Advantages of Digital Certificates. Digital certificates are well supported in the current Web environment. All the major Web servers support the use of digital certificates. Web servers can operate in a secure mode where all information sent and received by a Web server is encrypted through the activation of Secure Sockets Layer (SSL). Web servers generally require the installation of a digital certificate issued by a CA before SSL and encryption can be activated.

The current generation of Web browsers supports the use of digital certificates. Both Microsoft Internet Explorer and Netscape Navigator support the use of personal digital certificates. These certificates are currently used for such applications as secure electronic mail, but can be incorporated into other applications.

Digital certificates are just beginning to be used in the library environment. Some libraries establish themselves as Certificate Authorities and issue digital certificates to their users. These digital certificates are used to validate users by an authentication system maintained by a library. The library could channel a user authenticated in this way to a proxy server that, in turn, connects the user to information resources restricted by IP address. The use of digital certificates becomes the local authentication sufficient for access to a proxy server.

Disadvantages of Digital Certificates. The management of digital certificates poses the greatest obstacle to their wide implementation in the library environment. Commercial Certificate Authorities charge for each digital certificate they issue, and the software necessary for an institution to issue its own certificates is expensive. The process of installing digital certificates in Web browsers, though not difficult, requires some level of education and training for library users.

It is also necessary to make secure backup copies of each user's digital certificate. If the hard drive of a computer fails, it may become necessary to reinstall the certificate from the backup. Digital certificates can also be problematic for users who use multiple computers. Many organizations will store each user's digital certificate in a private network directory on a file server. In this way, the certificate is protected by the local authentication system and can follow users when they use multiple computers. Digital certificates are especially problematic in cases where multiple users share a single computer.

Digital Certificates—Expectations. In the current environment, few of the information resource vendors that specialize in library-oriented products directly support the use of digital certificates for authentication. In the overall infrastructure of the Internet, however, digital certificates have emerged as the preferred method for user authentication and for secure communications. Despite their current sparse implementation in library environments, if their use continues to expand in the commercial sector of the Web, it is likely that libraries and library vendors will eventually adopt their use.

Conclusion

Although IP address filters continue to dominate as the practical solution to the security problem, the technique has many limitations. Proxy servers and password scripts fill some of the gaps, and account-based systems with usernames and passwords are an alternative. The emerging technology involves digital certificates. Although this has become a mainstream technology in the commercial arena, libraries have not yet widely adopted it.

Wireless and Ubiquitous Computing

Steve Cavrak

Steve Cavrak (*Steve.Cavrak@uvm.edu*) is the assistant director for academic computing in the University of Vermont's Division of Computing and Information Technology Services. He is professionally interested in all things computing—hardware, software, and mindware—and is especially interested in studying the impacts of technologies on cultural life. One of his home pages can be found at *http://www.uvm.edu/~sjc/*.

In this chapter, we'll discuss a natural phenomenon called electromagnetism—what it is, how it's measured, and why we can use it for communicating with one another. Then we'll explore the concept of the wireless network—a structure that allows for the transmission of data between two or more geographical locations, without cables. We'll look at several varieties of wireless networks, from the simplest—a handheld TV remote control—to the most complex—an earthbound computer communicating through an orbiting satellite to another earthbound computer. Finally, we'll touch on how this technology may shape the future.

But first let's think about this incredible technological evolution. Fifty years ago, newspaper articles described computers as gigantic, room-filling, electronic brains called Univacs. Meanwhile, a cartoon depicted Dick Tracy using his wrist radio telephone to chase criminals, foil plots, and promote peace. Most of the enthralled readers did not see that these two technologies were on a collision course.

Today, we are still enthralled, but less amazed, to find that fiction and reality have merged. At the 1998 Winter Olympics, Nippon Telephone and Telegraph outfitted forty visitors with the latest wristwatch "handyphone." Teenagers cruise the shopping malls hoping to "find love just a beep away" with a pocket-sized dating game device called "Lovegety." Truck drivers routinely check their e-mail and stock portfolios with wallet-sized networked computers. Gas pumps at the service station use "smart pass" technology to recognize your car and begin a credit-cardless sale. Cellular phones are so popular and convenient that many customers are abandoning the traditional landline service.

Eventually, these technologies will be so commonplace as to not attract notice. Mark Weiser, formerly of the Xerox Palo Alto Research Center (PARC), has called this evolving computing and communication environment "ubiquitous computing." Ubiquitous computing refers less to particular technologies than to a technological climate packed with easy-to-use devices that are "smart," cheap, useful, and practically invisible. As Weiser's 1991 article illustrates, some of these devices are small and portable; others might be as large as rooms, and might even be the room themselves.[1]

The emergence of ubiquitous computing is being hastened by advances in wireless communication technologies. Although often digital, and often themselves based on computer technologies, these wireless technologies are based on physical principles so well understood that they are considered part of "classical physics"—the variety of electromagnetic radiation described as the radio spectrum.

Electromagnetism and the Radio Spectrum

We take much wireless technology for granted already—TV remote controls, cordless telephones, Walkmen, Watchmen, boom boxes, pocket pagers, satellite TV, cellular phones, radar speed traps, remote microphones, microwave ovens, garage door openers, air traffic navigation, Doppler radar weather maps, electronic fences for our pets—enough to make our heads spin. S. B. Morse's 1844 telegraphic "What hath God wrought" seems more appropriate today than he imagined.

All these devices use "electromagnetic radiation," waves of linked electrical and magnetic fields that traverse an ethereal vacuum at the speed of light. Sometimes these waves travel in wires, other times in the air, and still other times through the nearly perfect vacuum of space.

Electromagnetic waves include visible light as well as the wide array of radio signals, which range from AM, shortwave, FM, TV, and microwave to infrared, visible, ultraviolet, X-rays, and gamma rays. Radio waves may be labeled by their wavelength, commonly measured in metric units (meters), but often by their characteristic frequency, specified in Hertz (a per-second measurement, abbreviated as Hz or hz). What are some of these frequencies? Based on the "orders of magnitude" (units of ten), the characteristic frequencies are shown in table 1.

Are the megahertz shown in the table the same as those in my personal computer? Unfortunately, yes! All active electronic devices emit radio waves. Just as we call flowers growing out of place "weeds," electromagnetic radiation emitted out of place is called "noise" or "static." If you have any doubt, place a small FM radio close to your computer and tune it to a place where you have nice static. Then start doing typical computer

TABLE 1

The Electromagnetic Spectrum

Frequency Megahertz	Wavelength Meters	Application
1 Mhz	300 meters	AM radio
10 Mhz	30 meters	Shortwave radio
100 Mhz	3 meters	FM radio, broadcast TV
1,000 Mhz	0.3 meters	Microwave
Gigahertz	**Millimeters**	
1 Ghz	300 mm	Microwave
10 Ghz	30 mm	
100 Ghz	3 mm	Millimeterwave
1,000 Ghz	0.3 mm	
Terahertz	**Micrometers**	
1 Thz	300 μm	
10 Thz	30 μm	Infrared
100 Thz	3 μm	Infrared
1,000 Thz	0.3 μm	Visible light

things—typing, moving and clicking the mouse, reading and writing to disk, rebooting the system, and so on. All the while, your radio will beep and squawk and whistle and hiss; soon you will recognize the squawk of a mouse click and the hiss of a disk drive in action.

Another measurement of electromagnetic waves is frequency. The higher the frequency, the more information that can be handled. This means that the higher frequencies in the spectrum are not only the most useful, they are also the ones with the most capacity, which is why one of the biggest competitors of wireless communications is another form of "wire"lessness—fiber optics, or plastic wires that transmit light.

What makes the megahertz in a computer different from those used for radio and TV? One of the important differences is "power"—the strength of the signal. Radio power is measured in "watts." The power radiated by your PC is tiny, measured in "milliwatts" or even "microwatts"; if you move your test radio across the room, the noise from the PC vanishes. A handheld cellular phone has a power rating on the level of 1/2 watt (500 milliwatts). Commercial stations, however, operate transmitters that broadcast signals measured in "kilowatts" or even "megawatts." The more powerful a signal, the farther it travels.

A second important difference is the way the radio is used to encode signals. The signals coming out of your computer are fairly raw—nothing is really being done to them except perhaps turning them on and off in gross ways. The signals coming from devices designed for communication are modulated in very strict ways so that the encoding at the transmitting end can be correctly decoded at the receiver. For example, the "AM" in AM radio refers to signal "amplitude modulation"; the "FM" refers to "frequency (shift) modulation."

	Application	Frequency
TABLE 2	Cordless telephone	46–49 Mhz
	Cellular telephone mobile	824–849 Mhz
Assigned Radio	Cellular telephone site	870–894 Mhz
Spectrum	Unlicensed radio device	902–928 Mhz
	Common carrier paging	959 Mhz
	GSM (PCS)	1,800 Mhz; 1,900 Mhz
	Digital cordless telephone	2,400 Mhz
	NII Supernet	5,250 Mhz
	Police X band radar	10,525 Mhz
	Police k band radar	24,150 Mhz
	Police Ka band radar	34,200 Mhz

Keeping the radio signal "wheat" separated from the chaff is the task of civil authorities. In the United States, this is assigned to the Federal Communications Commission, the FCC. In Europe, the national bodies are coordinated by the Conference Européenne des Administration des Postes et des Télécommunications (CEPT). Global coordination is provided by the International Frequency Regulatory Board.

The regulation of signaling method is usually a technical matter left to the users of the spectrum. These users work together, generally following the procedures of national and international standards organizations. In the United States, the Institute of Electrical and Electronic Engineers (IEEE) plays the preeminent role in setting radio standards. Globally, the International Organization for Standardization (ISO) fulfills this role.

Sprinkled throughout the spectrum are special "bands," parts of the spectrum assigned to a particular class of users by the Federal Communications Commission. Table 2 lists the bands for certain applications.

Varieties of Wireless Networks

Wireless technology has been a part of computer networking essentially from day one. Today's most common form of wired networking—Ethernet—owes its origin to a radio-based "ALOHAnet" created by Norman Abrahamson at the University of Hawaii. ALOHAnet used radio transmission between the islands to provide terminal connections to a mainframe computer; satellite-based connections were used to link the islands to the mainland-based "ARPAnet" (Advanced Research Projects Agency Network, the predecessor of today's Internet).

The ALOHAnet story also nicely illustrates the basic design criterion for a network—the network has to carry data over a specific geographical area. Knowing what to network and where allows various technologies to be examined and combined to provide the biggest bang for the buck. For the most part, this means that any specific network will be a mixture of technologies—some wireless and some wire-based. The slogan should be "different networks for different folks."

Infrared Networking

One of the simplest wireless technologies is infrared light. The underlying technology is compact, low in cost, low in power, and quite safe. Infrared networking is generally based on the same "light emitting diode" technology found in most electrical devices that have an on/off indicator. It is also completely unregulated—all of which leads to a wide variety of possible networking niches.

The most popular use of infrared technology is the universal remote control. Click here to change a channel on your TV, click there to zap a commercial, click, click again to pause or rewind the VCR, click again and your TV is silenced and your stereo kicks in with the evening jazz program. Although not a particularly earthshaking invention, the remote control is one of the more user-friendly technologies available—so easy to use that it is almost indistinguishable from a toy. This is a harbinger of the qualities that characterize ubiquitous computing.

One of the earliest uses of infrared signaling in a computer setting was the IBM PCjr remote keyboard. The PCjr was designed for home rather than office use. Many of its users did not have a desk to keep the computer on, and, even if they did, it was probably not a very big one. Sometimes the desk would be the kitchen table, sometimes a counter top, sometimes the floor. The cordless keyboard provided an easy way to set up a unit without a cabling mess.

Wireless keyboards are often envisioned as part of the "set top" generation of home computers—computers the size of a VCR or a CD player that sit on top of a TV set and allow a viewer to interact with the TV in computer-like ways: perhaps voting along with the audience for the funniest video, or virtual cheering at a hockey game, or cruising the Web when nothing else is on, or taking advantage of a "buy now, pay later" offer on a cubic zirconium ring.

Several steps up in level of sophistication are the communication tools built into the PalmPilot and some handheld calculators. The PalmPilot III pad includes an infrared link that allows messages, notes, and phone numbers to be sent back and forth across conference tables. The PalmPilot has a special feature to exchange electronic business cards! Similar infrared capabilities are found in business, engineering, and scientific calculators to promote the exchange of data, formulas, and programs.

Infrared beaming works in a point-and-click fashion automatically; no network engineer is needed to assign network numbers, to install drivers, or to add special software. A main limitation of this style of networking is that it requires good aiming.

Something similar to more traditional computer networking services is provided by other vendors. IBM, for example, offers an infrared network that behaves just like Ethernet. The IBM technology uses diffuse infrared radiation, bouncing signals off ceilings and walls to connect computers that might otherwise be blocked from direct view of each other. Technologies like this have been tested in conference, seminar, and classroom settings, and, because they are self-organizing, they have met with a good measure of success.

Cordless Networking

Infrared is unregulated because it is so easily controlled and managed; it is really a lighting application. Radio, however, easily penetrates walls and invades space and is treated a bit differently. Very low powered applications are often unlicensed; they impact a room or, at most, a backyard. Increase the power a bit, and the radio signals can affect a whole building or even a close neighborhood of buildings.

The cordless telephone illustrates wireless networking. The cordless phone allows people to chat on the phone while walking around the kitchen, or perhaps walking out to the patio and sitting down and relaxing. The original cordless telephones had several channels—not because a person might be talking to several people at once, but because several cordless phones might be operating nearby, creating an unintentional party line. Newer phones have more channels, cutting down on the chance of interference but not guaranteeing that a particularly nosy neighbor can't eavesdrop. The latest generation of digital cordless phones include scrambling (encryption) technology to help provide the degree of privacy that people expect. These phones have also triggered anxieties in government that there might be a generation of untappable telephones in the future.

With a slight increase in power and a bit of sophistication in operation, the party line effect can be turned into a feature rather than a side effect. Wireless networks can be built for small and medium-sized businesses, for school classrooms, for library reading and reference rooms, for warehouses and factories—in fact, for a very large number of environments.

These private networks are licensed to operate in what is commonly referred to as the industry, science, and medicine (ISM) arena. Finally, there are popular subscriber services that operate regulated businesses as Radio Common Carriers (RCC).

The devices available in the RCC market are evolving very rapidly. Most of the new devices operate in the 900 Mhz region; the older, specialized-service niches are slowly being abandoned, partly because of cost and partly because of capacity. Most are also migrating to newer digital technology, making each device more and more like a computer, less and less like a unique piece of hardware.

Ethernet technology has been one of the most popular of wireless LAN (local area network) technologies. Wireless Ethernet is essentially plug-compatible with the most popular LAN network and provides a reliable, high-speed networking solution. Wireless Ethernet is popular where traditional wiring solutions are not viable—perhaps because the building belongs to someone who is not willing to remodel, the offices span properties with no connecting "right of way," hazards may prevent remodeling, the use of the space may be so variable that hard wiring is impossible, or the wiring itself might constitute a hazard.

In January 1997, the FCC approved an unlicensed service as part of the emerging National Information Infrastructure. This U-NII (unlicensed NII) spectrum assigns a 5-Ghz band to unlicensed data networks at a low cost, providing high performance and offering self-management.

Cellular Networking

Cordless technology works best in an environment where there is really "one" telephone, or at least one telephone number, per person—in a home, in an office, in a building, or perhaps in a neighborhood.

In many environments, however, this is not always possible. On a university campus, for example, a faculty member may have one phone number on campus, a different phone number at home, and maybe even a third phone number when going between the two. With students, it's even more confusing. Sometimes they are in an apartment off campus, sometimes in a classroom or study room on campus, sometimes at a workplace office, sometimes studying at a friend's place, sometimes at home on vacation or break, and sometimes somewhere else altogether. In industry, it's really not much different.

When networks begin to ooze out of the bounds of a particular organization in a dynamic way, the local area networking model begins to break apart, and some form of third-party networking organization has to step in.

The cellular network uses several fixed-location facilities to service spatial "cells." Clients are free to move between these cells without interrupting a conversation, their network connection following them from place to place even when they cross state boundaries.

Personal Communications Services

As the cellular networks become digital networks, cellular "telephone" services are evolving into "personal communication services"—different forms of service for different types of messages in different situations—for example, beepers, pagers, reminders, messengers. Often PCS accessories are credit-card-sized devices allowing a one-way series of messages, from the form "You have a call" to "You have a call from 987-6521" to "Mr. Watson, Come here. I want you. Alex." Messages may be stored, deleted, transferred to computer, and recalled later.

Each reiteration in the pager marketplace adds more features, more message power, and more capacity. The pager marketplace is led by its low cost, with basic service in the $15-a-month range and sophisticated services at $30 a month.

As each iteration of pager technology adds more two-way interactivity to the device, so each generation of cellular telephone adds more paging and information capabilities to the telephone. We may see the two markets converge, or we may see the emergence of a new one altogether. E-mail conferencing and World Wide Web browsing may generate a third stream.

Wireless Internet Services

Several U.S. universities on the West Coast have experimented with extending their campuses into metropolitan networking models, for example, those based on Metricom. Students use the same internetworking technology at home as they do in class, and they can send e-mail and voice mail to their parents at no additional cost. "Look ma, no telephone!"

The Telluride (Colorado) InfoZone provides an experiment in public-access community networking. Wireless terminals provide Internet access at the Bank of Telluride and the Steaming Bean Cafe to this community of tourists, transient workers, and hard-core locals. The *Raleigh* (North Carolina) *News and Observer* organizes its community network around a newspaper model.

Yet another twist on metropolitan networking is packaged under the interesting name of "wireless cable." Cable TV began when rural areas found that they were being left out of the television era; the expensive antennas needed to receive very weak signals could be "shared" under the sponsorship of a small company. As more TV networks began to deliver their product through satellite broadcast, the cable companies found that they could receive better signals and more channels by installing big dishes. Soon, cable companies began to install cables almost right under the town's TV broadcasting station.

Eventually, cable companies found that they could make more money rewiring cities than wiring farms and rural communities, which found themselves again being left out. This time, however, microwave technology had come down in price, and a small entrepreneur could use it to rebroadcast TV without having to lay cable. Because the new signals are in the microwave spectrum and not in the standard TV channel area, wireless cable was able to secure a new niche.

Direct Satellite Networking

In today's world, people move and the technology stays fixed. That is the model for desktop wiring, for the cellular telephone system, and for our geostationary satellite broadcasts. Need this be the case?

The low Earth-orbiting satellite approach says no. Satellite communications systems often form the backbone of networks—TV networks are satellite-based, international telephony is still satellite-based, and even the most popular paging service by far, SkyTel, is satellite-based. The network of uplinks and downlinks as well as the launching cost of the satellite itself forms a substantial cost component of ordinary communications.

It's possible to build a communication system in which a large number of small, nearby, and low-powered satellites pick up and route signals sent by handheld transceivers. The satellites themselves would be cheaper to manufacture and launch, and a significant part of the ground-based support system would be eliminated (perhaps the only part to be left on Earth would be the billing system).

Two low-Earth-orbiting satellite systems have been proposed. The Iridium project, headed by Motorola and consisting of sixty-six satellites, began commercial operation on November 1, 1998. Iridium supports a variety of personal communications services—voice, data, facsimile, and paging messages—to anyone from anywhere on earth through handheld wireless telephones and pagers.

In 2001, the Teledesic system will become available. Teledesic, headed by Bill Gates (Microsoft) and Craig McCaw (McCaw Cellular Communications), will be a similar system consisting of 840 orbiting satellites. As with Iridium, this proposal would work by grabbing signals from the Earth, passing them between satellites, and then beaming them back to the intended recipient, signaling another interesting challenge to the wired, wired world.

What Next?

Where is all of this going? What is the networking environment going to look like in ten years? The ubiquitous computing environment described by Mark Weiser is slowly taking shape. The technology curve of smaller, faster, cheaper, and more convenient devices couples with the growing acceptance and resources of network services, such as the World Wide Web. George Gilder's "Into the Telecosm" foresees a vigorous, entrepreneurial future, one that is so dynamic that his book by the same title resists traditional publication and instead appears as an ASAP serial from *Forbes* magazine.[2]

Nicolas Negroponte takes an enthusiastic but somewhat more sobering approach in *Being Digital*.[3] The essence of ubiquitous computing is still computing—the ability to mechanically process information in intelligent and useful ways. Often, however, underlying social and political concerns hinder the development of intelligent utility. Negroponte's monthly column in *Wired Magazine* provides a continuing appraisal of the state of the art.

The real impact of these technologies will be felt, however, as they begin to change the work, study, and play habits of the people using them. Will telecommuting eliminate rush hour traffic? Will online shopping put a dent in suburban sprawl? Will online information services erode public libraries? Will the recording industry be able to suppress digital music technologies? Will distance learning opportunities transform schools and colleges?

The crucial impacts, then, are less technological and more cultural and much harder to predict and appreciate, all of which promises an interesting if not exciting beginning of the twenty-first century.

Resources

Print

Davis, Peter T., and Craig R. McGuffin. *Wireless Local Area Networks: Technology, Issues, and Strategies.* New York: McGraw-Hill, 1994.

Muller, Nathan J. *Wireless Data Networking.* Boston: Artech House, 1994.

Nemzow, Martin. *Implementing Wireless Networks*. New York: McGraw-Hill, 1995.

Online

The World Wide Web teems with sites related to wireless networking projects, taking on the characteristics of an "infoswamp." The following list is a tiny sample focusing on current awareness items as well as a few key background sites.

alt.2600
    The alt.2600 FAQ is a fine starting point for understanding the nitty gritty of computing and communication. The FAQ was recently found at *ftp://rtfm.mit.edu/pub/usenet-by-hierarchy/alt/2600/*; the newsgroup itself is at news: alt.2600.

http://www.teledotcom.com
    The online version of a weekly trade newspaper

http://www.cemacity.org/
    Consumer Electronics Manufacturing Association, the sponsors of the annual Consumer Electronics Show

http://www.fcc.gov/
    Federal Communications Commission

http://www.iridium.com/
    The Iridium Network

http://www.metricom.com/
    Metricom, a manufacturer of wireless LAN and MAN components

http://www.mot.com/
    Motorola, a manufacturer of pocket pagers and cellular telephones

http://www.wired.com/wired/
    Wired Magazine, news of the wired and wireless

Notes

1. Mark Weiser, "The Computer for the 21st Century," *Scientific American* (September 1991): 94–110, at *http://www.ubiq.com/hypertext/weiser/sciamdraft3.html*.

2. George Gilder, "Into the Telecosm," *Forbes*, at *http://www.forbes.com/asap/gilder/*.

3. Nicolas Negroponte, *Being Digital* (New York: Knopf, 1995).

Push Technology: Something New, Something Old

Amira Aaron

Amira Aaron (*aaron@faxon.com*) is the director of Academic Services at the Faxon Company.

As librarians and information managers, we have been delivering customized bits of relevant information to our users for many years. The selective dissemination of information (SDI) in various forms has been an important part of our tool kit as we try to satisfy the individual information needs of our end users. In essence, we have manually been "pushing" information to those who request it, and patrons who select a book from a shelf have been using "pull" technology.

Today, new technologies and intelligent software agents are being used to bring this concept into the twenty-first century and to deal with the overwhelming amount of information available on the Web. It remains to be seen whether these sophisticated programs and technologies can, on their own, prove to be as effective and efficient as the intelligence and dedication of a trained information professional.

Definition of Push and Pull

The common definition of push technology is the delivery of information on the Web to the user, initiated by the information server rather than by the information user. Broadcast information, e-mail, and discussion lists are all forms of push technology according to this definition. In many cases, the information pushed from a server to a user actually comes as the result of a programmed request or profile, which is usually stored on the user's own device. The program captures the user's profile and then periodically initiates requests for information on his or her behalf from the server. You can check *http://www.whatis.com* for a more extensive definition.

For the sake of this discussion, we can think of push technology as the process by which content providers send information to the computer desktop or mobile device where it can immediately be viewed by the user. Pull technology, on the other hand, allows users to select information that is updated on a regular basis or upon request and then "pulled" down by the user to the desktop for viewing. Most push applications today still combine aspects of both push and pull technology—and most users still prefer it to be that way.

Some critics contend that most push applications available today are not "true" push, but instead simulated push. They argue that in order to be considered true push, the application must be event-driven versus update-driven. The pushing out of information must be triggered by a particular event or change in circumstances. The recipient must have a persistent link to the alerts, regardless of the connection used. It is not sufficient for the user to occasionally check to see whether new information is waiting to be pushed. Push technology must be integrated into the normal user experience and not be viewed as something out of the ordinary. It must also be modular and customizable; the information to be delivered should be aimed at the specific information needs of one user or a particular group of users.

Origins of Push Technology

We have seen an exponential growth rate of the Web since it was born in 1989 within the scientific community. In some ways, it has become the victim of its own success, attracting the attention of content providers ranging from those with individual home pages to major economic players. The amount and variety of content on the Web is now staggering. In many cases, traditional models of obtaining information from the Web are proving to be inefficient, and new methods of using technology to filter and deliver customized information are being sought. The push technology model is still in its infancy, being less than three years old!

Push technology is being looked to as a solution to the overload of information and limits to searchability on the Web. Slow connections frustrate users in search of a specific piece or type of information. Users, both individual and commercial, now demand and are willing to pay for customized delivery of information. "Resurfing" is no longer an acceptable activity; users definitely do not want to constantly surf the Net, checking for updates.

Benefits and Outgrowths of Push Technology

Push technology obviates the need for the user to search and re-search; it removes the requirement for the user to do anything overtly to obtain information. It provides an aggregation of content on the desktop and moves "bits" of data closer to the end user. Properly executed, it should reduce the overload of information and eliminate that which is not relevant to the user. Push technology is the first medium that lets content providers get feedback on the use of the content and then make further use of the feedback in providing future content.

The use of push technology allows the provision of real-time alerts and event-driven notification. It extends the reach of the Net to mobile users. Push technology gives us the ability to receive virtual software updates and to develop zero administration systems. Valuable specialized information can now be automatically delivered to targeted users, and content providers can more easily aggregate users by interest and preference. And push technology provides an extension of existing content systems, or databases.

Concerns about Push and Issues to Consider

Several very real concerns exist about push technology and the information it delivers. First, who selects the content to be pushed and what are their qualifications and motives? What is the quality of the content? Is it valuable, authorized content or does it consist merely of free teasers to entice users to pay for further, in-depth information?

There is a valid concern that push technology gives power to those who can afford to broadcast or select information, whether qualified or not. In addition, reliance on intelligent agent software may not offer the most relevant, scholarly content available and may also compromise the privacy of the user's research. There may be no true evaluation of the information on the part of the user; he or she may assume that it is valid because it has been pushed from the Internet. The user may also miss information found in other ways through serendipity. Often, there is an abundance of advertising, and there are also concerns about bandwidth and stretching of system resources.

There are thus several issues to consider when selecting or recommending a push application. The content must be evaluated, among other factors.

What is the content, and who is its author? What is the quality, timeliness, and relevance of the information? How complete is it?

Who is the publisher? Is it an aggregator or an individual? What do you know about the publisher's track record? Who selects the information to be pushed? What are their credentials? Who pays for the information—what effect does advertising have on the information being pushed?

What type of connection is used—is it persistent and active, or just occasionally linking? Is the link to a specific location or can the user retrieve it from any available computer?

What device is used—are there special hardware needs in order to receive the data? What hardware and software platforms are necessary? And what is the interface like—how does the user actually receive the information?

What does the application learn about the user's behavior and needs—does it make use of this feedback in supplying future information? How does it protect the privacy of the user's research?

It is the role of the librarian and information manager to attempt to answer some of these questions and to ensure that push technology applications being used are actually meeting the stated information needs.

Proprietary Push and Examples

One set of push technology companies developed proprietary products that offer very different approaches to delivering content; some of these, in fact, have already come and gone. Most take the approach of selling technology to content providers; others make their revenue primarily from advertising. Software and hardware environments vary greatly. Some products are designed for use on intranets or extranets or both. Some contain applications for screensavers, desktop tickers, wallpaper, and so on. The method of connection and delivery medium vary widely as well.

One of the first and best-known examples of a proprietary push application is PointCast, which delivers stock information, sports, business news, headlines, and more to the desktop according to the profile set up by the user. Proprietary client software is required. PointCast offers a ticker and screensaver in addition to the normal application. Updating can be scheduled on a regular basis or at the user's request. PointCast also has an application that can be mounted on a company's central server.

Another proprietary application is BackWeb, which delivers "infopaks" in low priority when the user is connected to the Internet. It also provides wallpaper and screensaver capabilities and has channels in over eighteen categories. AirMedia offers wireless satellite transmission that needs a special receiver. Marimba's Castanet is written entirely in Java, so it is platform independent.

For comprehensive, updated information on proprietary push applications, check out David Strom's site, *Push Publishing Technologies*, at *http://www.strom.com/imc/t4a.html*.

Browsers and Channels

In 1997, both Microsoft and Netscape introduced business and entertainment push technology channels as part of their new Web browser versions. The channel concept was the next step in the evolution of push technology applications, and the significant advances here were technological. At the time, Microsoft and Netscape were in major competition for attractive, big-name channel providers, including Bloomberg, Disney, Knight Ridder, Reed Elsevier, and ZDNet. The advent of these channels, however, did not seem to make as great an impact on the mass audience as was intended. In addition, scholarly and research applications were few and far between.

Each browser had its own version of standards for the technology, which were inconsistent with each other. Microsoft offered the Internet community the most robust standard for coding and formatting data to be used in channel applications, called the Channel Definition Format, or CDF. The intended result was to produce an environment where any content provider could create and deliver information using push technology.

With the implementation of Internet Explorer 4.0, Microsoft made it relatively simple for those with some programming knowledge to create active channels, multiple screensavers, desktop tickers, and more. In the same vein, the user could easily subscribe to a channel and indicate what parts of the channel he or she was interested in receiving and on what schedule. Channels on specific topics of interest could be located in the Active Channel Guide accessible from the Channel Bar on the active desktop.

The push technology environment provided by Netscape (Netcaster) was not as sophisticated, functional, or easy to use as the Microsoft channel technology. Using Netcaster, a user's favorite main channel page could be viewed as a Webtop that occupied the entire screen. The Channel Finder was present on the user interface, and users could subscribe to channels, specify cache size and number of pages to download, update schedules, and so on. No screensaver feature was provided.

With the development of the Windows 98 operating system, Microsoft began to phase out channels, their underlying technology, and the Active Channel Guide itself. The company now offers mobile push channels that can be received either on the standard computer desktop or on mobile, handheld PC devices. A mobile channel can be thought of as a small-scale website designed specifically for off-line browsing, with the unique form factor and capabilities of a Windows CE-based device in mind.

Users can subscribe to mobile channels through Internet Explorer 4.0 on their desktop computers. They can then synchronize the mobile channel content to their mobile devices. With mobile channels, Microsoft is fulfilling some of the true capabilities of push technology—the ability to receive and take with you the most up-to-date news or information. More information on mobile channels is available at the Microsoft website.

Sample Push Applications

Push applications are now being used in several educational and commercial organizations to deliver timely information to users. Companies are finding push aids useful in providing customer service, retaining clients, gathering information about clients, and keeping a remote sales force properly informed. Sample push applications are as follows:

- A stockbroker delivers up-to-date information to fifty clients with the same stocks.

- Drug companies send the latest information to health care professionals.
- Airlines send notification of flight changes to passengers.
- Automobile manufacturers distribute parts manuals, prices, repair procedures, and recalls to dealers and service stations.
- A software company distributes virtual software updates.
- Teachers use a service that delivers updated information to students' mailboxes.
- The insurance industry distributes timely information about variable annuities for use by life insurance agents.
- An executive receives critical graphical information on a Web TV in a hotel exercise room.
- A vendor sends publication updates to multiple libraries.

Filtered Push and Intelligent Agents

In order to be effective, push technology should lead to tailored, customized, personalized bits of information delivered in a real-time environment. Users should be able to specify, either explicitly or implicitly by their search and use behavior, what they want and how they want it delivered. Sophisticated intelligent software agents can learn on their own by following the user's example.

Intelligent software agents are programs that perform a variety of tasks. In general, an agent is a program that gathers information or performs some other service without the user's immediate presence and on some regular schedule. Typically, an agent program, using parameters the user has provided, searches all or some part of the Internet, gathers information in which the user is interested, and presents it on a periodic basis.

Other agents have been developed that personalize information on a website based on registration information and usage analysis. Some types of agents include specific site watchers that tell you when the site has been updated or look for other events, and analyst agents that not only gather but also organize and interpret information for you. Intelligent agents can learn from the behavior of the user and customize future delivery of information accordingly.

An agent is sometimes called a bot (short for robot). For thorough information on bots and intelligent agents, refer to BotSpot (*http://www.botspot.com*) and "Intelligent Agents Project at IBM T.J. Watson Research" (*http://www.research.ibm.com/iagents/*). Also, take a look at Gerry McKiernan's CyberStacks site, LibraryAgents (sm): *Library Applications of Intelligent Software Agents* at *http://www.public.iastate.edu/~CYBERSTACKS/Agents.htm*. Or visit the excellent site on *Intelligent Software Agents* by Sverker Janson of the Swedish Institute of Computer Science at *http://www.sics.se/isl/abc/survey.html*.

In a recent paper on push technology (July 1998), Marilyn Geller, a well-known information professional and consultant, describes an intelligent agent application that is very relevant to the library community and holds great promise:

> Closer to home, librarians have access to an application called NewsAgent. As part of the eLIB program, the NewsAgent project debuted early in 1998 with the intent of creating an alerting and current awareness service for librarians and information professionals. It is a collaborative project that brings together technology developers, content providers and librarians. Users of this experimental service can select from a variety of channels including publications, research, products, events and more.
>
> Within each channel, there are subject topics that can be selected to tune the customization of a user profile. Even more customization is possible by creating a Personal Topic. Users can select the channel and subject topics and fine-tune the scope of a personal topic by adding subject keywords and Boolean Logic connectors. . . . There are two ways that users can access material tailored to their profiles. They can request to have an alert sent to their email address daily, weekly or monthly, or, alternately, they can log into the NewsAgent web site with a user ID and password and pull down information in each of their tailored categories.
>
> Behind the scenes, NewsAgent uses a variety of technologies, standards, content sources and partnerships to support the service. At the heart of the system is a Virtual Content Store, which houses both data and metadata as defined by the Dublin Core standards. Data can be stored locally or remotely, and can be added either manually or through a variety of automated mechanisms. Information resources, as of this writing, include several electronic journals and electronic mailing lists related to information management. In July of 1998, this project is still defined as a trial service, but it comes closer to being a model for meeting the information needs of the scholarly and research community than others that have gone before it.[1]

Libraries and Push

Push technology and intelligent software agents can be used effectively in internal library business procedures as well as becoming an important part of the information dissemination function. As librarians, we traditionally deliver information to our end users in multiple formats. Push technology can simply be viewed as an extension of our standard SDI services. It is a way for libraries to become more relevant, effective, and timely. Push technology is a new way to realize an existing concept.

What are some examples of potential or actual push technology applications in libraries?

- New-title alerts
- Subject alerts from online public access catalogs (OPACs)
- Overdue and availability notices from circulation systems

- Articles of topical interest from a database
- Publisher dispatch data about the status of issues
- Tables of contents of selected journals
- Title changes and publication status changes

Questions to Ponder

As librarians, we need to be shaping the future of new information technologies. In our deliberations, we should be considering such questions as the following:

What uses could you make of push technology and intelligent agents in your own institution in delivering information to your users?

As librarians, what information would you like to see pushed to you from publishers or vendors or both?

Can you cite any push applications being used now in libraries and information centers?

What advantage could push technology have for staff members within your organization?

How do you feel about the concept of push versus that of pull?

What concerns, if any, do you as a librarian have about these new technologies?

How do these new technologies and intelligent agents affect traditional concerns about user privacy?

How do you feel about using advertising to pay for push applications as opposed to having the user pay for the information?

The Future of Push

Until this time, push technology has not had an extensive impact on the academic and scholarly research community. It has been more prevalent in the business and entertainment sectors. Librarians and information professionals must be closely involved in the adaptation of the new information technologies and intelligent agents, where appropriate, to the scholarly communication process. Push technology has the potential to simplify and automate many of the tasks involved in the customized delivery of information to the end user, but the applications must be developed with intelligence and with true concern for quality, ethics, and accuracy.

For More Information

Printed articles appear from time to time on the topic of push technology and intelligent agents; these can be located and obtained through literature searches and alerting services (yes—push technology). Many excellent informational sites exist on the Web and have been mentioned in this chapter. For links to these and other resources, consult the Push Technology and Intelligent Agent sections of the Faxon Institute Industry Resources Page, Advanced Technology category, at *http://www.faxon.com/html/fi_intag.html*.[2]

Notes

1. Marilyn Geller, "Pushing for a Place on the Internet: Push Technology for the Scholarly and Research Community," paper presented at the International Online Conference, London, December 1998.

2. I wish to acknowledge the support and contributions of my colleague and friend, Marilyn Geller, to this discussion.

Virtual Reality Primer for Cybrarians

David Mattison

David Mattison (*dmattison@home.com*) is an access services archivist with the British Columbia Archives where he has worked since 1981. He was formerly a librarian and an audiovisual archivist at the BC Archives. He has published widely, principally in the field of photographic history. A strong believer in lifelong learning and the Internet communications revolution, he has devoted hundreds of volunteer hours to maintaining the Victoria Telecommunity Network, which he cofounded in 1992 as the Victoria Free-Net. He has conducted workshops and presented papers on the Internet and the Web and is currently exploring VRML. His home page is *http://members.home.net/dmattison/index.html*.

The One True Thing

The antecedents of virtual reality (VR) exist in oral tradition, scientific concepts, obsolete technologies, and entertainments, such as magic and illusionist effects, stereoscopic photography, and motion pictures. True virtual reality is as close as you can get to the essence of reality. Were the George Eastman Company of Kodak camera fame to create a slogan for VR, it might be "You press the button, we will take you there." VR is emerging as a significant current in the cultural mainstream because of several factors, among them the ubiquity of the Net; the proven track record of image-based VR in the fields of science, education, commercial research, medicine, and entertainment; and the establishment of an international standard for the management of three-dimensional data.

Virtual reality for the purposes of this primer has two basic meanings: an artificially created, immersive reality that engages one or more of the senses; and virtual reality computer worlds created with the Virtual Reality Modeling Language (VRML) and distributed over the Web. For com-

Figure 1   A Virtual Reality Time Line

1962:	Documentary filmmaker Morton Heilig's "Sensorama" motorcycle VR ride attraction
1965:	Computer science doctoral student Ivan Sutherland's "Sketchpad," the first display of visual images on a computer monitor
1969:	Myron Krueger demonstrates his interactive GLOWFLOW room.
1970:	Myron Krueger coins the term *artificial reality.*
1984:	Jaron Lanier calls his "company" VPL Research Inc.
1989:	The term *virtual reality* is attributed to Jaron Lanier.
1989:	Mattel markets the PowerGlove for the Nintendo Entertainment System.
1991:	Cyberspace author and thinker Howard Rheingold publishes the book *Virtual Reality*, documenting two years of VR research.
1991:	Virtual Reality Studio software released for personal computers in the United States by Superscape, Inc., of England; known as 3D Toolkit there
1992:	Arcade-based entertainment unit "Virtuality" introduced in the United States by W Industries of England
1994:	Virtual Reality Modeling Language (VRML) 1.0 specification published
1995:	Nintendo introduces the Virtual Boy VR game, a table-mounted head display for 3-D play.
1997:	VRML97 (VRML 2.0) specification published as International Standard ISO/IEC 14772-1:1997
1998 April 26:	First live Internet multimedia streaming VRML performance of Shakespeare's *A Midsummer Night's Dream* at SHOC Interactive (Toronto, Canada)
1998 June:	First DisneyQuest virtual reality theme park opens at DisneyWorld
1998 November 21:	Avatars98, first conference of artificial personalities inside cyberspace

parison, the WWWebster Dictionary (*http://www.m-w.com/netdict.htm*) defines virtual reality as "an artificial environment which is experienced through sensory stimuli (as sights and sounds) provided by a computer and in which one's actions partially determine what happens in the environment."

The first basic meaning of VR is sometimes described as "artificial reality" (coined by arts scholar and technology author Myron Krueger in 1970), yet is more commonly referred to as virtual reality, a phrase traced to 1989 and Jaron Lanier of VPL Research. His company, cofounded with Thomas Zimmerman, was the first to commercially market such VR products as headsets and the DataGlove invented by Zimmerman.

For the purposes of this primer, the two types of VR treated are: a computer-generated environment entered through sensory devices (headsets, data gloves, and so on) or a visually immersive structure, and a computer model of an environment designed for Web access and created with the Virtual Reality Modeling Language (VRML) and other three-dimensional (3-D) tools.

Both types of VR may be utilized by one or more persons simultaneously. Although they are considered part of the VR realm, mechanical simulators, such as flight simulators or the Disneyland *Star Tours* attraction, are not included here because they are more or less self-explanatory. Graphical multiplayer games played over the Web, descended from world-based strategic and adventure games such as MUDs (Multi-User Dungeon or Dimension) and MOOs (MUD-Object Oriented), are beyond the scope of this chapter. Figure 1 highlights some of the interesting developments in virtual reality since 1965. Also, check the Online Resources section at the end of the chapter under General Guides to Virtual Reality.

Virtual Reality Software

While specialized hardware is normally worn for the "true" VR experience, computer simulations or models of real and imagined worlds complete with virtual people or avatars represent the other aspect of VR research. Although some of the retail market software released in the early 1990s could drive VR hardware, the software itself was intriguing enough to take on a life of its own, in a virtual sort of way.

The core of image-based VR is the realistic representation of three-dimensional (width, height, and depth) space through a two-dimensional surface. VR software (and this includes anything based on the VRML standard) must also allow the programming of object behavior and user interaction with the virtual world. The world should also be able to "sense" the presence or proximity of the user, and the world can even run on its own clock to let time-based events occur. Attaching multimedia components (still images, video, and audio) to any part of a world is also permitted.

Three-Dimensional (3-D) Graphics in Virtual Reality

The increasing popularity of 3-D as a design tool for websites is strengthening the entry-level and mid-range market for 3-D modeling software. Most of the VRML authoring programs or the manufacturer's website, however, provide libraries of 3-D objects that may or may not be editable within the program.

Even though the major VRML authoring programs include 3-D modelers, stand-alone 3-D modeling programs should also be capable of saving directly to or exporting to the VRML97 file format. Avoid 3-D graphics programs, even if inexpensive, that save in or export to only VRML 1.0 because you will then need to convert the VRML 1.0 file to VRML 2.0, and it will more than likely not resemble what your 3-D model masterpiece originally looked like.

In 1999, the Web3D Consortium announced its plans for development of X3D. Promoting X3D as another next-generation standard, initial specifications define X3D as combining XML, VRML97, and Internet broadcast streaming technology. For more information, see 3-D Websites in the Online Resources section at the end of the chapter.

From VR to VRML

The emergence of the Internet and the World Wide Web in particular as a new, ubiquitous form of communication drew attention to the lack of an open standard for representing 3-D objects and for the interchange of proprietary 3-D objects. The explosion of interest in VR in the mid-1990s also drove the international standardization process. Many interesting and workable 3-D/VR programs were released to the retail market and through the shareware distribution process.

The Web3D Consortium (*http://www.web3d.org/*) is the intellectual and commercial arm of VRML, guiding its evolution into one component of interoperable 3-D Internet content software. Charter members of the consortium include Apple Computer, Microsoft Corporation, Mitsubishi Electric Corporation, Oracle Corporation, Platinum Technology, Silicon Graphics, Sony Corporation, and Superscape, Inc.

Development of an open (nonproprietary), standardized markup language for 3-D Internet content occurred in two phases. Between 1989 and October 1994, employees of Silicon Graphics, Inc. (*http://www.sgi.com/*) were involved with that company's development of interactive 3-D applications. As the Web emerged in the early 1990s, the element of network accessibility became more critical. The first release of the VRML 1.0 specification (*http://www.vrml.org/VRML1.0/vrml10c.html*) in November 1994 was based on SGI's own product, Open Inventor.

VRML 1.0 worlds, however, were static 3-D scenes; nothing in them moved and a user could not interact with them. Development of VRML 2.0 took place throughout 1996 and early 1997. The specification was based on a proposal called "Moving Worlds" from SGI, the Sony Corporation, and Mitra; discussions of this open standard occurred only on the Net through the *www-vrml* mailing list.

Animation, object behavior, and user interaction, all delivered through the Web, were the focus of the VRML 2.0 specification. The International Organization for Standardization, for the first time, published the VRML97 specification (*http://www.vrml.org/technicalinfo/Specifications/VRML97/*) electronically as an HTML document.

The Basics of VRML

VRML files are ASCII text files that may be compressed. A binary file format for VRML is under development by the Web3D Consortium. VRML files are normally compressed using GZIP. The uncompressed VRML file extension is .wrl (pronounced "world"). A compressed VRML file may have file extensions such as .wrz or .wrl.gz. The original MIME type for a VRML file is x-world/x-vrml; the ISO MIME type is model/vrml. VRML 2.0 is not backwardly compatible with VRML 1.0, but free file translation programs exist (see The VRML Repository at *http://www.sdsc.edu/vrml/*).

A VRML scene is also known as a *world*. Scenes are composed of *nodes*. Each node spells out in great detail how a specific object is modeled and interacts with other nodes. There are more than fifty nodes; among them are ones that describe an object's coordinates, geometry, and appearance; nodes that control lighting, sound, and the general appearance of the world; and sensor nodes that create interaction or react to a viewer's or other object's behavior. Custom nodes can also be created through the use of prototypes.

Reuse of nodes by defining them with names partly accounts for the compactness of VRML worlds where every aspect of a 3-D object is mathematically prescribed. Nodes can also be grouped or nested in a parent-child pattern. Information flows between the nodes through *routes*, which is how objects are programmed to exhibit behaviors (rotating, moving, growing, shrinking, and so on) or simulate interaction with a user or appear to act independently of any user control.

In a graphical VRML authoring program, a VRML scene is usually displayed as a hierarchical tree similar to a Windows Explorer (File Manager) tree. An ordinary VRML file, however, very much resembles the programming language C. VRML worlds also support scripted events, and the default language for scripting is either Java or Netscape Corporation's JavaScript or both. Figure 2 highlights some of the pros and cons of VRML.

Viewers

Viewing VRML worlds with a Web browser requires only a plug-in or a VRML-compliant browser. Originally developed by Silicon Graphics, Cosmo Player (*http://www.cosmosoftware.com*) is a leading viewer for the Intel/PC platform. VRML viewers for the Macintosh include Cosmo Player and WorldView.

Superscape, Inc. (*http://www.superscape.com/*) offers a free Internet Explorer and Netscape Navigator browser plug-in called Viscape Universal. Both VRML97 and Superscape 3-D worlds (file extension of .svr) created with Superscape's own authoring tools can be viewed. Viscape, however, is required to view .svr content on the Virtual World Wide Web (*http://vwww.com/*) site, which hosts "over 500 independently owned 3D Web Pages." As is the case with MIME-specific plug-ins, Viscape cannot coexist with Cosmo Player. All Superscape authoring tools can save 3-D scenes or worlds in either VRML97 or .svr formats.

| FIGURE 2 | Pros and Cons of VRML |

Pros

- VRML97 is an international, stable, platform-independent standard.
- VRML is a 3-D file interchange format.
- VRML worlds are scalable in performance, meaning that, as computers and networks improve in speed, network transport and rendering of VRML worlds will improve.
- VRML worlds are scalable in size because they are vector-based; all information about a world except for external textures and multimedia attachments is stored as a series of detailed instructions.
- Like HyperText Markup Language (HTML), VRML files can be produced with any text editor; graphics capability, however, is required to view a VRML world.

Cons

- VRML is much more complex to understand and utilize in its native text state than is HTML.
- VRML currently lacks a high-compression binary file format. Compressed VRML files use the GZIP format.
- One vendor's implementation of the VRML97 specification may not always be compatible with that of another vendor.

VRML Authoring Programs

These programs all produce VRML 2.0- or VRML97-compliant worlds. Because the software is produced to a specification, interpretation of that specification has resulted in incompatibility between some VRML viewers and authoring programs. Except for VRML tools operating on Silicon Graphics hardware, all the authoring programs listed in the Online Resoures section at the end of the chapter operate only in the Windows 95/98/NT environment. However, even more VRML97 authoring programs can be found through The VRML Repository.

Virtual Communities

Established in 1995, The Palace (acquired in 1998 by Electric Communities) uses proprietary software to create virtual communities accessible through the Internet and through corporate intranets and public websites. The Palace software has also been used to create educational communities, such as TechLINC (*http://www.lcc.gatech.edu/techlinc/index.html*) at the Georgia Institute of Technology's School of Literature, Communication, and Culture.

As more companies reposition their Web applications to accommodate 3-D Internet technology, we can expect to see more examples of interactive 3-D worlds, such as Cryopolis (*http://www.cryo-networks.com/*) from CryoNetworks, Paris, France. Internet users of Cryopolis can create avatars to navigate the city and converse with one another through the keyboard, a microphone, or a video camera. Hyperlinking to external websites and viewing multimedia content are possible from within Cryopolis.

Print Resources

Ames, Andrea L., David R. Nadeau, and John L. Moreland. *VRML 2.0 Sourcebook*. 2d ed. New York: Wiley, 1997.

Carey, Rikk, and Gavin Bell. *The Annotated VRML 2.0 Reference Manual*. Reading, Mass.: Addison-Wesley Developers Press, 1997.

Marrin, Chris, and Bruce Campbell. *Teach Yourself VRML 2 in 21 Days*. Indianapolis: Sams.net Publishing, 1997.

Roehl, Bernie, ed. *Late Night VRML 2.0 with Java*. New York: Ziff-Davis, 1997. Available at *http://ece.uwaterloo.ca:80/~broehl/vrml/lnvj/index.html*.

Online Resources

General Guides to Virtual Reality

Hot Virtual Reality Sites: *http://www.itl.nist.gov/div894/ovrt/hotvr.html*.
One might call this the official U.S. government site on VR as it's maintained by a staff member of the Information Technology Laboratory, National Institute of Standards and Technology (NIST), and is part of the Open Virtual Reality Testbed Project (*http://www.nist.gov/itl/div894/ovrt/OVRThome.html*). The Frank and Ernest cartoon by Bob Thaves alone is worth the visit.

On The Net: Resources in Virtual Reality: *http://www.hitl.washington.edu/kb/onthenet.html*
A remarkable compendium of websites, even more in-depth than Yahoo! site (*http://dir.yahoo.com/Computers_and_Internet/Multimedia/Virtual_Reality/*). On The Net has its own search engine: keywords or data field, your choice.

Virtual Institute of Information, Columbia University, New York: *http://www.vii.org/*
The mission of VII is to track issues and maintain an industry watch on telecommunications, cybercommunications, and mass media. To this end it has links to resources on virtual reality and VRML.

Virtual Reality Association Inc. (VRA): *http://www.vr.org.au/*
International organization based in Australia; operates multiuser virtual world ElectraCity.

Virtual Reality Society (U.K.): *http://www.vrs.org.uk/*
International society founded in 1994; publishes *The VR Journal.*

General and Specialized Guides to VRML

The Mining Co. Guide to VRML: *http://vrml.miningco.com/*
A wide variety of resources, including a chat board.

3DWorld News: *http://www.tcp.ca/gsb/VRML/index.html*
Offers up-to-date news releases and educational resources on VRML and 3-D applications.

Java3D and VRML Working Group (Web 3D Consortium): *http://www.vrml.org/WorkingGroups/vrml-java3d/*
Java went 3-D in December 1998. This group is formulating the interface of the VRML and Java3D programming languages and creating "a *complete* Java3D-based VRML browser."

The VRML Repository: *http://www.sdsc.edu/vrml/*
Major resource organized by topic with a search engine.

VRMLworks: *http://hiwaay.net/~crispen/vrml/*
Much useful background information, educational resources, and links to other sites.

VRMLion: Objects and Resources for VRML 2.0: *http://www.km-cd.com/vrml/*
Excellent source of free 3-D objects, textures, sounds, educational tools, and links to other sites.

VRMLSite Magazine: "3D on the Internet:" *http://www.vrmlsite.com/*
Significant works and sites about VRML are all on one page.

VRweb: Ultimate VRML Directory Service: *http://www.vrweb.net/*
Superb resource with its own search engine and categories of VRML resources. Includes a changing sample world.

Guides to 3-D on the Web

Graphic Sites on the Net: *http://desktoppublishing.com/graphicsites.html*
Hundreds of links to any commercial, technical, scientific, or artistic aspect of visualization. A pick list contains further specialized areas, such as Apple Computer and Windows graphics products.

3D ARK: *http://www.3dark.com/*
Includes chat boards or forums, educational resources, links to other 3-D sites, and job information.

3DSite: *http://www.3dsite.com/*
Claims it has "the largest dedicated 3-D links database on the World Wide Web." The links database is also browsable by topic, including

Virtual Reality, VRML, and VR on the Web. Other useful features include general and specific 3-D authoring products, chat boards, and job hunting tools.

Ultimate 3D Links: *http://www.3dlinks.com/*
Similar to 3D ARK and 3DSite.

Authoring Programs

Community Place Conductor (Sony): *http://vs.spiw.com/*

Cosmo Software (Platinum Technology): *http://cosmosoftware.com/*

VRCreator 2.0 (Platinum Technology): *http://www.platinum.com*

Realism 3D (iDREAM Software, L.L.C.): *http://www.idreamsoftware.com/*

Spazz3D: *http://www.spazz3d.com/*

3DWebmaster (Superscape, Inc.): *http://www.superscape.com*

Guides and Conferences on Virtual Worlds

Active Worlds: *http://www.activeworlds.com/*
Requires download of free client software to link to hundreds of 3-D worlds.

Contact Consortium: *http://www.ccon.org/*
Everything you want to know about life inside cyberspace as virtually experienced by real people and their avatars can be found here.

The Palace: *http://www.thepalace.com*
Probably the most successful virtual community developed in North America.

Quitting the "Technology of the Month" Club

Ray Olszewski

Ray Olszewski has worked as an economist, a statistician, a network manager, a Web software developer, and a teacher of writing, computer programming, and mathematics. He is currently an independent consultant. He can be reached at *ray@comarre.com*.

"Okay, everyone, time to move out. Dumke, take the point!"
"Sure thing, sarge."

We've all seen movies about World War II with dialogue like this. And we all know what it means: Private Dumke is about to die. In the next minute or so, he'll be shot by a sniper, or step on a land mine, or turn a corner and walk into a German patrol. All as predictable as sunrise.

Fast forward to the nineties. Computer use, LANs, and the Internet are growing at explosive rates. New technologies appear weekly, and the term *Internet year* (meaning a couple of months) becomes commonplace. Businesses, schools, libraries, consumers—we all need to stay abreast of the newest developments, keep our equipment and software up to the minute, to realize the enormous benefits that will come from the new capabilities that are moving us into the Information Age.

Yeah, right. Take the point, Dumke.

Technology Acquisition Is Not Like a Book Club

Although some vendors allow clients to try out their products, more often than not problems do not arise until you've already invested time, effort, and money. Of course, exploring new technologies and opportunities is fun, or it is so central to our work that we have no choice but to do it. For many of us, though, staying at the leading edge of technology (these days commonly called "the bleeding edge") is a cost without commensurate benefits.

The process repeats itself regularly. Interesting technical ideas are painted as first-order breakthroughs, either by overzealous programmers or self-serving marketers. The trade and popular press expand on the idea—why not, since these people are paid to use high-end equipment, look at new products, and spend their time fiddling with their systems instead of simply using them. Products are rushed to market or, increasingly, to widespread distribution in so-called "beta" versions (*beta* is a Greek word that means "infested with bugs"). Seminars are offered and books are published in the effort to be first.

Then reality sets in. The idea dies, or retreats to the specialized niche where it really is useful. We, or our organizations, end up with burdensome equipment expenditures, orphaned equipment and software, and skills in using systems that promised much but never delivered. We become cyber-Dumkes, recycled characters in a computer game in which we go out to be shot, only to start over next time and get shot again.

There's an alternative, though. Conservative use of technology, motivated by a healthy cynicism about the promised benefits of the latest "new and improved" software and hardware, can provide most of the benefit of new technology without much of the waste and pain.

Consider two recent examples of technologies that promised the moon but delivered almost nothing.

> *VRML.* Virtual Reality Modeling Language (VRML) is an extension to the World Wide Web that allows Web-content creators to instruct a browser to display images that have the appearance of 3-D. Visually, it's a very cool technology, and about five years ago, it was touted as the next big thing for the Web. In the end, it came to nothing and now occupies a tiny and shrinking niche. The major browsers didn't provide easy support for it, it demanded a lot of bandwidth, and real users of the Web just didn't find it very useful. (See the chapter titled "Virtual Reality Primer for Cybrarians," on page 252 in this book, for more on VRML.)
>
> *Push.* Another Web technology, Push lets Web-content providers send pages to your browser at their initiative, instead of waiting for you to ask for them. About two years ago, it was the next big thing for the Web. In the end, the application looked trivial, and LAN managers saw it as a burden because of the bandwidth it consumed and the degree to which it soaked up employee time in incidentals. (See the chapter titled Push Technology: Something Old, Something New for an in-depth discussion of push technology.)

Both these technologies, and many others, survived their brushes with stardom, settling down into small, niche roles. But almost anyone who made a significant investment in software to support these capabilities wasted his or her money and time.

Even technologies that ultimately become successful can be adopted too soon. The various versions of the Windows operating system certainly are a successful technology now, but early adopters struggled. Versions prior to

Windows 3.1 were buggy on the desktop and too prone to crashes and compatibility problems to be anything but a headache for the people who used them. Until Version 4.0 (some would even include 4.0), the same was true for servers using Windows NT.

And what about the World Wide Web itself? In hindsight, its emergence as a centerpiece of the Internet can appear inevitable, but six years ago, when the Web was still new, its success was not apparent. In 1993, at least three technologies—the Web, Gopher, and WAIS (Wide Area Information Server)—were competing for the central role in information transfer over the Internet. Each had its strengths, each its weaknesses. Exactly why the Web emerged the winner remains unclear, but the answer lies in the fact that its limitations were overcome, not that it was, initially, decisively superior to the alternatives.

In this case, early adopters of Web technologies prospered, while others found themselves with orphan investments (such as WAIS-based or text-based library catalog front ends that were difficult to retool for the Web).

The key to minimizing the waste of time and money is to focus on near-term needs, adopting technologies that will deliver real value to your organization and its patrons over a fairly short planning period, say, two years at the outside. Avoid strategies that are based on more distant goals, or on metaphoric objectives like "get ready for the Information Age" or "be ready for the twenty-first century."

The details of this strategy are familiar to the point of being clichés. In areas outside technology adoption, you would surely follow them as routinely as you breathe. The key is to avoid suspending your critical judgment when technology is the focus.

What to Do?

First, always focus on concrete, realizable benefits that will accrue to your organization or its clients within a reasonable time frame—best under a year and never more than three years out.

Second, whenever you evaluate a technology option, consider all the costs of introducing it—not just the direct costs of the acquisition, but additional support needed in the form of a faster LAN, new servers, more training and support time, and the like.

Third, focus on personnel requirements up front. This is especially important for technology decisions, as qualified technical personnel are currently scarce and expensive, with strong competition from the private sector.

Finally, be willing to invest in areas where the technology seems to be stable. For example, when I helped design the LAN for a former employer about six years ago, we intentionally minimized investment in areas where we saw change to be rapid and uncertainty high. At the same time, we saw the site as difficult to wire physically, so we installed what was then a very high end system, all ready for 100-megabit transmission. Looking

264   CUTTING EDGE OR BLEEDING EDGE: YOU MAKE THE CALL

back, that emphasis proved right. When the site moves from 10-megabit to 100-megabit Ethernet, it will need only to replace the electronics and make some small changes in the wire terminations.

How do you do this? Let's look at a few more examples, this time with technologies whose outlook is still uncertain.

Example 1: Server Operating System Choices

Until three years ago, if you operated a LAN or an Internet site with servers, your choices were easy. For local file and print services, you used a PC running NetWare (or a Mac running AppleShare, for the Macintosh sites). For Internet services, you ran some variant of Unix (or, for the largest sites, a minicomputer or mainframe operating system). If you ran a specialized application, such as a library circulation, cataloging, and public-access catalog system, you used NetWare or Unix, whichever ran the package you chose.

Then Microsoft began pushing Windows NT as the server operating system of the future, and it began to make major inroads into both the NetWare and Unix markets. The timing was good for Microsoft because Novell, the company that makes NetWare, was distracted by an effort to acquire a wider range of applications software companies, and its poor customer-support policies seemed designed to alienate its client base. Unix was fragmented, with most suppliers committed to specialized, expensive hardware. For a time, it looked as if NT would achieve in the server market the dominance that Windows already had on the desktop.

This didn't last. To say that NT has its problems isn't to pick on Microsoft; all operating systems (OS) have strengths and weaknesses, and you need to understand each operating system's best use. Windows' historical strength is in its interface, important on the desktop but fairly unimportant in servers. Continued delays in the release of NT 5.0 highlighted the problems with NT—problems with security, remote maintenance, scalability, and basic reliability.

These problems were especially troubling when contrasted with the improvements released for NetWare and Unix in 1998. Novell released NetWare 5 and a set of related products that addressed the most serious shortcomings of NetWare. Thanks largely to Linux, a freeware variant of Unix, the Unix market grew by providing a reliable version suitable for use on Intel-based hardware.

While NT remained an important server OS, both NetWare and Unix (including its freeware variant Linux) were making strong comebacks in the server market by the end of 1998. I expect that all three choices will soon be viable, able to provide the core functions that any LAN/Internet server needs to provide.

How does a conservative, skeptical information technology (IT) manager deal with this market uncertainty? In many ways, this is the toughest area in which to be cautious, since LAN and server upgrades are common. The most important thing to consider is that the cost of replacing your existing system with a totally new one is high, and the benefits, however compellingly presented, probably will not outweigh the total costs, including new equipment, consulting time to deal with the unanticipated problems, retraining of system users, and retraining or replacing of technical support personnel.

If you are equipping a new facility or adding fundamentally new services, incremental upgrades will not be an option. In this case, your biggest problem will be finding the expertise you need to evaluate the alternatives. While I can urge caution here, I cannot suggest a good solution.

Every systems expert I have known (including me) knows more about some alternatives than others. The familiar ones may have as many problems as the unfamiliar ones, but the expert knows those problems and how to solve them, while the unfamiliar server systems present new, puzzling challenges that can seem worse than the familiar ones. Users, too, have their biases, whether in favor of the familiar or the new, supposedly "trouble-free" replacement for a system known to be flawed.

In the end, you have to work hard to make sure that comparisons are fair, that all costs are included, and that a vendor will stand behind its assurances and cost estimates.

Above all, do not view a system upgrade or replacement as more than a small step in a continuing process. The uncertain time will never end. We have not yet had a single server operating system that dominated the market, and we are unlikely to get one soon. Therefore, assume that your LAN will always have to be upgraded incrementally in situations where OS choices have to be made and build in the flexibility to accommodate a mix.

Example 2: Thin Clients

Once upon a time, there were no desktop computers. Desktop access to computers was achieved with CRT-based terminals. Applications ran at a distance, and the computers were maintained by specialists.

In the past fifteen years, improvements in desktop computer technology have moved more and more routine work from remote computers onto the desktop. This shift had substantial benefits, but it came at a price. In large and small organizations, the costs of maintaining desktop computers grew, and the increasing frequency with which software updates were released added to the complexity. Rapid improvements in the underlying hardware shortened the useful lives (or at least the apparent useful lives) of desktop computers, creating pressures for constant upgrades.

To address these problems, we began hearing a few years ago about the idea of a "network computer." The idea was simple: An uncomplicated, inexpensive computer would sit on the desktop, connected to servers that would provide most services, either directly or by downloading needed applications on the fly. The desktop computer would be easy to maintain and need replacement infrequently, while the focus on servers would make upgrades easier to manage.

Though the idea had an attractive sound, many were skeptical. Critics questioned the ability of the industry to deliver low-cost desktop boxes, even ones as limited as this plan called for. They noted that much, perhaps all, of the saving on the desktop would be offset by the costs of faster LANs and more powerful servers. Perhaps most tellingly, they noted that the primary advocate of the network computer was Larry Ellison, CEO of Oracle, a company that specializes in database software and doesn't manufacture any computer equipment.

Though a few models were announced, network computers as such never entered the market in a significant way. But they left a legacy of focus on the total life-cycle cost of computer systems, including initial cost of hardware and software; length of service of the hardware; frequency, cost, and complexity of software upgrades; and training and maintenance. This new focus has achieved little as of yet, though a few so-called zero administration tools have appeared to simplify maintenance of desktop computers.

At this point, the balance between desktop-based applications and server-based applications, or the mix between "fat" and "thin" clients, remains elusive. Once again, for now, the key is to remain flexible, committing only when absolutely necessary and adopting only solutions that have a proven track record.

Example 3: Java

Java is a programming language that was designed to be "platform independent"—that is, to run in the same way on many different types of equipment, including Intel-based PCs running Windows, Macintoshes, and Unix workstations. Though touted by its developers at Sun as a breakthrough, it really continues a decades-long search for the Holy Grail of workable, cross-platform programming and development tools.

Variants of this idea go back at least to the late 1970s, when the "p-system," an implementation of Pascal developed at the University of San Diego, tried to deliver a development and execution environment common to several platforms. It failed to do so, for reasons that I suspect are common to these development efforts: poor performance, a focus on the convenience of developers over the needs of end users, and the proliferation of platform-specific extensions that hampered platform independence.

As Java developed, we saw the same problems emerging with it. Compared to applications developed using compilers that generate machine-specific code, Java applications tended to be slow. Some features were lacking, including at first the provisions needed to address security issues. Most seriously, though, Microsoft challenged the Java standard, first with a competing technology (ActiveX), then by developing a Java variant that incorporated extensions specific to Windows.

At this point, it looks unlikely that Java will realize its initial promise. Although usable on servers and workstations, it offers no compelling advantages over established programming languages. Its main strength lies in the sophistication of its interface with Web browsers, which makes it a serious niche player for the development of improved Web services.

At this point, the cautious network manager would make little or no commitment to Java. Unless you need a commercial application that comes only in a Java version, stay away from supporting Java on your servers. If you need to develop custom software, stay with more established languages for now (C, C++, Visual Basic on Windows systems, Perl on Unix systems).

The major Web browsers already support the running of Java "applets" (programs designed specifically to run within a browser), so this use requires little effort on your part. Until Java applets begin to provide important functions to your clientele, blocking their use is a reasonable course based on their potential to cause security problems.

Conclusion

Your organization is not about technology; it is about providing services effectively to patrons. However, your sources of information about technology are, mostly, people and businesses whose focus is on technology, who are biased to think that a steady stream of technical novelties is critically important.

The rapid pace of improvement in computer hardware and software over the past two decades has, in broad brush, validated the views of the technophiles. That time is changing, as the industry matures. In recent years, we have seen more style than substance, and careful users of technology have the opportunity to control the cost and disruption of upgrades by being selective about their use of new technologies.

8 As the Librarian Turns

ON THE LIGHTER SIDE: ...AND A SMALL CHILD SHALL LEAD THEM

Jim Johnston

I was working on a fresh load of binding the other day. I had just checked materials in, same as every month, when I decided to take a break to stretch my legs. As I was walking through the lobby, something odd struck me. After a moment of standing there, slowly revolving (and getting some pretty strange looks), it dawned on me that the lobby did not match with my childhood memories of just how library lobbies looked. Something important was missing.

Remember the good old days, when every library, regardless of its size, shape, or religious background, had a Card Catalog File sitting majestically in its lobby? If books were your religion, those old massive whacks of semi-fine carpentry were your altars.

Roughly two billion drawers with dull brass fittings, each drawer stuffed to overflowing with little typed cards that listed every single book and volume in the building, cross-referenced under its Dewey Decimal number, title, author's name, and subject.

Remember how it worked? How the patrons would come in and head straight to that looming edifice of information. Once there, they would look up their selection, pinpoint its location in the stacks, and set off to wander through the labyrinth of shelves in search of knowledge.

Those simple days are pretty much gone forever and most of those huge Card Catalog Files have been converted to cheap on-campus housing for college students (I once resided in "Asimov-Azur," myself). Worse than that, their function was replaced by (shudder) computers! Today one is hard pressed to find a library, even a small one, that doesn't have the

---

Reprinted from *College & Undergraduate Libraries* 5, no. 1 (1998): 37–43. Copyright held by Haworth Press. Used with permission.

little plastic tan box of a computer sitting somewhere in the lobby, serenely flashing some sort of screen saver program. A patron comes in, heads for it . . .

. . . And all hell breaks loose.

To begin with, most adult patrons have absolutely no idea what to do with a computer. They either punch keys at random, generally crashing the entire system, or just stand in front of the machine, willing it psychically to do their bidding until one or the other breaks out in tears. (It's a terrible thing to see a Mac cry . . .)

After a few minutes, they seek out the nearest employee to demand information, retribution, or a stiff drink.

Unfortunately, most library employees also have little, if any, knowledge of how to work the damn things. (Many have small children visit their homes weekly to program their VCRs.)

Thankfully, most do know how to make a stiff drink (taught, I am told, as part of the graduate library studies at most major universities), so it's not a total loss.

(Perversely, the most frequent exceptions to this scenario are small children. They seem to be born with a master's degree in computer technology, and generally, after only a few seconds, have not only located their selection, but have updated the programming, done their parents' taxes, played a few games of *Marathon,* and reprogrammed the library's entire system to display various vulgar words on every screen in flashing Day-Glo colors . . . but I digress.)

By the time the patron of yesteryear would be well on his or her way home, today's patron is leaning at a cockeyed slant, his or her fourth martini spilling onto the counter, while frantic employees call around, trying to locate . . . that's right . . . a small child to either find the adult client's selection or to explain the latest vulgar words.

I watched this change occur in various libraries over the years and, although I pitied the hapless librarians desperately trying to adapt, I really sorta enjoyed observing this Keystone Kop method of technology intrude into the Pearl Buck world of the printed word. Loads of laughs and, bottom line, what did I care? I certainly wasn't a librarian and I strongly doubted I'd ever work in a library.

However, this is exactly the situation in which your humble author found himself unwillingly—and unwittingly—thrust, ten years later.

When I was first hired for the position of Binding Assistant, my library had just recently surrendered to Bill Gates and his rabid techno-wienies and changed over to computers. As a matter of fact, I won the position only because my resume listed my fifteen years of working with computers in the military and they were desperate for experienced people. (Another example of why lying on one's resume is generally a bad idea, to be punished at a later date by a whimsical deity.)

Did this faze me? Never! I found the beginner's computer books I needed, with the help of a small child who happened to be passing by. It was a fair trade: I taught him all the vulgar words I had learned in a career of military service.

Thankfully, my screen faced away from the office at large and I was able to fool my coworkers into believing I knew what I was doing by making sure the computer was unplugged and then spending hours hammering on my terminal's dead keyboard. When nobody was looking, I switched in reports I had typed the night before at home on my manual Royal. With the addition of some occasional colorful language and the odd slap to the side of the terminal, it was readily accepted that I, too, was locked in mortal combat with a terminal.

Meanwhile, I studied hard after working hours, cramming years of knowledge into weeks, and in only one month's time was able to locate the "on" switch at my terminal. Bathed in the sickly green terminal light of success, I found it easier to pretend to be using the keyboard. I also found myself getting numerous headaches. (I briefly considered the possibility that the light from the screen might have been killing me . . . then a coworker explained that it wasn't *that* sort of terminal. Who knew?)

Not willing to settle for this small victory, I pressed on and, before I (and, more importantly, my boss) knew it, I had learned enough to transfer all my routine paperwork to the computer. More than that, I also learned how to find any given book in the library, how to do all of my statistics and charts, and how to access the Internet to "surf the Web." (That led to my learning some pretty amazing things regarding sex and First Amendment Rights at some of the darndest sites a man ever spent several weeks of work hours surfing!)

Soon I had converted my position from a "simple pencil and paper, anyone with a high school diploma could do it" job to a "sophisticated, computer-based, only Steve Jobs need apply" cyberjob. From the moment I sat down in the morning, to the second I left at the end of the day, every job involved the computer to some extent.

Although this conversion has ensured my continued employment (I didn't bother writing down any instructions or notes when I made the change, you see), it has, unfortunately, caused a few minor problems with my coworkers, who I like to refer to as "The Gray Haired Mafia."

These are the dear ladies who have been working at the library since its primary function was to store scrolls. (One of my coworkers claims to have had a torrid affair with Dewey, of the Dewey Decimal System, but she's forgetful and might mean Admiral Dewey . . . opinion varies. Another spends her off time trying to serve an overdue bill to descendants of the yutz she claims is responsible for losing the Dead Sea Scrolls in the first place.) They are the unofficial power of library back rooms across the country.

These ladies know how a library should be run. With pencil, paper, and billions of little white cards, to be exact, and without any newfangled devices, i.e., computers.

Needless to say, when I started keeping all my various bits of information and paperwork on the computer, their consensus was that I was either a heretic or a freethinker—either offense deserving of their ultimate punishment: death by lecture. Over hot cups of tea and cold mah-jongg tiles, they plotted nefarious plans of revenge.

They converged on my desk one special afternoon, when none of them had any medical appointments, and attacked in force! Blue hair to the right of me, dentures to the left. . . . I was trapped! Stories from the Spanish Inquisition flashed through my mind and I wished I could have been facing something as simple as that. I started to gnaw on my right leg in self-defense. Then . . . it happened!

While the Gray Haired Mafia was trying to convince me of the error of my ways through the vicious use of tag-team remembrances of better times, the computer—wisely and correctly deciding that its continued survival depended on staying on the good side of the majority—decided to step out for a smoke until the dust settled. Sensing a possible diversion, I quickly phoned for help, but the National Guard was not available, and I had to settle for just getting my terminal fixed.

As the Gray Haired Mafia slowly danced in victory and told each other how my computer crashing at that precise moment proved that "Man Was Never Intended to Input," the Campus Computer Clowns pedaled their little red car to my side of the office and started tumbling out. I stared, aghast, at their bright costumes, rubber noses, floppy feet, and gag pocket protectors. This was a rescue?!

Little did I know that the CCC consisted of some of the most knowledgeable first-year computer science students our noble institution possessed, all of whom were dedicated to service, passing grades, and sucking up to their professors in a big way (I'm talking black hole type suction here, folks). A Day-Glo colored scatological obscenity flickered briefly on my screen; I agreed with it wholeheartedly and quickly moved away from my terminal in alarm.

They came, they tested, they squirted each other with seltzer and honked their large red noses. They fixed my terminal, gave me a joy buzzer handshake and left.

After which, of course, my terminal was even more messed up than before. Oh, the original problem was fixed . . . but their "fix" trashed two other needed functions, including my beloved Web surfing program. When I called them back, I quickly learned the first rule of using a computer in a university library. To wit, "Leave well enough alone!" (The second rule, I understand, is, "Never try to warm your cappuccino by setting it on the monitor.")

Unfortunately, I was but a babe in the woods and had not learned those infamous rules. I made the mistake of calling the Clowns back in to fix their fix. (And wondered how I could keep my cappuccino from going cold so fast.)

When they arrived, I explained what wasn't working now, and the head Clown—hearing of the loss of my Web surfing application—asked me if I had remembered to stand while waiting for it to load. "Stand?!?" I replied. "Why on earth would I have to stand while waiting for it to load? Static electricity interfering with the program opening or loading from the hard disk or some such?"

"Naw . . . tradition." At my blank look, he continued, "Haven't you ever heard that 'they also surf who just stand and wait,' dude?" and dissolved into disturbingly demented giggles. I refrained from strangling him, but only because I still needed my terminal fixed.

Two custard pies and a whoopee cushion later, they departed and I had learned my lesson. "Leave well enough alone" was firmly embedded in my mind. When I attempted to boot up my terminal, I also gained an intense appreciation of the phrases "program crash," "hardware crash," and "Where do the librarians keep the martini fixings?"

My terminal was now a five-thousand-dollar paperweight, with only the occasional vulgar word flashing across its screen to indicate any activity. Worse, my cappuccino was ice cold.

I contemplated calling the CCC back in . . . for all of ten seconds. Then I eyed my old typewriter with resigned consideration. Perhaps a step backwards . . . ?

No. I turned back to my terminal with renewed determination. The work must go on! The books must be cataloged! The computers must be up and running! The nervous breakdowns must be experienced!

I took matters into my own hands. I fell back on twenty years of military training and discipline. I confidently took charge of the situation, calmly appraised the difficulty, wisely considered my options and smartly performed the appropriate action needed:

I went out and found a small child.

Now my computer even gets ESPN!

Rupert Giles, Techno-Terror, and Knowledge as the Ultimate Weapon

GraceAnne A. DeCandido

GraceAnne A. DeCandido (*ladyhawk@well.com*), MLS, is a writer, teacher, speaker, and consultant in her own company, Blue Roses Editorial and Web Consulting. She has been a book reviewer for twenty-five years, worked in public, academic, and special libraries, and held editorial posts at several major library periodicals culminating in the editorship of the late, lamented *Wilson Library Bulletin*. She has spoken about Giles at Oxford University, his alma mater, and at the California Library Association, his state professional group.

I am not alone in the belief that the role of school librarian Rupert Giles on television's *Buffy the Vampire Slayer* has done more for the image of the profession than anything in the past fifty years, with the possible exception of former American Library Association President Patricia Glass Schuman's appearance on *Larry King Live*. We now have a hero librarian in Giles: a pop culture idol whose love of books and devotion to research hold the key to saving the universe—every week.

For those who might inexplicably have missed it, here is a brief summary of the dramatis personae in the "Buffyverse." Giles is the Watcher: the source of training, counterintelligence, and guidance for high schooler Buffy Summers, the one of her generation chosen as the Vampire Slayer. Giles is the librarian and Buffy a student at Sunnydale High School, set in a balmy southern California town. Sunnydale is notable for being situated on the Hellmouth: a place where vampires, demons, and the forces of darkness gather as bees to honey. Buffy, a small, delicate-looking blonde, relies on Giles not only for adult support, but also for the research necessary for her to do that for which the Vampire Slayer has been chosen.

A version of this chapter appeared as "Bibliographic Good vs. Evil in *Buffy the Vampire Slayer*," *American Libraries* 30, no. 8 (Sept. 1999): 44–47.

Buffy's buddies (called, affectionately, the Slayerettes) include the never-cool Xander; his best friend, the brilliant and fashion-impaired Willow; Xander's reluctant sweetie, the gorgeous airhead Cordelia; and Willow's occasional genius (and occasional werewolf) boyfriend, Oz. They comprise Buffy's support group. They meet and conduct much of their research in the school library. Giles, whose collection development policy must be an extraordinary document, has access in the stacks to a vast number of volumes on vampire and demon lore, the occult, witchcraft, spellcasting, and other rarities not usually found among the copies of *Huckleberry Finn* and *Weetzie Bat.*

Others in the cast definitely come from the dark side. Buffy's boyfriend (and, later, ex-honey) is a brooding, beautiful, 200-year-old Irish vampire named Angel, who has been cursed with a conscience. There are many vampires, demons, and Evil Guys, some of whom make multiple appearances.

Giles: Our Great Sage and Sex Symbol

It is a heady experience for any profession to find itself an integral part of a wildly popular TV series. How much more so for librarians, who have been bedeviled with a poor public image since at least the nineteenth century. Giles, of course, moves across the stereotype in other, not necessarily positive ways—he is both male and technologically inept.

Giles is tweedy, occasionally befuddled, and very wise, with a certain amount of darkness in his own past. He dropped out of Oxford to pursue magick, but then moved to the British Library, and thence to Sunnydale where duty called him. He comes from a family of Watchers, reads a number of languages, and, until her untimely death, had a passionate relationship with the Romany technopagan computer instructor, Jenny Calendar.

We have a librarian model who is elegant, deeply educated, well if fussily dressed, handsome, and charged with eroticism. In a world of teens where parents rarely make an appearance, he is a stable, friendly, and supportive adult. He lives the faith that answers can be found, and, most often, found in the pages of a book.

Giles is icon and image for us; in him we see our quotidian struggles to provide the right information and the right data resolved into a cosmic drama with the forces of darkness, some of which are extremely attractive, by the way. We love Giles because at last we have a pop image for our uneasy relationship with dark and light, information and story, books and technology.

We love Giles and we loved his romance with the computer instructor cum Romany Wiccan. We mourned when—and this is as emotionally complicated as can be—the vampire with a soul who loved Buffy murders Jenny, whom Giles loved. We see Giles struggle valiantly with information sources, we can see his love of story, we can see, as Xander says, that "knowledge is the ultimate weapon" and that format is the least of our problems when there are vampires and demons about.

Giles: "I Believe the Subtext Here Is Rapidly Becoming Text"

The librarians who follow Buffy find a great deal of library lore and information-seeking behavior, as well as an occasional drop of genuine wisdom, in the words of Giles, Buffy, and the denizens of Sunnydale. We can deconstruct some dialogue from the show (with citations to episodes) for our own delectation and amusement, as follows.

Willow: "How is it you always know this stuff? You always know what's going on. I never know what's going on."
Giles: "Well, you weren't here from midnight until six researching it."
—"Angel"

The plodding nature of most research cannot be eliminated, even by brilliance and magic. It is Giles's particular gift to cast a glamor over the kind of dogged reference we practice daily. He invests the methodical search for the fact that will solve the problem at hand with a kind of fierce joy, but he never underestimates its cost in time or care.

Giles: "I'm sure my books and I are in for a fascinating afternoon."
—"Phases"
Giles (echoing Buffy): "'Get my books. Look stuff up.'"
—"The Pack"
Willow: "I'm sure he will. He's like . . . Book Man!"
—"Passion"

Books are central. It is in books that Giles, as the Watcher, finds the images, the information, the incantation, the lore that will assist Buffy in her struggle against the Hellmouth and its universe of monsters. Although Giles relies upon Willow to search the Internet for materials not easily accessible in print, like newspaper records and police logs, Giles believes that what he needs to know for Buffy's sake lies in his many volumes at home and at work.

Giles also makes that necessary leap of faith common to all good librarians: He bridges the chasm between the information as it lives in the text and the transfer of that information into a form the Slayerettes and Buffy can actually use. Sometimes that means literal translation, other times it means recasting what he reads into stories or tag lines or aphorisms that make sense to the teens he serves. The sacredness of the book, the literal power of words, underscore the action in Buffy's world. They form the matrix and latticework for all that terrific Pow! Kick! Stake! stuff that happens later.

Xander: "He's like SuperLibrarian. Everyone forgets, Willow, that knowledge is the ultimate weapon."
—"Never Kill a Boy on the First Date"

Although snide comments about Giles's profession abound, the core belief that knowledge is the answer underlies all. This is apparent from

Xander's remark even though he and the others are often cavalier about regular school assignments. What can be found in the library is central. There are many weapons to be had in Sunnydale. Buffy uses the classic silver cross and stake, among others. Giles has an array of medieval weaponry, and the Slayerettes have a very high level of rapier teen wit, peppered with pop-cult references and sly asides.

The thirst to know, however, is at the core of it all: to know the forces of darkness, to name them, and hence to defang them; to know themselves, as they dance on the edge of maturity; to search out the specifics of how to overmaster a particular demon along with the principles of how knowledge can lead to larger truths. What a message for us to emblazon on our t-shirts and on our hearts.

Angel: "They're children, making up bedtime stories of friendly vampires to comfort themselves in the dark."

Willow: "Is that so bad? I mean the dark can get pretty dark. Sometimes you need a story."

—"Lie to Me"

Willow places her hand precisely on a central truth of Buffy, and of librarianship. Sometimes these teens need a story to cover themselves for a lost assignment or a lost weekend. Sometimes, though, they need a story to tell themselves to get through the latest horrific vision or ghastly demise. Sometimes, it is the story itself that brings both comfort and information: In the beginning of the third season, a voiceover from Jack London's *Call of the Wild* was used to great effect.

We know this as we work. We know the reference desk as a continuing story with cliché and banality along with a flashy denouement or a trailer for next week. We know the story of staff meetings where we wish a wooden stake could turn misbegotten shape to dust. We know the stories we tell ourselves when one more technical problem threatens the simplest task. And sometimes those stories hold a goblin, because how else could the machines on which so much of our work lives are predicated be so damnedly recalcitrant?

Buffy also identifies her role as a storybook hero in "Killed by Death," when she tells the child in the hospital, "We both know there are real monsters. But there are also real heroes that fight monsters. And that's me." The story enables us to see not only the teen Buffy as a true hero, but Giles, Book Man, SuperLibrarian, as a hero also.

Jenny (to Giles): "The divine exists in cyberspace the same as out here."

—"I Robot, You Jane"

Giles has definite issues with computers and online technology. He is a living metaphor for what those of us *d'un certain âge* might have gone through as the profession we thought we had joined transmuted itself into something very, very Else.

The core of librarians who got their MLS degrees twenty-five years ago and more are now doing things professionally that were unimaginable to the selves we were then. We came to librarianship because we loved the sound of words talking to each other, rubbing up against each other; or because the world inside a story was far more real to us than the world inside our neighborhoods; or because we loved chasing an idea around. For many of us, librarianship originally was a choice to separate ourselves from workplaces that were less humane, less involved in the drama of people's lives.

It came as a shock to some of us, as it does to Giles, that the glass box (the computer Jenny calls "the good box") could also be a tool in the search for knowing, and an increasingly indispensable tool. In "I Robot, You Jane," Giles tells Jenny, "If it's to last, then the getting of knowledge should be tangible" in the smell and texture of old volumes. In the same episode, Giles confesses to Buffy that computers fill him with "childlike terror." Jenny gently chides him for living in the Middle Ages, and assures him he will enter the new century with a few years to spare.

Buffy: "You're the Watcher, I just work here."
Giles: "Yes. I must consult my books."
—"When She Was Bad"
Giles: "I'd best head to the library. Research beckons."
—"Killed By Death"
Buffy: "But, Giles, it's one thing to be a Watcher and a librarian . . . The point is, no one blinks an eye if you wanna spend all your days with books."
—"What's My Line (Part 1)"

Giles takes a lot of kidding because of his perceived stuffiness, his single-minded approach to problems, and his apparent lack of current awareness. However, the kidding doesn't negate how fully the Slayerettes are invested in Giles as both a mentor and a symbol of adult comfort and reassurance. He knows what his job is, so do they, and so do we.

Young adult and reference librarian Lesley Knieriem of the South Huntington Public Library (New York) said it well in an e-note: "Giles is appealing to librarians in that he portrays us as we like to think we are: enormously intelligent, literate, genteel, sensitive, devoted to our patrons, with a sexy, ferocious 'ripper' concealed within, only to be let out when needed to slay the demons of ignorance. Yes, he does fit many of the stereotypes: bookish, stuffy, reserved, technophobic (this last isn't any of us!). Giles embraces his stuffiness, pokes gentle fun at it, and transcends it."

Giles: "To forgive is an action of compassion, Buffy. It's not done because people deserve it. It's done because they need it."
—"I Only Have Eyes for You"

We have all had supervisors who have done unforgivable things to us; we may have done a few ourselves to those we supervise. We have all had patrons who have fought their particular demons right in front of the checkout desk, and we wanted to avert our eyes. Giles, given to pronouncements but rarely to exhortation, here states a truth as cleanly as any prophet. We hope it comforted Buffy; it can certainly comfort us.

Giles: "You mean life?"
Buffy: "Yeah. Does it get easy?"

Giles:	"What do you want me to say?"
Buffy:	"Lie to me."
Giles:	"Yes, it's terribly simple. The good guys are always stalwart and true. The bad guys are easily distinguished by the pointy horns or black hats. And, uh, we always defeat them and save the day. No one ever dies, and everybody lives happily ever after."
Buffy:	"Liar."

—"Lie to Me"

We have seen that the books and materials that provide us with information and textual analysis of the bad guys can also provide us with stories wherein we conquer the demons and go forth. Giles reminds us that some days, the dragon wins. And that good and evil are rarely so separate that we can distinguish them clearly without the white light of study and analysis. Finally, we might look at the words of another character who, we might say, knows that self-knowledge is the ultimate weapon. His name is Whistler.

Whistler:	"Bottom line is, even if you see 'em coming, you're not ready for the big moments. No one asks for their life to change, not really . . . The big moments are gonna come, can't help that. It's what you do afterward that counts. That's when you find out who you are."

—"Becoming, Part 1"

Whistler:	"There's moments in your life that make you. That set the course of who you're gonna be. Sometimes they're little, subtle moments. Sometimes . . . they're not."

—"Becoming, Part 2"

Whistler, nominally a demon, has as his function to maintain the balance between good and evil—a metaphor for technical services if ever there was one. It is he who provides Angel with the opportunity to even the odds for Buffy, and brings them together. Whistler indulges in a bit of philosophy that might be as useful in our lives as in our so-potent art. Change will come, and it is what we do when it comes that matters. We have our tools.

Indispensable Buffy References

Golden, Christopher, and Nancy Holder with Keith R. A. DeCandido. *Buffy the Vampire Slayer: The Watcher's Guide.* New York: Pocket/S&S, 1998.

The Episode Guide included (written by my son) gives the writers credit for all these great lines, episode by episode.

There are many Buffy websites, official and not-so. For Giles groupies, however, there is nothing like Sonja Marie's The Official Giles' Appreciation Society Panters Home Page (*http://www.geocities.com/Television City/7728/gaspers.html*) and its Words of Wisdom from the Watcher (*http://www.geocities.com/TelevisionCity/7728/quotes.html*). The official *Buffy the Vampire Slayer* site is *http://www.buffy.com/*.

Overcoming Image: Strategies for Librarians in the New Millennium

Jan M. Houghton and Ross J. Todd

Jan M. Houghton (*jan.houghton@uts.edu.au*) is a senior lecturer in the Department of Information Studies, University of Technology, Sydney. She has extensive experience in teaching future library and information professionals and setting them on the path for continuing their own professional development. Teaching and research interests include the development of the information infrastructure, the role of information agencies, and changes in the information industry.

Ross J. Todd (*ross.todd@uts.edu.au*) is head of the Department of Information Studies, University of Technology, Sydney. He teaches and researches in the information user behavior area. He is also deputy chair of the Board of Education of the Australian Library and Information Association, which develops educational policy for the library and information sector.

Something about the idea of a new millennium is causing us to stop and take stock of where we are now and where we would like to be in the grand scheme of things. Many in the library profession are also choosing this time to reexamine the role of librarians and libraries in the twenty-first century. Rapid developments in information and communication technology are also acting as catalysts for change as librarians both welcome the benefits and fear becoming irrelevant in the electronic environment. Bound up with this is a concern about professional image; professions have long recognized that a strong, positive image is important for obtaining status and power in the community generally and in specific organizations.

Writing and talking about image has been a preoccupation, even an obsession, for the library profession. However, more energy, ink, and outrage have been invested in bemoaning what is seen by many librarians as a negative image than in providing constructive and workable strategies for addressing it. The writing is repetitive—telling and retelling that librarians are sorely misunderstood by the media and the general population—and the result of this is to reinforce the stereotype without providing any real guidance for the future.

What do librarians really think about themselves as professionals? How do they think the public sees them and why? How would they like others to see them? What is the reality of the public image of librarians and their role? What is the profession doing about its image?

To find some answers, we analyzed over one hundred items on image published between 1970 and 1997 (the full report was commissioned by the Australian Library and Information Association in 1997). One thing became obvious very early in our research—a perceived negative image of librarians and libraries is a pervasive and perennial part of the culture, literature, and practice of librarianship. In other words, many in the profession believe it has a low public image; this perception is long-standing and influences practice in a substantial way.

In this chapter, we will describe briefly the main findings from our literature analysis and then discuss some broad strategies for enhancing the image of the profession and for marketing it as one with a dynamic future. A more detailed discussion of images that exist within the profession (self-image) and as expressed by its clients and the general public can be found in an earlier paper.[1]

Writing On Image

The material examined ranged from detailed historical overviews, empirical research findings, and other scholarly analyses to other types of material reflecting the experiences and views of practitioners (you will find a short reading list at the end of this chapter). As expected, much of the writing about image is by librarians and is published in the library literature; very little appeared elsewhere.

We found several conferences that had focused on the question of image and status and some large-scale surveys. Although much of the material originated in the United States, particularly in the 1980s and 1990s, the concern with image is international and ongoing. New items are found each time a search is done, and there are several websites now that focus on image. Interestingly, there is also a substantial amount of material about how librarians and libraries are portrayed in literature (novels, poetry, drama) and in the media (film and television) and a large body of humorous material.

What Is Meant by Professional Image?

Image relates not only to individuals but also to what they do and where they do it; in this case, to librarians, library work, and libraries. Perceptions of image are made up of many factors; roles, titles, capability, behavior, social status, and pay levels are some of those mentioned.

Perceptions are influenced very much by the experiences of the individual. Academic and corporate librarians, for example, are more likely to take a positive view than public and school librarians, who do most of the writing about the negative image or stereotype. Why this should be so would make an interesting study in itself, as would the fact that much of the writing is from male librarians out of proportion to their numbers in the profession. Another curious finding from our analysis was that, although many people write about image, very few attempt to define what is meant by it. (Koren is a useful reference for this; a standard dictionary is also a good starting point.[2])

What Are the Myths and Realities of the Image of Librarians and Libraries in the 1990s?

First, the stereotypical image certainly exists because we see it frequently in fiction, commercial film, television, advertising, and cartoons. Although considerable variation exists in the portrayal of the image of the librarian, stereotypical characteristics relate both to occupational role and personality and include positive as well as negative views.

Reported descriptions of personality include negative terms, such as *spinster, snooty,* and *authoritarian,* and positive terms, such as *kindly, helpful,* and *smart;* on occupation, terms include *tedious, clerical,* and *technical* as well as *people-oriented, reliable,* and *valuable.* Such stereotypical images are coupled with the general view in the literature that people are puzzled by what librarians actually do for a living, aside from retrieve and stamp books and collect fines.

There are some interesting historical accounts of the development of the stereotype, particularly the feminine aspect (see Newmyer for an example).[3] However, there is a clear difference between what librarians see as their public image based on this stereotype and what research has found to be the public image. Librarians perceive themselves generally as undervalued, not recognized, and not appreciated; they tend to convey a self-defeating image, and it is hard to find examples of positive writing from librarians other than those in the corporate world. Surveys conducted by library professional bodies have found mixed responses on self-image; for example, the 1988 study by the United States Special Library Association found that librarians thought fairly highly of themselves but didn't believe others did.[4]

What little research there is shows that, though there is a range of public perceptions, library users are generally positive in their assessment of libraries and librarians. Librarians are seen by many as effective and intelligent problem solvers with a high level of research, technical, and specialist skills; they are seen as socially important and their work essential.

Libraries are accepted as a part of the social infrastructure now and for the foreseeable future. There is almost no research-based evidence that suggests members of the public believe the negative stereotypical image is the reality; they laugh at it and reproduce it, but have no trouble distinguishing the real from the cartoon. This positive research evidence is neither referred to nor cited in the bulk of the literature on image written by librarians, who appear to be unaware of this research.

Research studies of individuals and groups who use library services indicated that most formed an opinion of librarians in childhood, specifically in schools. Findings vary but generally respondents reported positive experiences with librarians, and portrayed them as educated, with considerable expertise and skills, and with positive personal attributes, such as dedicated, responsible, responsive, approachable, and imaginative. Some examples of this research are listed at the end of this chapter.

Librarians writing about what they perceive as being a negative public image and its impact on the development of the profession offer many suggestions for why this situation exists. Some of the more common reasons are listed here with an interpretation in parentheses.

Public lack of knowledge of the role and importance of library work. (Members of the public don't appreciate us because they don't know what we do so it's their fault.)

The label of *librarian* and title of *library* are old-fashioned and reinforce negative ideas. (If we give ourselves a sexy modern name, image problems will go away.)

The nature of library work is the problem. (We think it's boring so it's no wonder the public does, too.)

Professional indifference to social and political issues. (We will seem more relevant if we start taking sides.)

Poor service delivery. (It's the fault of those other libraries and librarians who haven't jumped on the technology bandwagon.)

Poor marketing. (All we need to change our image is some good public relations.)

Although there is probably a grain of truth in all these suggestions, they are at best speculative and based on anecdotal experience rather than research. We assume there is an image problem without clearly defining it, and we come up with reasons for it—the public for not understanding, the media for not making us look good, those other librarians who resist change, or our organizations for not providing enough resources. However, there is no systematic research evidence that supports particular causes or identifies specific effects, and, without that, libraries can waste money and librarians can waste time with marketing strategies that have little effect.

Strategies for Developing a Positive Image

As with the volume of writing on aspects of image, the writing on strategic approaches to addressing the stereotype and improving professional image tends to be superficial. Practitioners write about what they think should be done or what they did in their library; however, there is no evidence of careful planning or systematic evaluation of alternative approaches.

A range of strategies and marketing initiatives are suggested as solutions without any real analysis of the problem that is meant to be solved and of what the strategy is meant to achieve. This is partly due of course to the limited research on image itself and to the lack of any clear or consistent idea within the profession of what the preferred image is. If we don't want to be seen as the stereotype, what do we want to be seen as? A study by the Benton Foundation in 1996 found library leaders themselves unable to agree on what should be done for the future.[5] Remember, when next reading a report of "how we did good in our library" or "how we changed our image," ask yourself what evidence there is that the activity had any impact on image or established the library's reputation with its client group.

Outlined here are some general approaches to developing the image of librarianship that we found had some basis in the research and from which specific strategies can be identified, implemented, and, most importantly, evaluated. Obviously, there will need to be differences in approaches depending on the type of library—public, school, academic, or corporate—but generally these are ideas to think about as individual librarians and as a profession aiming to move beyond the stereotype.

Make Visible the Benefits, Rather Than Roles, Tasks, and Genders

One survey asked users in a range of libraries to list what they thought librarians did.[6] The top three answers were: issue and return books, shelve books, and help readers—all highly visible and routine tasks. This suggests that there is a need to rethink the visible work practices and recognize that image is a reflection of what is seen as much as what is known. If people perceive librarians as clerical assistants doing routine tasks and enforcing rules and regulations, it is because that is what they actually see librarians doing—charging out books, collecting fines, looking up catalogs, and so on.

Improving the public face of librarians will contribute to a more positive public image; for example, focusing on the client's needs rather than managing the collection, explaining rather than rigidly enforcing rules, remembering that most people develop their image of libraries from childhood experiences. Rather than trying to "educate" members of the public by telling them what we do, show them through their own experiences.

Be Clear about the Role of Libraries and Librarians

There is some evidence that confusion and ambiguity within the library profession about its own role and priorities is partly responsible for the apparent failure of libraries to claim a central position in the information society. There is, for example, often a mismatch between mission statements about meeting needs and the domination of day-to-day activities. How many librarians see themselves as information experts and put themselves forward as information leaders in their organization or in the community?

According to Miller, the history of librarianship is clouded by the absence of clearly defined priorities.[7] Miller asks: What is the priority? Is it preservation or service? Is it educational? Informational? Recreational? Cultural? Is it to preserve and affirm a country's indigenous culture? Or should the library diversify and specialize its holdings? Should it be based on popular appeal or social good? Miller suggests that in an attempt to be all things to all people, the library has failed to establish a real purposeful identity, and public indifference and perceived low image have been major outcomes. So, establish the purpose of the library, determine the priorities, and then sell the message.

Encourage Proactivity Rather Than Reactivity in the Workplace

Some research suggests that the characteristics of conservatism and passivity often attributed to librarians arise because they appear to be indifferent to political and social issues—described by one writer as supplying information that nobody wants but failing to supply answers to the real puzzles of life.[8] Librarians have followed a code of ethics that says they should demonstrate neutrality and objectivity and be value-free, not allowing personal values to affect the quality of service.

There is an argument that treating all users as equals and providing services in a fair and nonjudgmental way discourages librarians from giving priority to those most in need of services; that is, librarians fail to get involved in the real information needs of people as they try to administer to all.[9] Something to think about here!

Rethink Your Marketing of Library Services to Promote Real Benefits

Libraries need to effectively market their benefits in very tangible ways and to lobby and campaign to increase public visibility. Traditionally, librarians have not always been good marketing protagonists for their services, arguing that the public is supposed to know what librarians can do for them. Many library marketing campaigns seem to focus on trivia—for example, a poster campaign that asked "What is arachibutyrophobia? Have a question? Call your librarian"; others focus on special events, such as Children's Book Week, but fail to reach the public consciousness with the full extent of library information services. Libraries are at the forefront of the information and communication revolution and should be trumpeting the benefits of this to the world.

Public relations needs to be built into the management structure of libraries to ensure effective publicity, coordination of public relations functions, the fostering of links with user groups, informing the client community, and identifying and promoting benefits. Use of local press and exhibitions (not in the library) are presented as possible strategies. Also suggested is the establishment of a local publicity advisory committee that networks with other organizations to publicize their activities.

Publicize Image Solutions, not Image Problems

The profession needs to stop writing and talking about the stereotype, stop claiming that this contributes to and reinforces the poor self-image, stop proclaiming that the stereotype is the fault of any one individual or segment of the community, and work out and publicize a preferred identity that is definitive, easily understood, and lived out in actions. We need to learn to laugh much more at the stereotype, accept that all professions have one, and get on with clearly articulating the message of what we do.

Each member of the library profession should take to heart this message: Stop criticizing the profession and begin speaking about it in a positive way.[10] We need to clarify the issues and begin working on them, and, most importantly, we need to publish more research-based material rather than continue with opinion and anecdote only.

Be Proactive about Image

Librarians need to be more proactive about image and respond in a proactive way when harmful stereotypes are presented in the media or organizations—for example, by sending letters to companies that exploit negative images. The reaction should not be just to complain but to point out that the organization may be alienating its consumer base by such action.

At the same time, evidence can be provided of enlightened librarianship as vital, active, and beneficial. It may be that negative stereotypical images persist because individual professionals have neglected to act in unison to eradicate them.[11] The body of literature analyzed showed little evidence of librarians reporting what they had actually done to deal with instances of negative images or evaluating the outcome in the short term or long term.

Put the User at the Center of Public Relations, Not the Library nor Librarian

Marketing should focus on achievements and on the benefits of information services to the community. Emphasis should be on showing users the benefits they will obtain from the relationship; this is likely to be more helpful than being preoccupied with technical skills and the use of technology.

Similarly, the average customer is not particularly interested in hearing how important librarians are to the community, or what skills they possess, or what complex roles they play, or how misunderstood they are, or how they should be appreciated for the expertise they provide. A library full of computers will not automatically command respect; people will respond to the real benefit of getting information.[12] This puts more emphasis on marketing the library in terms of benefits to individuals and groups—that is, moving the focus from the collection to information and the user.

Understanding clients' needs and matching services to needs is seen as critical to improving both performance and image. By focusing on the benefits to their clients, librarians will demonstrate how important they are to the well-being, decision making, and success of the community and organizations. It is no longer enough for libraries to be social, friendly, and useful places; they must also be seen as good value for the money.

Pay Appropriate Wages and Provide Developmental Career Paths and Opportunities

One research study concluded that librarians perceive that they have a career path that doesn't lead far and that they have difficulty accepting that their jobs have limited horizons.[13] Comparative studies on occupational status often show librarianship as having a low status as a prospective career. It is seen as socially important but lacking power because it is a "helping" profession; others link low occupational status to relatively low salaries and poor career progression.

Another problem is that our profession usually promotes the library and not the librarian. These are issues for the profession as a whole to address, but individuals have a role to play in lobbying professional bodies to take action.

Moving Forward

The most important messages coming out of our analysis of the literature on image can be summarized in the following list of action points:

Take direct action. Individual librarians need to confront perceived negative images through direct action rather than through rhetoric. Although image is a collective problem, it will not improve unless individuals deal with it at their own work level. This includes lobbying your own professional associations.

Clarify roles and priorities. Focus attention primarily on improving direct interaction with clients. Work from the grassroots up to change the stereotype. Give your clients positive experiences, and the positive image will follow.

Avoid library bashing. Librarians need to avoid becoming their own worst enemies, particularly through their own professional literature. Celebrate and promote user-centered benefits. Write about positives, not negatives.

Encourage research. Examine findings from good research studies and surveys and use the positives to promote a better image. Support research that will investigate and evaluate library practices and provide a guide to how libraries and librarians can best move forward to the new millennium.

Resources

Bowden, R., and D. Wijasuriya, eds. "The Status, Reputation and Image of the Library and Information Professional." *Proceedings of the IFLA Pre-Session Seminar, Delhi, 24–28 August, 1992.* The Hague: IFLA Publications, 1994.

Carmichael, J. "The Male Librarian and the Feminine Image: A Survey of Stereotype, Status, and Gender Perceptions." *LISR* 14 (1992): 411–446.

Scherdin, M., and A. Beaubien. "Shattering Our Stereotype: Librarians' New Image." *Library Journal* 120, no. 12 (1995): 35–38.

White, J. J. "A New Criterion to Measure Librarianship." *Libri* 36, no. 4 (1986): 276–281.

Notes

1. J. Houghton, B. Poston-Anderson, and R. Todd, "From Obsession to Power: Changing the Face of Librarians," *Pathways to Knowledge, Proceedings, 5th Biennial Conference* (Adelaide: Austrilian Library and Information Association, in press).
2. J. Koren, "Towards an Appropriate Image for the Information Professional: An International Comparison," *Libri* 41, no. 3 (1991): 170–182.
3. J. Newmyer, "The Image Problem of the Librarian: Femininity and Social Control," *Journal of Library History* 11, no. 1 (1976): 44–67.
4. F. H. Spaulding, "Image of the Librarian/Information Professional; A Special Libraries Association Presidential Task Force," *IFLA Journal* 15, no. 4 (1989): 320–323.
5. *Buildings, Books, and Bytes: Libraries and Communities in the Digital Age* (Washington, D.C.: Benton Foundation, 1996).
6. A. Stevens, "Do They Mean Us . . . ?" *Assistant Librarian* 88, no. 5 (1995): 75–77.

7. L. Miller, "The Self-Image of the Library Profession," *International Library Review* 21, no. 2 (1989): 141–155.
8. C. Curran, "The Astronomy and Sociology of Unpower," *Wilson Library Bulletin* 7, no. 7 (1989): 47–48, 140.
9. Miller, "The Self-Image of the Library Profession."
10. M. Paul and J. Evans, *The Librarians' Self-Starter* (Camberwell, Victoria: Freelance Library and Information Services, 1988.)
11. B. MacDonald, "The Public Image of Libraries and Librarians as the Potential Barrier to Rural Access," *Rural Libraries* 15, no. 1 (1995): 35–57.
12. M. A. Leary, "Books, Microforms, Computers, and Us: Who's Us?" *Microform Review* 21, no. 2 (1992): 57–61.
13. I. Fleck and D. Bawden, "The Information Professional: Attitudes and Images: Examples from Information Services in Law and Medicine," *Journal of Librarianship and Information Science* 27, no. 4 (1995): 215–226.

Finding Things and Telling Stories

Judy Myers

Judy Myers (*jm@uh.edu*) is assistant to the Dean at the University of Houston Libraries. One of the developers of Reference Expert, an expert system for reference work, she has written extensively about applying the knowledge of librarians in the online environment.

Imagine that you are suddenly transported to a new world. It seems benign, although quite different from what you are used to. There are trails to follow, but often just a few steps along the trail take you in an unexpected direction. The colorful space appears to have been constructed by some human sensibility, but in quite a random way. Some parts of the world are dull or even dark and wicked, but there are bazaars and flea markets and dancing bears, and after a while you learn how to make the music play.

Just as humans have done forever in new worlds, you learn to retrace your steps, to remember and make note of the places you liked so you can revisit them, and you begin to learn how to find the sustenance you want and need. Perhaps you begin to want to impose order on this world (also as humans have done forever) by making up stories to explain it, and even by rearranging it, putting things where you think they should be.

As you gather with other people in this space, you begin to share ideas about the world and what it means. If you are a librarian, some of these thoughts will probably be about how to find things and how to arrange the world to make things easier to find. At this point you see that your story about this world is different from everyone else's story. Some see the world as built, others as a happening. People don't agree about arrangement, either. Where should we put the scissors? You have put them next to the paper; I come along and look for them next to the needle and thread.

No world is like any other. People who go to new worlds find that many of their strengths and skills are useful, but many of their specific tools and practices are not. It's human nature to bring our old tools to the new world, just for comfort if nothing else, and to see if they will work. If they do work, they are likely to do so in new ways. If you are camping in the woods, a triangular metal punch for opening cans might not seem to be of much use once the cans run out, but in a pinch it makes a great scraper and a minimal saw. And, things that were discovered but not much used in the old world may be just what is needed in the new—more about this later.

So, this is a fable/rumination about human nature, librarianship, and the Web. About a time, perhaps *this* time, when we are comfortable enough to give up some of the talismans we have brought from the old world and begin to think about how to really live as part of this new space. About what it takes to create an information space, and the particular slant of librarians on this matter.

What do we need from the Web? It's simple, really. We need to be able to put things where the people who want them can find them. We'd like the things we find to look like sensible responses to our queries.

Vannevar Bush and the Scissors

The scientist Vannevar Bush wanted to be able to put things away and find them again. We may think libraries have developed a good way of doing that, but Bush didn't agree. He criticized library classification systems, saying:

> [I]nformation is found, (when it is) by tracing it down from subclass to subclass. It can be in only one place, unless duplicates are used; one has to have rules as to which path will locate it, and the rules are cumbersome. Having found one item, moreover, one has to emerge from the system and re-enter on a new path.
>
> The human mind does not work in this way. It operates by association. With one item in its grasp, it snaps instantly to the next that is suggested by the association of thoughts . . . the speed of action, the intricacy of trails, the detail of mental pictures, is awe-inspiring beyond all else in nature.[1]

The power of Bush's dream of finding information in a meaningful and intuitive way has drawn us back to his article ever since it was first published in 1945.

Bush hypothesized a device called a memex, which would store images and find information by association. The memex was to be built into a desk for the use of a single researcher. It included a rather ingenious pair of eyeglasses with a camera attached to capture and store images on microfilm, and a mechanical device to retrieve and display desired parts of the film. Bush imagined himself snapping images as he read articles and

FINDING THINGS AND TELLING STORIES   293

books, appending his handwritten notes, and having the memex copy the images onto film that was stored in the desk.

Bush proposed two means for retrieval, the first being a keyword index generated by the memex and the second using associative trails. The trails were to be built by the researcher, who would display two images on the screen, then press buttons on a console to make a link between them. Additional items could then be linked to build a "trail of [the researcher's] interest through the maze of materials available to him." Bush imagined encyclopedias and other resources available for sale with associative trails already built, and a "new profession of trailblazers, those who find delight in the task of establishing useful trails through the enormous mass of the common record."

A bit earlier, S. R. Ranganathan made a discovery that did not catch fire at the time, but that may have bearing on Bush's first problem, of unwanted paths in library classification systems. In 1924, Ranganathan traveled from Madras, India, to London to study librarianship at the University College. Ranganathan quickly became bored with the traditional curriculum and requested permission to undertake a special project. The College granted his request, and he set out to study the classification schemes available in print in the College library, and the use of classification schemes in about a hundred libraries.

At the time, library classification schemes were quite new, in a very experimental stage, and there was quite a variety of them. Yet, Ranganathan found that every one of them had the same problem. They were all enumerative schemes; they all sought to provide a slot for each bit of knowledge. These enumerative schemes were already breaking down because the writings of the twentieth century were less about observation (such as the discovery of new plant species or rock forms) and more about actions that involved compound subjects (such as the use of technology to transform raw materials into products).

In the nineteenth century, enumerative schemes had worked well for biologists, whose world changed rather slowly as new bugs and body parts were discovered. But other fields of knowledge are not like biology, and, in the new century, areas of inquiry were being created at a ferocious rate by *combining* elementary ones. There were works on teaching mathematics, on teaching mathematics in elementary schools, on the history of teaching mathematics in London in the elementary schools. Each new melding of knowledge spawned many others—the history of teaching history in the elementary schools, the use of steel in road bridges, in machines, in dentistry, ... The classification schemes could not be revised quickly enough to keep up. Although Ranganathan did not comment on this, the classification schemes also had the problem that Bush later found: Each complex topic was slotted into only one place. If the works on the history of teaching mathematics were with the works on education, they were not with the other works on history or mathematics.

That Christmas, Ranganathan visited Selfridge's Department Store where a salesman was demonstrating a Meccano set. With several lengths of slotted metal strips, rods, and wheels, and a few bolts and nuts, the salesman could construct an infinite variety of toy models. This led Ranganathan to the idea that a library classification could be made with only a few short schedules, with the classification number for any particular work being constructed by combining parts. To connect the numbers for the various parts, he envisioned the colon (:) and other punctuation marks in place of the bolts and nuts of the Meccano set.

Ranganathan set to work developing his idea into a classification scheme, and, on the way back to Madras in 1925, he applied his new Colon Classification to the books in the ship's library. In Madras, Ranganathan classified the books in the Madras University Library and its new acquisitions for the next several years.[2]

At first glance, the Colon Classification[3] may look like a simplified version of Dewey or LC; it begins with a list of main subjects, each followed by subdivisions. But the schedule for each subject is quite short—the one for Medicine (L) has only six pages. The list can be so short because it has to contain only the kit parts, not the compound subjects. The scheme has entries, called *facets,* for each of the basic components of medicine—there are entries for kidneys (L51), diseases (L14), treatment (L6), and pediatrics (L9C). Ranganathan called this list of headings specific to a subject its *personality.* For example, the personality of Mathematics (B) includes algebra (B2), analysis (B3), and calculus (B36). Personality is the first of the five main classes of the Colon Classification.

Any particular work can be described by adding the number for each relevant topic or facet. For example, a book on treating kidney diseases in children would be classified by giving it the numbers for children, kidneys, diseases, and treatment: L9C,51;14:6.

Instead of making subject divisions for time periods and places, such as Politics and Government—United States—1850, in the Colon Classification, the classes for *places* and *time periods* appear elsewhere in the book, and only once. If a book or an article covers a particular place or time period, the appropriate numbers are bolted onto the rest.

In addition to personality, space, and time, Ranganathan's other main classes are *energy* and *matter,* the dominant concepts of the industrial age. If a book was not specific to some of these concepts, then it was simply not classified with regard to them.

The Colon Classification did not spread, perhaps because it loses its advantage over other systems just at the point where the call numbers are assembled and put on the books. Because there is still only one copy of the book, it has to be in only one place. The rules for assembling the class number are complicated and rigorous, and they have to be. The many parts of the class number have to be written in the same order every time in order to put together all the books on treating kidney diseases in children, and to put these books with the other books on pediatrics. Of course, the system could have been designed to put the books on kidneys together, and some researchers would have preferred to do so. However, in the physical world, we can see only one facet—we lose the chance to arrange the books in more than one way.

The problems of assembling call numbers and putting writings in only one place disappear in the electronic realm. The parts of the number no longer have to be in a particular order because we are only indexing the work, not shelving it. Electronic searching is very well suited to faceted classifications. When any part of the class can be the main search term, any of the facets can be turned to catch the light. In an enumerative classification, such as Dewey or LC, putting together the books on road-building materials separates these books from the rest of the books on asphalt and brick and stone and concrete. In a faceted system, the topics can be searched independently, and a search can gather all the materials on road-building techniques, or all the materials on brick, or all the materials on costs of petroleum products. The scissors can be next to everything.

The Web as Story

If anything should fulfill Bush's dream, it is the Web. But we are not there yet. The Web is useful for finding things, but I want even more. I want a story, or at least the parts from which to build one. I had toured the White House, and wanted to know more about the sculpture garden—what was in it now and how it had evolved. I had toured the FDR Memorial, had seen the statue of Franklin Roosevelt with his dog Fala, and wanted to know more about the presidents and their pets. (What does their relationship to their pets say about them as people? As presidents?) I had read *All the President's Men* and wanted to follow Deep Throat's advice to "follow the money" through some more recent presidencies.[4] The Web wouldn't do any of these for me. Instead of a story, or an associative trail that Bush would have appreciated, I got a haystack of links. For all its content and links and search engines, the Web is not a memex. It takes more than a mechanism to build sense into a world.

Stories are our oldest and most powerful means of making sense of our world. We may think that as modern adults we see the world as it is, that we have outgrown stories, but we have not. The behavior of quarks, the latest management theories, are all stories. In order to get a story out of the Web, we need to have a story *about* the Web.

Stories do more than explain our world. Once we believe in a story, we act in accordance with it. We can share the story and act toward a common vision. It matters which story we tell. What is our story of the Web?

Think of your own story of the library. It probably encompasses much more than the physical setting of books (and computers) and people using them. Perhaps to you the library is a quiet place that allows room for thought. Perhaps it is the place where you see your friends studying, which helps you get in the mood to study. Or, perhaps it is a place to find answers, or to lay claim to the time of an intelligent and helpful professional.

We've tried to fit our existing stories onto the Web; we've looked at the Web as a library, as a bazaar, as a circus. Each of these stories is a partial fit, but in each case there are leftover parts of the story and leftover parts of the Web. Perhaps we need to go deeper, to begin with even more fundamental stories.

Two of the profound stories people tell about their worlds are the Native American Coyote stories and the stories from India of Ganesh, the god with the head of an elephant. Coyote and Ganesh are in the tradition of the trickster, the random element of life. Coyote stories are often humorous, even whimsical, but they have a very dark streak. Although there are stories of how Coyote creates the world, in the broadest stream of Coyote stories there is no change made in the world and the story has no tidy ending. At the "end" of a Coyote story, everyone is humbled, probably several of the characters are dead or maimed, Coyote himself is quite ragged, and life goes on in its uncertain way. Coyote stories are not about people changing their lives or building a better world—they are about surviving, but not about progress.

In his trickster stories, Ganesh is a bit lazy and survives by his wits, as does Coyote. But Ganesh lives in a human-made world and his stories are about building it. With his large ears, Ganesh can hear everything, and with his large brain, he knows what is relevant. But his special talent is to remove obstacles by thinking about problems in a simpler way—today we would call it "thinking outside the box," a flatfooted term that just shows how dull our society has become. Ganesh is associated with new beginnings, while Coyote is associated with timeless existence. (Both of these character descriptions are, of course, much too sparse and tidy for myth.)

Here are typical stories of Coyote and Ganesh:

One day, Coyote was going along and he saw Rabbit. Rabbit saw him too and ran into a hole. Coyote said, "Now let me think. How can I get you out? I'll pick some grasses and set them on fire. Then you will come out of the hole and I will eat you." Rabbit laughed. He said, "That won't work, Coyote. Before you can set the grasses on fire I will eat them." Coyote said, "Let me think. Do you like to eat sagebrush?" "Oh," said Rabbit, "I *love* sagebrush." "Piñon pitch!" said Coyote, "I'll use Piñon pitch!" Rabbit was worried. "You will kill me. I don't eat Piñon pitch." Coyote was happy. He started a fire with the pitch, right over the hole where Rabbit was hiding. Rabbit began to cough. "Come closer," said Rabbit. "Blow on the fire! I am nearly dead, but your pitch is almost gone." And then Rabbit could feel Coyote very close, blowing as hard as he could. Rabbit kicked very hard with his strong back legs and threw hot rocks and pitch into Coyote's face. Rabbit ran away. Laughing very hard.[5]

One day Ganesh's parents called their two sons to them. "We love both of you very much," they said, "but now we must decide which of you we love the very best. We have thought about how to decide and we have agreed upon a test. The first one who rides around the world will be our favorite son." Ganesh's brother was very fit and sleek. He said, "How wonderful, to get to see the whole world and to be the favorite son as well!" He oiled his body. He stretched his muscles. He mounted his peacock and sped away toward the sun. Ganesh, not very fit and sleek, finished the sweet he had been eating. He took from his pocket his small pet mouse. He stroked its silky fur and set it on the ground. Then he settled himself upon the back of the mouse. Slowly, the mouse began to carry Ganesh toward the sun. After they had gone only a few feet, they turned and began to circle Ganesh's parents. After some time they had come back to face the sun again. Ganesh rose carefully from the mouse. He stroked his silky fur and placed him gently in his pocket to rest. Then he looked at his parents and smiled. Ganesh's parents smiled back, but quizzically. Ganesh said, "But don't you see, my beloved parents, you are my whole world. I have traveled around my whole world." Ganesh's parents enfolded him in their arms and said, "You are our favorite son."[6]

Stories such as these help us to understand the cultures that produced them. Far more importantly, they serve their own cultures by sharing a worldview among the citizens of the culture. People make up stories to explain their worlds, and they also build their worlds to match their stories. It may be that stories, such as these of Coyote and Ganesh, are fully sufficient to explain the differences (and similarities) between these two civilizations.

The story we tell of the Web will do more than explain it. Our story will create the Web. Tinkering with our existing tools will not be enough— even tinkering with the wonderful story of the memex will not be enough. To find out what the Web means, and is, and can be, we need to get closer to the stories that define us as a people.

Perhaps at this point librarians need more Coyote *and* more Ganesh. Ganesh encourages us to think of ways to change the world, while Coyote can help us live in the ragged parts of it. Both make good use of ideas and tools that do not seem to apply. The trickster is best able to see the world anew.

Notes

1. Vannevar Bush, "As We May Think," *Atlantic Monthly* 1 (July 1945): 101–108. Reprinted in *CD ROM: The New Papyrus* (Redmond, Washington: Microsoft Pr., 1986), 3–20.
2. A. Neelameghan, "Colon Classification," in *Encyclopedia of Library and Information Science*, vol. 5 (New York: Marcel Dekker, 1971), 316–340.
3. S. R. Ranganathan, *Colon Classification*, 6th ed. (Bombay, India: Asia Publishing House, reprinted with amendments, 1963).
4. Carl Bernstein, and Bob Woodward, *All the President's Men* (New York: Simon and Schuster, 1974).
5. This is my telling of one of the more common Coyote stories. Versions of this and other Coyote stories may be found in:

   Richard Erdoes and Alfonso Ottiz, eds. *American Indian Trickster Tales* (New York: Viking, 1998).

   Robert A. Roessel Jr. and Dillon Mitchell, eds. *Coyote Stories of the Navajo People* (Phoenix, Arizona: Navajo Curriculum Center Pr., 1974).

6. Most of the information on Ganesh comes from the program notes for the performances of the Christmas Revels in Houston, Texas, December 11–15, 1998. The story is my telling of one from that performance. My thanks to N. Shamsundar for reviewing my comments on Ganesh and pointing out that what I have said of Ganesh is only a small part of the whole. For more on Ganesh (also called Ganesha), see:

   http://www.compulink. co.uk/~ganesh/ganesha.htm and *http:// freeindia.org/ack/Ganesha/ganesh01. shtml.*

   Thank you to Neomia C. Lowe for the second source.

Acronyms and Initialisms

AACR2: Anglo-American Cataloguing Rules, 2d edition
AASL: American Association of School Librarians
ACL: Access Control List
ACRL: Association of College and Research Libraries
AFL-CIO: American Federation of Labor–Congress of Industrial Organizations
ALA: American Library Association
ALCTS: Association for Library Collections and Technical Services
AM: Amplitude Modulation
AMC: Archive and Manuscript Control
ANS: Advanced Network and Services
AOL: America Online
APA: American Psychological Association
ARCnet: Attached Resource Computer Network
ARIADNE: Alliance Remote Instructional Authoring and Distribution Networks for Europe
ASCII: American Standard Code for Information Interchange
AT&T: American Telephone & Telegraph
ATDnet: Advanced Technology Demonstration Network
ATM: Asynchronous Transfer Mode
BARRNet: Bay Area Regional Research Network
BBN: Bolt, Beranek, and Newman
BMP: Bitmapped
BSML: Bioinformatic Sequence Markup Language
CA: Certificate Authority
CAIRN: Collaborative Advanced Interagency Research Network
CCC: Copyright Clearance Center
CDF: Channel Definition Format
CD-ROM: Compact Disc, Read-Only Memory
CEPT: Conference Européenne des Administration des Postes et des Télécommunications
CERIAS: Center for Education and Research in Information Assurance and Security
CERN: European Laboratory for Particle Physics
CIT: Center for Institutional Technology
CIX: Commercial Internet Exchange
CML: Chemical Markup Language
CNN: Cable News Network
CNRI: Corporation for National Research Initiatives
COD: Cash on Delivery
CONFU: Conference on Fair Use
Conser: Cooperative Online Serials
CPU: Computer Processing Unit
CRES: Computer-related Eye Strain
CRT: Cathode Ray Tube
CSMA/CD: Carrier Sense Multiple Access with Collision Detection
CSN: CompuServe Network Services
CSS: Cascading Style Sheets
DARPA: Department of Defense Advanced Research Projects Agency
DC: Dublin Core
DHTML: Dynamic Hypertext Markup Language
DNS: Domain Name System
DOI: Digital Object Identifier
DOM: Document Object Model
DOS: Disk Operating System

DREN: Defense Research and Engineering Network

DSSSL: Document Style Semantics and Specification Language

DTD: Document Type Definition

EAD: Encoded Archival Description

EASI: Equal Access to Software and Information

ECMAScript: European Computer Manufacturers Association Script

EM: Electromagnetic

ESnet: Energy Sciences Network

FAQ: Frequently Asked Question

FCC: Federal Communications Commission

FDDI: Fiber Distributed Data Interface

FGDC: Federal Geographic Data Committee

FIX: Federal Internet Exchange

FM: Frequency Modulation

FTC: Federal Trade Commission

FTE: Full-Time Equivalent

FTP: File Transfer Protocol

Gbps: Gigabits per Second

GILS: Government Information Locator Service; Global Information Locator Service

GSM: Global Standard for Mobility

GUI: Graphical User Interface

HDTV: High-definition Television

HTML: Hypertext Markup Language

HTTP: Hypertext Transfer Protocol

I2: Internet2

ICM: International Connections Manager

IEEE: Institute of Electrical and Electronic Engineers

IETF: Internet Engineering Task Force

IFLA: International Federation of Library Associations

IITF: Information Infrastructure Task Force

IMS: Instructional Management Systems

IP: Internet Protocol

IPng: IP Next Generation

IPv4: Internet Protocol Version 4

IPv6: Internet Protocol Version 6

IPX/SPX: Internetwork Packet Exchange/Sequenced Packet Exchange

IRC: Internet Relay Chat

ISBD(ER): International Standard Bibliographic Description for Electronic Resources

ISBN: International Standard Book Number

ISM: Industry, Science, and Medicine

ISO: International Organization for Standardization

ISSN: International Standard Serial Number

IT: Information Technology

LAN: Local Area Network

LC: Library of Congress

LCSH: Library of Congress Subject Headings

LDAP: Lightweight Directory Access Protocol

LDDS: Long Distance Discount Service

LII: Librarian's Index to the Internet

LITA: Library and Information Technology Association

MAE: *originally* Metropolitan Area Ethernet, *later* Metropolitan Area Exchange

MAN: Metropolitan Area Network

MARC: Machine-Readable Cataloging

MathML: Mathematical Markup Language

MBONE: Multicast Backbone

Mbps: Megabits per Second

MFS: Metropolitan Fiber Systems

MIDI: Musical Instrument Digital Interface

MIDnet: Midwest Network

MIME: Multipurpose Internet Mail Extensions

MLA: Modern Language Association

MLS: Master of Library Science

MONET: Multiwave Optical Networking Network

MOO: MUD-Object Oriented

MUD: Multi-User Dungeon

NAP: Network Access Point

NASA: National Aeronautics and Space Administration

NCSA: National Computational Science Alliance

NDS: Novell Directory Services

NetBEUI: NetBIOS Extended User Interface

NetBIOS: Network Basic Input/Output System

NEXRAD: Next Generation Weather Radar

NGI: Next Generation Internet

NIC: Network Interface Card

NII: National Information Infrastructure

NISN: NASA Integrated Services Network

NISO: National Information Standards Organization

NIST: National Institute of Standards and Technology

NOAA: National Oceanic and Atmospheric Administration

NOS: Network Operating System

NREN: NASA Research and Education Network

NSF: National Science Foundation

NYSERNET: New York State Regional Network

OC12: Optical Carrier 12

OMF: Observation Markup Format

OPAC: Online Public Access Catalog

OS: Operating System

OSHA: Occupational Safety and Health Administration

OSI: Open System Interconnection

PBS: Public Broadcasting System

PC: Personal Computer

PCS: Personal Communications Service

PDF: Portable Document Format

Perl: Practical Extraction and Report Language

PKI: Public Key Infrastructure

PTA: Parent Teacher Association

PURL: Persistent Uniform Resource Locator

Q&A: Question and Answer

QoS: Quality of Service

R&D: Research and Development

RAM: Random Access Memory

RCC: Radio Common Carriers

RDF: Resource Description Framework

RLG: Research Libraries Group

RSI: Repetitive Strain Injury

RTP: Real-time Transport Protocol

SAE: Society of Automotive Engineers

SDI: Selective Dissemination of Information

SGI: Silicon Graphics, Inc.

SGML: Standardized General Markup Language

SONET: Synchronous Optical Network

SSL: Secure Sockets Layer

STP: Shielded Twisted Pair

SURANET: Southeastern Universities Research Association Network

TCP/IP: Transmission Control Protocol/Internet Protocol

TEI: Text Encoding Initiative

TIGER: Topologically Integrated Geographic Encoding and Referencing

TLD: Top Level Domain

UCAID: University Corporation for Advanced Internet Development

UKOLN: United Kingdom Office for Library and Information Networking

UNC: University of North Carolina

U-NII: Unlicensed National Information Infrastructure

URL: Uniform Resource Locator

URN: Uniform Resource Name

USDA: United States Department of Agriculture

USIPA: United States Internet Service Providers Association

USMARC: United States Machine-Readable Cataloging

UTP: Unshielded Twisted Pair

vBNS: Very High Performance Backbone Network Service

VBScript: Visual Basic Script

VCR: Videocassette Recorder

VII: Virtual Institute of Information

VR: Virtual Reality

VRA: Virtual Reality Association

VRA CC: Visual Resources Association Core Categories

VRML: Virtual Reality Modeling Language

W3C: World Wide Web Consortium

WAIS: Wide Area Information Server

WIPO: World Intellectual Property Organization

WWW: World Wide Web

XML: Extensible Markup Language

XSL: Extensible Style Language

INDEX

3-D graphics, 254–55
3DTV, 86
6Bone, 54

A

AASL (American Association of School Librarians), 159, 164
Abilene project, 41, 55
access, long-term, 130
Access Control List (ACL), 226
access to information
    and children, 190–96, 198
    and copyright, 107
    and digitization, 134, 148
    e-journals, 157
    in licensing agreements, 156, 222
    policies for, 186–87
    and security, 224–25
accuracy in websites, 64
ACL (Access Control List), 226
acquisitions procedures, 129
acronyms, 299–302
    in netiquette, 17
ActiveX, 266
addresses in IPv6, 53–54. *See also* identifiers
adjacency searches, 12
administrative metadata, 92, 141
Adobe Acrobat Reader
    in course reserve, 171
    as plug-in, 78–79
Adobe Photoshop, 139
Adobe Portable Document Format (PDF), 185–86
Advanced Technology Demonstration Network (ATDnet), 56
agents, intelligent, 248–49
ALOHAnet, 236
Altavista, 13

America Links Up, 190–91
America Online (AOL), 46
American Association of School Librarians (AASL), 159, 164
American Library Association
    Access to Electronic Information policy, 187
    and e-journal licensing, 156
    Library Instruction Round Table, 212
    lobbying on copyright, 108
American Memory project, 147–48
American Psychological Association
    Electronic Style, 116–17
    Publication Manual, 114–15, 119, 120
Anglo-American Cataloguing Rules 2, 92–93
animation, 255
ANS Communications, 46
AOL (America Online), 46
Apache Web server, 183
Appletalk, 40
applets, Java, 267
application layer, 39
April Fools' jokes, 20
archival resources, 95
archives of online reference service, 163
ARCnet access method, 39
Ariadne Newsletter, 4
ARIADNE project, 96
armrests, 26
ARPANET (Advanced Research Projects Agency Network), 234–36
Ask Dr. Math, 167
Ask Shamu, 162, 167
"ask them first" training technique, 209
AskA services. *See* Reference services, online

AskERIC, 159, 162, 164
assistive technology, 163. *See also* visually impaired users
Association of College and Research Libraries Instruction Section, 212
associative trails, 293
Asynchronous Transfer Mode (ATM), 52
ATDnet (Advanced Technology Demonstration Network), 56
@Home Network, 48
AT&T, 45, 46, 48, 49
ATM (Asynchronous Transfer Mode), 52
audience
    for online reference service, 160
    for website, 62–63
authentication of users, 128, 222–32
    cross-institutional, 223–24
    digital certificates, 230–32
    IP source filtering, 225–27
    LANs, 36
    local systems, 223
    password scripting, 229–30
    proxy servers, 227–28
    user-account authentication, 228–29
authoring programs, VRML, 257
authority
    in digital libraries, 148
    in websites, 63
authorization for computer resources, 222

B

backbone network, 42, 44–46
Backbone Network Service (vBNS), 41, 52, 54

303

backrests, 26
BackWeb, 246
BARRNet, 47
BBN Planet, 45
"before and after" training
technique, 209
behavior problems around
Internet, 193
Berkeley Digital Library
SunSITE, 95, 130, 181
Berkeley Finding Aid Project,
95
Berners-Lee, Tim, 69–70
beta technology, 262
bias in websites, 63, 64
bibliography. *See* resources
Bioinformatic Sequence
Markup Language
(BSML), 73
bleeding edge technologies,
261–67
"Bob" (twenty-first century
cybrarian), 82–83
Boolean searches, 12
Bowker (R. R.) Digital Object
Identifiers, 101
browsers, 39, 73. *See also*
Internet Explorer;
Netscape Navigator
and Java applets, 267
and push technology,
246–47
BrowserWatch, 181
BSML (Bioinformatic Sequence
Markup Language), 73
Buffy the Vampire Slayer,
276–81
bus topology, 38
Bush, Vannevar, 292–95

C

CA (Certificate Authorities), 231
cable television, 240
cabling for network, 37–38
CacheNow!, 183
CAIRN (Collaborative
Advanced Interagency
Research Network), 56
California, Miller v., 203
call numbers, 294
camera, digital, 139
card catalogs, 206, 271

Carl Uncover, 65
carpal tunnel syndrome, 25
Cascading Style Sheets (CSS),
71
cataloging of electronic
resources, 129
CDF (Channel Definition
Format), 247
cellular networking, 239
Center for Education and
Research in Information
Assurance and Security
(CERIAS), 183
CEPT (Conference Européenne
des Administration des
Postes et des
Télécommunications), 236
CERIAS (Center for Education
and Research in
Information Assurance
and Security), 183
Certificate Authorities (CA), 231
chain letters in e-mail
messages, 18
chairs, ergonomic, 26, 31
Channel Definition Format
(CDF), 247
channels, 246–47
Chemical Markup Language
(CML), 73
Chicago Manual of Style,
115–16, 119
children
and filtering, 197–205
Internet skills of, 190–96
online reference service, 159
websites for, 62
CIT Infobits, 4
citations, 113–121
CIX (Commercial Internet
Exchange), 44
claiming electronic resources,
132
classrooms for Internet
training, 213
client, network, 36
client, thin, 265–66
client/server LANs, 38
CML (Chemical Markup
Language), 73
CNET, 6
CNRI (Corporation for National
Research Initiatives), 101

Collaborative Advanced
Interagency Research
Network (CAIRN), 56
collection development
e-journals, 153–54
electronic resources, 125–33
Colon Classification, 294
*Colorado Alliance of Research
Libraries Electronic
Journal Access,* 154
*Columbia Guide to Online
Style,* 117–18, 120
Commercial Internet Exchange
(CIX), 44
Communications Decency Act,
203–4
comprehensiveness of
website, 63–64
Compuserve, 46
Computers and Academic
Freedom, 187
Conference Européenne des
Administration des Postes
et des Télécommunications
(CEPT), 236
Conference on Fair Use
(CONFU), 172
confidentiality in online
reference service, 161
CONFU (Conference on Fair
Use), 172
connection options, 47
Connolly, David, 70
Conser Cataloging Manual,
92–93
consortiums and pricing,
131
content
currency of, 13
in push technology, 245
of website, 65
Content Standards for Digital
Geospatial Metadata, 96
contracts for electronic
resources, 127–28
CoolTalk, 85
copying e-mail messages, 17
copyright, 103–12
in digital libraries, 137, 148
e-journals, 155
in e-mail messages, 17
history and purpose, 104–5
international, 106–7

and libraries, 106–9
  in online reference
    services, 162
  and reserves, 172
  on websites, 67, 108–9
Copyright Clearance Center,
  172
Copyright Remedy
  Clarification Act, 104
cordless networking, 238–39
Corporation for National
  Research Initiatives
  (CNRI), 101
Cosmo Player, 256
costs. *See also* pricing
  of new technology, 263
  online reference services,
    162–63
  reserve systems, 173
Council on Library and
  Information Resources,
  136
Coyote, 296
cross-posting in e-mail
  messages, 18
crosswalking, 97
Cryopolis, 258
CSS (Cascading Style Sheets),
  71
currency of websites, 66–67
current awareness websites,
  3–5
Current Cites, 4, 181
customization of resources, 128
CyberAtlas: The Reference
  Desk for Web Marketing, 6

D

D-Lib Magazine, 4
databases, enriched, 87
DataXchange Network, 49
Defense Research and
  Engineering Network
  (DREN), 56
delivery of answers in online
  reference service, 163
descriptive metadata, 92, 141
design of websites, 64–66
DFC (Digital Future Coalition),
  107
DHTML (dynamic HTML),
  70–72

Dienst projects, 13
digital certificates, 230–32
Digital Future Coalition (DFC),
  107
digital imaging, 134–44
digital libraries, 145–51
Digital Library Initiative
  program, 147
Digital Millennium Copyright
  Act, 109
Digital Object Identifiers
  (DOI), 101
digitization
  of course reserves, 171
  planning process, 135–37
direct satellite networking,
  240–41
Directory of Electronic
  Journals, Newsletters, and
  Academic Discussion
  Lists, 154
disabled users. *See* assistive
  technology
discussion lists
  citations of, 115
  digital libraries, 151
  electronic reserves, 173–74
  electronic resources, 129–30
  ergonomics, 30–31
  frauds and hoaxes, 23
  online reference, 160
  training, 215
  web access in libraries, 181
distant users. *See* remote users
DNS (Domain Name System),
  99–100, 101
Document Object Model
  (DOM), 71, 73
Document Style Semantics and
  Specification Language
  (DSSSL), 69, 71, 73
Document Type Definition
  (DTD)
  archival materials, 95 (*See*
    also Encoded Archival
    Description)
  in SGML, 69
  Text Encoding Initiative,
    95–96
DOI (Digital Object
  Identifiers), 101
DOM (Document Object
  Model), 71

Domain Name System (DNS),
  99–100, 101
downloading from websites,
  66
DREN (Defense Research and
  Engineering Network), 56
drive-cloning, 182
DSSSL (Document Style
  Semantics and
  Specification Language),
  69, 71, 73
DTD (Document Type
  Definition). *See*
  Document Type
  Definition
Dublin Core
  intelligent agents, 249
  as metadata, 91, 93–94
dynamic HTML (DHTML),
  70–72
DynaText/DynaWeb, 95

E

e-journals, 152–58
e-mail
  citation of, 114–15, 116, 118
  copyright in, 106
  current awareness, 3
  in messaging systems, 86
  netiquette for, 16–19
  in online reference
    services, 165, 166
  and public access
    terminals, 186–87
e-mail programs, 19, 39
E-Res, 175
EAD (Encoded Archival
  Description), 68, 94–95,
  142
ease of use of websites, 64–66
ECMAScript, 71
EContent, 7
edutainment, 84
electromagnetic radiation, 27
electromagnetism, 234–36
Electronic Journals Resource
  Directory, 154
electronic picture frames, 86
Electronic Style: A Guide to
  Citing Electronic
  Information, 116–17, 119

Electronic Text Center, 96, 140, 141
emoticons, 17
Encoded Archival Description (EAD), 68, 94–95, 142
encryption
  cordless telephones, 238
  digital certificates, 230–31
  in security systems, 225
Endpage, 4
Energy Science Network (ESnet), 56
Equal Access to Software and Information, 185
ergonomics, 24–32
ESnet (Energy Science Network), 56
Ethernet, 39, 238
evaluation
  of instruction programs, 214
  of online reference services, 168
  of push application, 245–46
  of resources, 126
  of search results, 211
  of websites, 61–67, 211
exercises, hand, 28–29
expandability, 181
extensibility, 72
Extensible Markup Language (XML), 72–74
Extensible Style Language (XSL), 71
external users. *See* remote users

F

fair use, 105
  e-journals, 155
  and reserves, 172, 173
fax in messaging systems, 86
FCC (Federal Communications Commission), 236
FDDI (Fiber Distributed Data Interface), 39
Federal Communications Commission (FCC), 236
Federal Geographic Data Committee (FGDC), 96
Federal Internet Exchange (FIX), 44

Federal Trade Commission (FTC), 21, 22
federated searching, 11
fee-based services, 160
FGDC (Federal Geographic Data Committee), 96
Fiber Distributed Data Interface (FDDI), 39
file formats, 140–41
file migration, 141
file naming, 142
file server, 36
file transfer program (FTP), 39
filtering, 191, 199–203
  court decisions, 198–202
  technology of, 202–3
filtering messages in e-mail, 19
firewalls, 183
FIX (Federal Internet Exchange), 44
flaming in e-mail, 18–19
flat-panel television, 86
footrests, 26
Fortres, 182
forwarding of e-mail messages, 17
frames, 66, 70
frauds, 20–23
FreeWareWeb Online! Newsletter, 85
FTC (Federal Trade Commission), 21, 22
FTP (file transfer program), 39
Full-Text Archives of Scholarly Society Serial Publications, 154
Full-Text Electronic Journals Project, 154
funding
  charging for printers, 185
  digitization projects, 135
  online reference services, 162–63

G

games and Internet instruction, 216–18
Ganesh, 296–297
gateway mechanism, 157
Getty Information Institute, 136
"Giles, Rupert" (fictional librarian), 276–81

GILS (Government Information Locator Service), 96
glare reduction, 28
global directories for URNs, 101
Global Federated Searcher, 14
gopher, 263
governance of online reference service, 161–62
Government Information Locator Service (GILS), 96
government publications, 67
graphics on website, 65
Greenpeace, 64
grep searches, 12
GTE Internetworking, 46

H

harassment in e-mail messages, 18
hardware
  for digitization, 138–39, 141
  for online reference services, 162
  for public access, 181–82
helper applications, 78
hertz, 234
hoaxes, 19–20, 23
holography, 86
HotWired, 6
HTML (Hypertext Markup Language), 69–70
  compared to XML, 73–74
  in Dublin Core, 94
HTTP (Hypertext Transfer Protocol), 69, 70
hubs, 37
Hypertext Markup Language. *See* HTML (Hypertext Markup Language)
Hypertext Transfer Protocol (HTTP), 69, 70

I

I2. *See* Internet2
IBM PCjr, 237
ICM (International Connections Manager), 48
identifiers, 99–102. *See also* addresses

IETF (Internet Engineering
Task Force), 101
image manipulation, 142
ImageCast, 182
images, 96
IMS (Instructional
Management Systems)
Project, 96–97
Industry, Science, and
Medicine (ISM)
applications, 238
Information Infrastructure
Task Force, 107
Information Institute, 159,
162–63
information literacy, 193,
206–15
infotainment, 84
InfoWorld Electric, 6
infrared networking,
237–38
initialisms, 299–302
instruction, 206–15
Instructional Management
Systems Project (IMS),
96–97
intelligent agents, 248–49
interactive media, 84
interconnect level, 43–44
interfaces, 126–27, 132
International Connections
Manager (ICM), 48
International Frequency
Regulatory Board, 236
International Organization for
Standardization. *See* ISO
(International
Organization for
Standardization)
*International Standard
Bibliographic Description
for Electronic Resources*
(ISBD(ER)), 92, 93
Internet Conference, 85
Internet Engineering Task
Force (IETF), 101
Internet Explorer. *See also*
browsers
digital certificates, 231
and proxy servers, 228
push technology, 247
Internet Free Expression
Alliance, 203

Internet Multicast Backbone
(MBONE), 85
Internet Protocol Version 6
(IPv6), 53–54
Internet Resources, 5
Internet Service Provider (ISP),
48
Internet World, 6, 8
Internet2, 41, 51–52, 54–55,
56–57
Internet.com, 6
Internetwork Packet
Exchange/Sequenced
Packet Exchange
(IPX/SPX), 40
intranet-based metasearch
systems, 14
Introduction to Imaging, 136
IP source address
authentication, 128,
225–27
and password scripting, 230
IP spoofing, 226
IPng (IP next generation). *See*
IPv6
IPv6 (Internet Protocol Version
6), 53–54
IPX/SPX (Internetwork Packet
Exchange/Sequenced
Packet Exchange), 40
Iridium project, 240–41
ISBD(ER) *(International
Standard Bibliographic
Description for Electronic
Resources),* 92, 93
ISM (Industry, Science, and
Medicine) applications,
238
ISO 690-2, 118, 120
ISO 8879:9986, 69
ISO 10646 and XML, 73
ISO (International
Organization for
Standardization)
networking protocols, 39
and radio standards, 236
ISP (Internet Service Provider),
48

J

James Madison University, 65
Java, 10, 73, 266–67

JavaScript, 70
JPEG file format, 140
JScript, 71

K

*Kathleen R., et al. v. City of
Livermore,* 198–99
Kerberos authentication
system, 223, 227
keyboard, 27, 28, 31
KidsConnect, 159–68

L

LAN. *See* Local area network
(LAN)
LANtastic, 38
LaTeX plug-in, 79
LDAP authentication system,
227
legal issues
copyright (*See* copyright)
imaging, 137
licensing, 127–28
on websites, 67
LibLicense website, 127
librarians
"Bob," 82–83
career paths, 271–75
and change, 291–97
image of, 282–90
in television, 277–81
libraries
and copyright, 103–4
future of, 149
and multimedia
developments, 87–88
push applications, 249–50
role of, 15, 286–87
Library of Congress
American Memory project,
148
digitization, 137, 138
Encoded Archival
Description, 95, 142
MARC, 93
library web sites
and copyright, 108
making searchable, 15
in training, 211

licensing agreements, 127–28
and authentication, 222
e-journals, 155–57
lighting on monitors, 28, 32
LII New This Week, 5
"lingo bingo" training
technique, 209
links, 64, 67. *See also*
associative trails
listserv discussion groups. *See*
discussion lists
literacy, information, 193,
206–15
literacy, video, 87
*Livermore (City of), Kathleen
R., et al. v.,* 198–99
lobbying efforts, 108
local area network (LAN),
35–41
cabling, 37–38
definition, 35–37
wireless, 41, 238
local authentication systems,
223
LOEX Clearinghouse for
Library Instruction, 212
*Loudoun County Library
(Board of Trustees of the),
Mainstream Loudoun v.,*
199–202
Lynx, 185

M

Mad Scientist Network, 167
MAE (Metropolitan Area
Exchange), 44
mail-bombing in e-mail, 18
*Mainstream Loudoun v.
Board of Trustees of the
Loudoun County Library,*
199–202
management of web access,
187–88, 193–94
mapping data from one
schema to another, 97
MARC, 92–93
marketing and technology
news websites, 6–7
marketing of librarians, 285–89
markup languages, 68–76
massage, 29

Math Forum, 167
Mathematical Markup
Language (MathML), 73
MBONE (Internet Multicast
Backbone), 85
MCI and vBNS, 52
MCI WorldCom, 45, 46, 48,
49
memex, 292
mergers of national backbone
operators, 46
messaging systems, universal,
86
metadata, 91–98
and digitization, 141–42
metasearch systems, 11, 13–14
Metricom, 240
Metropolitan Area Exchange
(MAE), 44
Metropolitan Fiber Systems, 46
microwave technology, 240
MIDnet, 47
Miller v. California, 203
mirror sites, 66
mission statement of websites,
61–62
*MLA Handbook for Writers of
Research Papers,* 116,
119, 120
MONET (Multiwave Optical
Networking) network, 56
monitor
lighting of, 28
placement of, 26–27, 31
monitor tents, 209
mouse, ergonomics of, 27, 31
Multilateral Peering
Agreement, 44
multilingual searches, 12, 14
multimedia, 83–87
multimedia plug-ins, 77–81
Multiwave Optical Networking
network (MONET), 56
music videos, 84

N

naming scheme, 101
NAP (Network Access Point)
architecture. *See* Network
Access Point (NAP)
architecture

NASA Integrated Services
Network (NISN), 56
NASA Research and Education
Network (NREN), 56
NASA websites, 63
National Backbone level,
44–46
National Computational
Science Alliance (NCSA),
93–94
National Electronic Site
License Initiative, 157
National Federation of the
Blind, 185
National Football League,
195–96
National Fraud Information
Center, 21
National Information
Infrastructure, 239
National Institutes of Health,
56
National Oceanic and
Atmospheric
Administration (NOAA),
56
National Preservation Office,
138
National Science Foundation
(NSF), 42
navigation on Web, 208–9
NCSA (National Computational
Science Alliance), 93–94
NDS authentication system,
227
needs assessment survey, 207
Net-Happenings, 5
NetBEUI (NetBios Extended
User Interface), 40
Netcaster, 247
netiquette, 16–19
Netscape Navigator. *See also*
browsers
digital certificates, 231
and HTML, 70
and proxy servers, 228
push technology, 247
Netsurfer Digest, 6–7
NetWare. *See* Novell NetWare
Network Access Point (NAP)
architecture, 42, 43–44
network computer, 182,
265–66

network interface card (NIC), 37
network layer, 39
network operating system. *See* operating system, network
Network Solutions, 100
networking
  Internet, 42–50
  local area networks, 35–41
  public access terminals, 180–84
new users, 19, 208–9
NewJour, 154
NewsAgent, 249
Next Generation Internet Initiative (NGI), 52, 54, 55–58
NIC (network interface card), 37
NISN (NASA Integrated Services Network), 56
NIST WebBook, 63
NOAA (National Oceanic and Atmospheric Administration), 56
NODE Learning Technologies Network, 85
noise, electromagnetic, 234–35
Northwestern University reserve system, 171
Norton Ghost, 182
NOS (network operating system). *See* operating system, network
Novell Directory Services, 223
Novell NetWare, 40, 264
NREN (NASA Research and Education Network), 56
NSF (National Science Foundation), 42
NSFNET, 42, 44, 46, 49
NYSERNET, 46–47

O

OARNet, 47
object behavior, 255
obscenity, 203–4
OCLC
  Dublin Core, 93–94
  PURL, 101

OCR (Optical Character Recognition), 139–40
OMF (Weather Observation Definition Format), 73
Online, 8
online resources. *See* resources
online tutorials, 213–14
Open Inventor, 255
Open System Interconnection (OSI), 39
operating system, network, 36
  choice of, 264–65
  for LAN, 40
Optical Character Recognition (OCR), 139–40
OSI (Open System Interconnection), 39
Ovid, 65
ownership *vs.* access, 130

P

p-system, 265–66
pagers, 239
Palace software, 257–58
PalmPilot, 237
participatory publishing, 86
party-line effect, 238
password scripting, 128, 229–30
passwords
  on library websites, 163
  and proxy servers, 228
  scams, 21
  user-account authentication, 228–29
PCS (Personal Communications Services), 239
PDF (Portable Document Format), 185–86
peer-reviewed material on websites, 63
peer-to-peer networks, 36, 38
peering, 43–44
Persistent Uniform Resource Locator (PURL), 101
personal communications, citation of, 114–15, 116, 118

Personal Communications Services (PCS), 239
physical layer, 39
physical layout of website, 65
PKI (Public Key Infrastructure), 230–31
Plant Pathology Internet Guide Book, 64
plug-ins, 77–81
  in collection development, 79–80
  VRML, 256
  in website content, 80–81
PointCast, 246
policies
  collection development, 133
  Internet access, 197–205
  online reference service, 161
  public access, 187
pornography on Web, 194, 198–99
Portable Document Format (PDF), 185–86
PostScript, 69
power searching, training for, 210–11
prequery processing, 13
presentation layer, 39
presentation skills, 212
preservation and digitization, 134–35, 148–49
pricing. *See also* costs
  e-journals, 155
  electronic resources, 130–31
"Principles for Licensing Electronic Resources," 157
print server, 36–37
print vs. electronic resources, 131
printers on public access terminals, 185
printing
  options from websites, 66
  of reserve materials, 173
priorities on type of use, 187–88
privacy, 17, 204
prize scams, 21–22
procedures for online reference training, 166–67
programs for Internet training, 207–8

Project Gutenberg, 66
promotion
	Internet instruction
		programs, 213–14
	library services, 288
protocols for LANs, 38–40
proxy servers, 183–84, 227–28, 230
PSINet, 46
Public-Access Computer Systems Review, 5
public access to Internet, 179–89
Public Key Infrastructure (PKI), 230–31
public libraries, web access in, 193
public relations, 288
publishing, participatory, 86
pull technology, 244
PURL (Persistent Uniform Resource Locator), 101
purpose of website, 61–62
push technology, 243–51, 262
pyramid schemes, 21

Q

quality of service
	under Internet2, 54
	under IPv6, 53
	setting priorities, 57
question and answer services, 159–69
quoting in e-mail messages, 17

R

Radio Common Carriers (RCC), 238
radio spectrum, 234–36
radio waves, 234
Radius authentication system, 227
Raggett, Dave, 70
Ranganathan, S. R., 293–94
RCC (Radio Common Carriers), 238
RDF (Resource Description Framework), 93, 94, 97–98

reevaluation of electronic resources, 132
Real-time Transport Protocol (RTP), 85
RealAudio, 85
RealNames, 100
RealPlayer plug-in, 79
reference services, online, 159–69
regional network providers, 46–47
remote control, 237
remote users, authentication of, 128, 227–28, 230
repetitive strain injuries, 24–25
	hand exercises, 28–29
	keyboard, 27
Research Libraries Group (RLG), 95, 138
reserves, electronic, 170–75
resolution system, 101
Resource Description Framework (RDF), 93, 94, 97–98
resources
	6Bone, 54
	Buffy the Vampire Slayer, 281
	copyright, 109–11, 137
	digital libraries, 149–51
	digitization, 136, 143–44
	electronic reserves, 173–74
	ergonomics, 29–31
	evaluation of websites, 67
	filtering, 203
	hardware, 181
	image of librarians, 289–90
	intelligent agents, 248
	Internet connections, 50
	Internet indentifiers, 101
	Internet2, 54
	LANs, 41
	marketing and technology news, 6–7
	markup languages, 75–76
	metadata, 98
	multimedia, 88
	netiquette, 23
	online reference services, 168–69
	plug-ins, 79
	policies and procedures, 133, 187

push technology, 250–51
scams, 23
security, 182–83
site design, 184–85
style manuals, 117–18, 120–21
technology news, 7–8
training, 212, 213, 214–15
vBNS, 52
virtual reality, 258–60
web computer management, 180–81
wireless computing, 240–41
results-ranking methods, 210–11
retention policy, 130
reviews of websites, 3–9
rights management metadata, 92
ring topology, 38
RLG (Research Libraries Group), 95, 138
RTP (Real-time Transport Protocol), 85
"Rupert Giles" (fictional librarian), 276–81

S

safety for children on Internet, 195
San Diego State University reserve system, 171
satellite communications systems, 240–41
scams, 20–23
scanners, 139
schema, 91
Science Online, 63
scope of online reference service, 160, 161
Scout Report, 5, 66–67, 181
SDI (selective dissemination of information). *See* push technology
search engines, 11–13
	for multimedia, 87
	training on, 210
searching
	in digital libraries, 149
	training for, 210–11
	using URLs, 100

Secure Sockets Layer (SSL), 231
security
    and authentication of users, 221–32
    levels of, 224
    networks, 182–84
    public access terminals, 182
Seidman's Online Insider, 7
selection criteria
    e-journals, 153–54
    electronic resources, 126
selective dissemination of information (SDI). *See* push technology
serendipity and push technology, 245
session layer, 39
sexually explicit web sites, 198–202
SGML (Standard Generalized Markup Language), 68, 69
    DTDs, 95
    use on web, 72
Sherlock, 10–11, 14
Shneiderman, Ben, 13
Shockwave plug-in, 79
Silicon Graphics, Inc., 255
simulation games, 84, 85
site licenses and authentication, 222
SiteBuilder, 175
6Bone, 54
SkyTel, 240
software
    digitization projects, 139–40
    ergonomic adjustments, 29–30
    LANs, 40
    online reference services, 162
    virtual reality, 254–55
SONET (Synchronous Optical Network), 52
"sound off" training technique, 209
spamming, 22–23
speed of interconnections, 49
spelling, 193
spillage, 224–25
spoof messages, 20, 22
spoofing, IP, 226
Sprint, 48–49

SprintLink, 46
Squid, 183
SSL (Secure Sockets Layer), 231
stability of website, 66–67
staff
    and Internet technology, 195
    for new technology, 263
    for online reference service, 162, 164–65
    reserve services, 173
    training of trainers, 211–12
Standard Generalized Markup Language. *See* SGML (Standard Generalized Markup Language)
standards
    digital certificates, 230
    radio broadcasting, 236
    for URLs, 101
standards, lack of
    digitization, 138
    in search engines, 13
star topology, 38
STARTS project, 13
storage media for digitization projects, 140–41
story, 295
structural metadata, 92, 141
structure in markup languages, 72
stumpers in online reference services, 167
style manuals, 113–21
style sheets in DHTML, 71
subject directories, training on, 210
suggestion boxes, 207
supercomputers, 52
Superscape 3-D, 256
SURANET, 47
surfing and copyright, 106
.svr files, 256
Synchronous Optical Network (SONET), 52

T

T-1 connections, 47
TCP/IP (Transmission Control Protocol/Internet Protocol), 40

IP source address filtering, 225–26
TechLINC, 257
technical metadata, 92
technical options of website, 65–66
technical requirements for electronic resources, 128
technology, adoption of, 263–67
technology change
    on the lighter side, 271–75
    management of, 263–67
TechWeb, 7
TEI (Text Encoding Initiative), 95–96
Telecommunications Act of 1996, 240
Teledesic system, 241
telephone, cellular, 238
telephone, cordless, 238
television, developments in, 86
Telluride InfoZone, 240
terminals, public access, 180–84
terminals, task-specific, 188
TeX, 69, 79
text editor on web site, 185
Text Encoding Initiative (TEI), 95–96
text scan searches, 11–12
thin clients, 265–66. *See also* network computer
3-D graphics, 254–55
three-dimensional webspace, 86
3DTV, 86
TIFF file format, 140
TIGER mapping website, 63
time frame for technology benefits, 263
time limits on terminal use, 187–88
TLD (Top Level Domains), 100
token ring access method, 39
Top Level Domains (TLD), 100
traffic priorities in IPv6, 53
training
    and arcade games, 216–18
    for online reference service, 165

training—*cont.*
of trainers, 211–12
of users, 195–96, 208–11
transaction access, 131, 132
transport layer, 39
trial periods for software, 129
trickster stories, 296–97
Trusted Information Systems Internet Firewall Toolkit, 183
types of use of Internet, 187–88

U

U-NII (unlicensed NII), 239
ubiquitous computing, 234
ubiquitous television, 86
UCAID (University Corporation for Advanced Internet Development), 54
Unicode, 73
Uniform Resource Locator (URL), 92, 100
Uniform Resource Name (URN), 101
UnipriNT, 185
universities and Internet connections, 51–58
University Corporation for Advanced Internet Development (UCAID), 54
University of Michigan reserve system, 171
University of Texas at Austin, 66
University of Virginia Electronic Text Center, 96, 140, 141
Unix, 264
upgrades of hardware, 181–83
URL (Uniform Resource Locator), 92, 100
URN (Uniform Resource Name), 101
U.S. Nuclear Regulatory Commission, 64
usability tests, 184
usage statistics, 128, 132

user-account authentication, 228–29
user instruction, 195–96, 207–9
user interaction, 255
users in licensing agreements, 156
UUNET, 46

V

validation in markup languages, 72
vBNS (Backbone Network Service), 41
VBScript, 70–71
vector space search model, 11
video literacy, 87
video plug-ins, 79
VideoPhone, 85
viewers, VRML, 256
virtual communities, 257–58, 260
virtual reality, 86, 252–60
Virtual Reality Modeling Language. *See* VRML (Virtual Reality Modeling Language)
Virtual Reference Desk, 159–60
Virtual World Wide Web, 256
virus warnings as hoaxes, 19
Viscape Universal, 256
Visual Resources Association Core Categories (VRA CC), 96
visually impaired users, 185–86
VivoActive plug-in, 79
voicemail in messaging systems, 86
volunteers in online reference service, 164–65
VRA CC (Visual Resources Association Core Categories), 96
VRML authoring programs, 257, 260
VRML (Virtual Reality Modeling Language), 86, 254, 255, 256, 262
VRML97, 256

W

WAIS (Wide Area Information Server), 263
Washington Post, 63–64
Weather Observation Definition Format (OMF), 73
web auction frauds, 21
Web Developer.com, 7
web indexing, 11
web sites
design of, 184–85
evaluation of, 61–67
instructional, 211
for online reference service, 163–64
Web3D Consortium, 255
WebOnCall, 85
WebTV, 85
weeding of electronic resources, 132
White Paper on copyright, 107, 108
Wide Area Information Server (WAIS), 263
Windows for Workgroups, 38, 40
Windows NT, 40, 223, 264
Windows technology, 262–63
WinProxy, 183
WinU, 182
WIPO (World Intellectual Property Organization), 106–7
Wired, 8
wireless cable, 240
wireless communications, 233–42
wireless Internet services, 240
workplace ergonomics, 30
workstations, ergonomics of, 26–27, 32
World Intellectual Property Organization (WIPO), 106–7
world (VRML scene), 256
World Wide Web Consortium (W3C), 72, 97–98
World Wide Web Virtual Library, 154
WorldCom, 46

Worldview, 256
wrist rests, 27–28
wrist telephones, 233
.wrl files, 256
.wrl.gz files, 256
.wrz files, 256
W3C. *See* World Wide Web
    Consortium

X

X.509 standard for encryption,
    230

XML (Extensible Markup
    Language), 72–74
  in Dublin Core, 94
  Instructional Management
    Systems Project (IMS),
    96–97
  in metasearch systems, 14
  Resource Description
    Framework (RDF), 98
XML for the automotive
    industry, 73
XSL (Extensible Style
    Language), 71
X3D, 255

Y

Yahoo, 12–13
Yahoo Internet Life
    (magazine), 8
Yahoo Internet Life (website), 7

Pat Ensor is Director of Library Services at the University of Houston-Downtown. Ensor previously served for six years in the position of head of Information Services at University of Houston Libraries, including one year as the interim Assistant Director for Public Services. Prior positions include Coordinator for Electronic Information Services at Indiana State University and Reference Librarian at California State University, Long Beach.

Ensor has published and presented extensively in the field of information technology. She is coeditor of *Information Imagineering: Meeting at the Interface* (ALA, 1998). She is active in the national Library and Information Technology Association (LITA), where she serves on the Executive Board of Directors. She holds a master's in library service from the University of Alabama.